BABE RUTH'S

BABE RUTH'S AMERICA

by ROBERT SMITH

Thomas Y. Crowell Company
New York   Established 1834

Designed by Jill Schwartz

Manufactured in the United States of America

1 2 3 4 5 6 7 8 9 10

Library of Congress Cataloging in Publication Data

Smith, Robert. date
  Babe Ruth's America.

  1. Ruth, George Herman, 1895–1948. I. Title.
GV865.R8S64   796.357'092'4   74-8737
ISBN 0-690-00502-4

TO JANET
who knew it was good before she read it

CONTENTS

BABE RUTH'S
AMERICA

PART I

The Early Days

WHEN George Herman Ruth first came to Boston in 1914, his first year in professional baseball, he was just nineteen years old, a rangy, tall, bright-faced, rambunctious, profane, and thoroughly unregenerate product of St. Mary's Industrial School in his native Baltimore, from which he was still on parole. Because he had been drinking beer since he was eight years old and smoking cigars since shortly after that, because he took the name of the Lord in vain freely in any company, chewed tobacco and spat wherever he saw room, made after light ladies with the avidity of a sailor just in from the sea, and was given to roughhouse play in public places, he was not really fit company for proper Boston boys. Yet all his new teammates loved him, none recalls ever seeing him out of temper in those early days, and even his rivals knew him for a kid who bubbled good nature and would give you whatever he had in his pocket if you asked for it.

Babe was called Jidge by his teammates, that being the New England diminutive for George. After he had roughhoused his way around the locker room, ripping open trouser flies, knocking off hats, or wrestling to the floor any who opposed him, he was often hailed as the Big Baboon. For Babe was big. He was not at all the rotund figure on the toothpick legs that cartoonists pictured in his later years. He was broad, lean, solidly muscled, taller than average, with legs that were long and sturdy. His hair, ink-black, often fell over his forehead. His dark eyes seemed to own a special glow. He was outgoing, full of laughter, and easy to meet. It would be several years before he developed a "King of the Kids" attitude that would cause him to sulk if any of his clubmates failed to consult him on matters he thought might affect his position.

Babe did not stay in Boston that first year. He went instead to Providence, a cramped, raffish, but self-righteous little city with a good baseball club, a hundred places to drink, and just as many places where girls could be rented for money. Babe had come up from Baltimore, with his teammate Ernie Shore, in July and had pitched a few exhibition games in cities like Manchester, New Hampshire, and Lawrence, Massachusetts, and was not thought of as a hitter at all. But he hit a long home run in Providence, indicating that he might serve as a handy man to use as a pinch hitter when he wasn't working on the mound. As far as Babe was concerned, he was ready to do anything on a baseball diamond. He had been a left-handed catcher (with a right-handed glove) in the industrial school, had played first base at Baltimore, and could run the base lines with the best. Whatever needed doing, he would do it, as long as he could get back to Boston.

Boston in that age was a self-satisfied town, the wealthiest large city in the nation on a per capita basis, with more income per capita than New York and Chicago combined. But mere wealth was not of ultimate account in Boston. Indeed, those sly connivers who would promise to get *anyone* into "society" for a fee quickly gave up on Boston, where, they granted, wealth would never be accepted as a substitute for "breeding." The wealth of Boston was not flaunted in clamorous trading centers or glittering hotels or sky-high office buildings. The highest building in Boston in that day was the five-hundred-foot Custom House, that had been built on land scraped off a nearby hill and dumped into the harbor near the foot of the Long Wharf. And a man who climbed to the top of the Custom House one day said that all of Boston, except for its church towers, was notably flat—flat roofs everywhere, flat railroad sheds and factory buildings, flat-roofed apartments on Commonwealth Avenue and Beacon

Street, flat bridges over the Charles River, built on stone piers with no lofty suspension towers, and little squat ferries cutting back and forth over each other's wake to meet the narrow-gauge railroad in East Boston. Tooting and puffing, they plowed the harbor with their busy walking beams nodding up and down like the treadles of sewing machines.

But the quality of life in Boston was by no means flat, to Babe Ruth or to anyone else who lived there before the First World War. It was a more sedate town than New York, of course, with far less opportunity to waste one's substance through the night. But its politics was boisterous enough, its Red Sox the equal of any baseball team ever built in the other great Eastern cities, its fans as ardent, its young men as fervently patriotic, and its thinkers and speakers as free and full of heart as any in the whole land.

All that Boston lacked, some of its most openly devout people felt, was the light—the light, that is, that came with religious awakening. Almost two hundred years earlier, when Puritan Boston had seen its religion begin to degenerate into ritual, the light had come with the visit of Reverend George Whitefield, an evangelist from England who had brought "new light" to many a heart. (His visit, and his recruitment of a whole fellowship who called themselves "New Lights" very nearly coincided with the arrival from England of a set of lamps for Boston's pitch black streets.)

In 1915, there was no George Whitefield to come preach the doctrine of inward spiritual grace. There was instead Billy Sunday, a former outfielder for the Chicago baseball club, who had always, he said, used prayer to help him catch difficult fly balls. (He might better have applied it to his batting average.) Now he was using public prayer to persuade men and women by the hundreds to "hit the sawdust trail" to spiritual salvation. (Billy conducted his meetings in tents, public arenas, or temporary halls where sawdust was used to absorb spills or keep down the dust, as in a saloon or circus.)

Billy was not due to bring the Word to Boston until 1916. Now he was leading standing-room crowds in singing his trademark hymn, "Brighten the Corner Where You Are," in Paterson, New Jersey. But he spoke from time to time of his eagerness to visit Boston, to brighten the corners there, to put Sin to flight, and to down Demon Rum. He would most certainly, he vowed, speak sharply to the Harvard students about their habit of serving beer at their smokers.

On Billy's trail—not his sawdust trail but on the trail he and his re-

3

tinue had left as they carried the light from one town to another—there were a few who would have liked to speak to Billy about the personal habits of his crew. In Philadelphia, one Charles Keegan had rented his richly furnished home at 1914 Spring Garden to Billy and his followers. Now that Billy had left, Keegan charged that there was $1734 due him for damage done to the house, and he warned that if Billy did not pay up quickly, he was going to sue, salvation or no salvation. Billy's gang, said Keegan, had gouged walls, broken furniture, stolen glassware, and torn six doors off their hinges. Six oil paintings were missing, along with nine bath towels, three table covers, ten napkins, thirteen pillow cases, twenty-eight beer glasses, forty engraved water glasses, twenty-six whiskey glasses, ten bock glasses, five cordial glasses, and nine fancy beer steins, not to mention a wicker armchair, sundry embroidered scarfs, some silk curtains, a Turkish rug, a silver-plated syrup jug, and the shade off the front door.

When Philadelphia reporters found Ma Sunday taking off in her automobile, they climbed on the running board to question her about Mr. Keegan's charges. "All a lie!" cried the estimable lady. "A damnable lie!"

And was it not true that someone had broken into a locked trunk in the cellar and stolen a quantity of whiskey and gin? At this, Ma Sunday clenched her fists. "How dare you stand there and ask me such things?" she shrieked. "I'll punch you in the face!" When the wary reporter had stepped out of range, the good lady added, more calmly, that all this was "too lowdown for us to bother with." As for Billy himself, he declared that none of the names his enemies called him could even scratch his hide. "I could start a libel suit in every town I ever visited," he observed. "But I just haven't got the time."

Instead, Billy's time was taken up with exhorting the smug citizens of Paterson to awake and see themselves. "If Jesus were to come to Paterson today," Billy shouted, "you would crucify Him!" Whereupon men and women and adolescents by the dozen would tumble over each other to reach the wide middle sawdust-sprinkled aisle, to march in ranks down to the platform and, by shaking sainted Billy's hand, acknowledge their acceptance of Christ. One evening he even coaxed four hundred United States sailors and marines to march down the trail to salvation, meanwhile urging his ushers, who were charged with circulating the tin plates for the free-will cash offering, to "pass up the sailor boys." The sailor boys, however, refused to accept any charity conversions and handed their own hats about for their mates to drop contributions in to swell the evening take.

Another evening Billy took off on the Unitarians, who everywhere seemed most determined to thwart his crusade. "Jesus Christ was crucified by the Unitarians of his time!" Billy bellowed to the crowded hall. "They stoned Him and put Him on the cross and sold Him for thirty pieces of silver—about fifteen dollars in today's money, the price of a good hog!" As for any who, like the Unitarians, persisted in the delusion that a soul might reach Heaven through reading good books and doing good deeds—they were dippy! That stuff was all a lie! And any man who doubted the divinity of Christ was as low as those who drove the spikes into the Lord's hands!

While declaiming in this manner, Billy never kept to a pulpit, although he might sometimes bang his fist down on a desk. Instead he galloped up and down the wide stage, leaping, pounding his hands together, waving them high over his head, or flailing the air with the large handkerchief he used to mop the perspiration off his face.

Jeff Davis, self-crowned King of the Hoboes, who sat in the Paterson hall one night all unconverted, appraised Sunday as a "better comedian than Charlie Chaplin." What Charlie does with his feet, Jeff said, Billy accomplishes with his hands. But why, he wondered, should a clown like that be allowed to draw sustenance from the body politic scot free. "When a circus comes to town," said Jeff, "it has to pay a tax. But Billy comes free of charge and will be forty thousand bucks to the good."

Proper folk, however, gave no weight to the mouthings of a professional ne'er-do-well. And the men and women who inhabited the snug apartments on Beacon Hill or the swell-front flats along Commonwealth Avenue were acknowledged the most proper the nation knew. But there were improper Bostonians aplenty, not all as improper as Ruth himself—who had never learned to wear underclothes and who was as likely to use another man's toothbrush as his own—but in their own ways as reckless and unpolished as barnyard animals.

In 1915 when Babe Ruth first settled in Boston to stay, he lived at the Putnam Hotel on Huntington Avenue, close by the Opera House and Symphony Hall. A good share of his teammates dwelt there too—Joe Wood, Harry Hooper, Larry Gardner, Tris Speaker, Ray

5

Collins, and a number of lesser lights—so there was never any lack of company. Opera stars stayed here as well and sometimes discussed with the players ways of improving wind and stamina. But the ballplayers were interested chiefly in fun when there was nothing to do at the park. Happily, the hotel, although it owned no liquor license, did provide a back room with a full bar and a flowing supply of good liquor where selected patrons might partake of illicit good cheer. On playing days, Babe and his friends might walk to the field: for the city was small then and Fenway Park lay out on its edge, near the banks of the Muddy River, where muttering ducks still gather to be fed by passersby.

Most baseball fans, however, gathering as they did from Dorchester and Roxbury and Brookline and Jamaica Plain and Cambridge and Waban and Somerville and a dozen other towns thereabouts as well as from South Boston and the inner city, came most often by trolley cars that ran down Beacon and Boylston streets, along Commonwealth Avenue and on Huntington Avenue too, past the Putnam Hotel and past the Opera House and Symphony Hall, the Museum of Fine Arts, the Wentworth Institute, Peter Bent Brigham Hospital, the YMCA, and the Christian Science Mother Church and into Copley Square near the Public Library. In baseball weather, the open trolley cars would be so aswarm with men and boys, all in their wonted dark suits and caps or sporting sailor straws, that there seemed not a place left for a foot or a hand to hold; how the hapless conductor made his way up and down the running board to gather and ring in all the nickels, God alone could tell.

Babe Ruth of course would have been in the park long before the cars grew crowded. On his way to the park, and of course when he was playing, Babe never wore anything on his head but a cap, a size larger than most men wore, set perfectly straight on his head, making the top of his head seem flat and his face even broader than nature meant. Babe's face, even when he was young and relatively thin, always seemed nearly as broad as it was long, although of course it was not. When he smiled, as he seemed to do most of the time, his wide mouth gave his whole face an almost froglike character.

Ballplayers were not rich men in that day, not even the great stars like Tris Speaker and Ty Cobb, nor were their playgrounds much more splendid than some they had played in during school or when they performed in the minor leagues, except that in the big leagues

6

there were slat-back seats in the grandstand and turnstiles too intricate for a small boy to skip through. But even in the big leagues, locker rooms sometimes seemed no more inviting than a cellar. There were still a few with concrete floors or dirt floors, heated with potbellied stoves, and with lockers hardly big enough to hold shoes and a shirt. But of all the parks in the American League, ballplayers of that early day thought Fenway Park was the finest. The lockers were large enough to hold a man's entire wardrobe. The showers were roomy and always hot. The playing surface was well tended: never too muddy, never baked hard, never loose and sandy on the base lines. This was a sort of miracle, when one considers that the Back Bay earth had been hauled in a half century earlier on railroad cars from as far off as Needham, along with assorted fill from everywhere—old hoopskirts, bottles, and discarded oyster shells—to stifle the noisome tidal flats that had grown into an offense to the inhabitants.

Fenway Park was still nearly new in Babe Ruth's day. For a time while it was abuilding there was a question if baseball would ever be played there at all, it being so close to the Unitarian Church that, even though no baseball was permitted on a Sunday, the profane revelry the game gave occasional rise to might have offended the ear of some of the weekday faithful. But the Red Sox management forestalled any protest from that source by awarding the Unitarian minister a lifetime pass to the grandstand—a pass that some years later I made occasional use of in company with the minister's own little boy.

So there the park stood, a splendid place by baseball standards, with its sprawling stands and brick walls no boy could hope to scale, as men and boys had scaled the weathered board fences of the old grounds in the South End. There were open spaces around the park that gave room for small boys to gather and await the foul balls that occasionally flew back over the grandstand roof and bounded away across the leprous turf of the adjacent lot. What joy it was to scamper after those balls, all white and beautiful as leaping fish, to capture and hold one tight and use it then as a pass into the park with as many mates as you cared to admit had come in your company.

Words cannot describe how Boston fans then doted on the Red Sox. The club had grown close to them throughout its first years at the old park, where early ticket buyers might discover the great Cy

Young pushing out tickets from behind the wicket and could stand there a moment or two and jaw about the game Cy had pitched the day before. An ardent Roxbury crew, habitués of a tavern operated by one "Nuf Ced" McGreevey, a voluble little Irishman who put a cap on every argument by snapping " 'nough said!" to his antagonist, formed a cheering section of their own. They came to games carrying signs hailing all their heroes, as Mets fans have learned to do. They carried channel-buoy megaphones through which to yell their disagreement with an umpire or howl their delight at a mighty blow. And they adopted as their theme song, and sang it at every game, a popular tune called "Tessie," which had nothing to do with baseball at all.

Out of this movement grew the Royal Rooters, who sat always in a special section of the grandstand, all together, to sing "Tessie" and offer concerted cheering or derision, as the occasion invited. This crowd, who used to parade about the field before an important game sporting parasols or banners or signs inquiring "Are Ye There?," were almost as much a part of the Boston scene as the Red Sox themselves, who had won all the Irishmen in town to their side and away from the Beaneaters, now called the Braves, a club that had long nourished an anti-Catholic cabal in its ranks.

There was always a glorious excitement about the new park, where fans poured out their souls' anguish or ecstasy with far more fervor than they ever did at church. And even though a baseball player's lot was not yet a wholly lavish one, the glory it offered sometimes seemed recompense enough.

Babe Ruth's salary of $3,500 was almost six times what he had signed for with Baltimore and it was better than double his Providence pay. While it did not win Babe a listing among the city's top earners, it was twice what my uncles earned from working six days a week on the railroad. Those were days when a ballplayer, or anyone with the change, could buy a hearty breakfast at the Hotel Brunswick—with fruit and cereal and eggs and toast and coffee—for thirty-five cents. A man who laid out half a dollar for lunch in a one-arm joint might shake his head at the way prices were mounting. A new six-cylinder automobile could be bought then for $800. An apartment in a decent neighborhood could be rented for twenty-five dollars a month. The finest beefsteak was sold for thirty-five cents a pound, while three dollars would buy a man as good a straw hat as

8

he could find in the city. So a salary of better than sixty dollars a week could make a man feel like a king.

Babe was not yet a king in anyone's eyes. But he was becoming the best pitcher in town, now that he had learned to make a baseball go where he wanted it to. (In a game against Lawrence his first year up, he had allowed eight walks while striking out five.) He threw hard. He owned a sharp curve. And his control was matchless. He gave up only eighty-five walks against 112 strikeouts in 1915 and brought his earned-run average down to 2.44, while winning eighteen games. If he went on this way, old-timers were saying, this fresh kid from Baltimore would be right up there with the big guys—earning $10,000 a year.

Babe himself felt flush enough when the season was over to take his final paycheck home to Baltimore and open up a saloon in partnership with his father. The saloon did not prosper, nor did Babe's attachment to his father or his old home town really flourish. He was a Boston boy now. Hardly anyone ever heard him talk about his family—except when he once, in Washington, begged Manager Bill Carrigan for a night off "to visit his folks in Baltimore." Carrigan let him off and late that night observed Babe visiting somebody else's folks in a local saloon. There were no more nights off to see the family and no one ever recalls seeing Babe's father at a ball game except once, in New York. Yet Babe, in his heart, remained devoted to his father and wept bitterly at his funeral in 1918, perhaps counting over all the woe he had brought him when he was the wildest kid in town. Babe's mother had died eight years before, when he was fifteen.

Now, with his wages growing fatter and his skill as a pitcher sharpening from week to week, Babe was earning title as the wildest young man in Boston. He was always in search of locomotion. As a youngster in the Baltimore Orioles' training camp at Fayetteville, South Carolina, Babe had been wont to hop aboard any unwatched bicycle and go scorching off at top speed until he grew tired. Once he commandeered a saddle horse and, untrained at steering such a vehicle, rode it into a fruit stand and sent apples and oranges scattering. In Boston, nearly grown up now, he kept borrowing automobiles, usually from young ladies whose charms he had sampled.

One night he talked his companion of the evening into letting him drive her Packard back to the hotel, or somewhere. He drove it down to where the streetcar tracks converged just west of Kenmore Square, at the confluence of Beacon Street and Commonwealth Avenue. Usually the big streetcars would wait for one another here, allowing the car that had priority to go first on to the tracks that led into the subway. Babe, driving along about 2 A.M. in a state of euphoria, set out to dodge around the standing car and found himself suddenly wedged against it by a moving car he had not noticed. The Packard was ingloriously flattened at its front end and Babe had a hell of a time pulling himself free. Once out, he made his way back to the Putnam on foot, leaving the wrecked car there, disowned and disabled, for the police to fret about.

The Boston police, all of them devout followers of the Red Sox, were habitually indulgent with their heroes. When Larry Gardner parked his Stutz Bearcat in front of the Touraine Hotel, effectively blocking traffic, Captain Good of Station 16, the Fenway precinct, sent word to forget it. And no one was about to put the arm on Babe Ruth.

There were far more portentous matters for the police to deal with in the more densely settled reaches of the city. One observer of that day, digesting the crime statistics, reported that the closer to City Hall one carried his reckoning, the higher the crime rate grew. Of course a man could get himself arrested in Boston a sight more handily than he might in less straitlaced environs. Martin Lomasney, Democratic overlord of Ward Eight in Boston, for instance, once found himself busted for using profanity in public. "No such gosh darn thing!" Lomasney declared in court. "I never use bad language in public! I have a reputation to uphold." The judge nonetheless found Martin guilty, then discreetly filed the case.

More scarlet wickedness was rampant elsewhere, as few knew better than Babe himself, who was no man to rest content with after-hours card games or a few drinks on the quiet. To him, good times meant girls. And who wanted an army with him when he set out on the prowl? According to the notations of the Watch and Ward Society, which had taken the city's conscience into its keeping, there were houses of ill fame throughout the South End, and they were so well guarded that the society could not to save itself get an operative into them to garner evidence. One must needs apparently know a waiter or a bartender or an official steerer of some sort to get past the door. But Babe had no such difficulties. Having long since learned what girls were good for, he had early discovered how to make his way into the hideaways where girls could be had in any number. His own list of addresses must have been every bit as extensive as that of the Watch and Ward Society, which had listed suspected bordellos on Lower Tremont Street, on Shawmut Avenue, on Compton Street, on Aberdeen Street, and at 228 West Canton.

Babe's teammates were none of them eager to follow in the youngster's footsteps. To most of them, a merry time was a visit to the amusement park at Revere Beach, where there were "rides" on wildly undulating tracks guaranteed to lift your heart into your throat, shooting galleries and games of every sort where stuffed animals and china dolls were offered as prizes, wheels that defied a man to stand upright while they whirled faster and faster, and even a Tunnel of Love where boys could cuddle with girls in the dark, with demons popping from the walls occasionally to prompt the girl to clutch you about the neck. Then there was beer or "tonic" to drink, hotdogs and popcorn or salt-water taffy to assail one's stomach with, and a long sandy beach to loll on.

This was kindergarten play to Babe, and no one ever caught him among the crew who traveled there of a Sunday. And of course the ballplayers occasionally sought rougher pastimes—steady drinking, card games, and late visits to the burlesque shows, all of which were regularly monitored by the Watch and Ward Society to make sure no breasts, no navels, and no naked thighs were exposed on the stage and that there was not even any "apparent nudity" to stir young men's baser passions. But outside the theater, and despite the alertness of the society's investigators, it was possible to lay hold of a handful of obscene pictures for fifty cents—to take back to the hotel and pass around among one's teammates.

There came a time when Babe began to center his attention on one special girl, to whom he paid court every morning. She was from Texas, a waitress at a small restaurant on Huntington Avenue a hundred yards or so south of the hotel, across Massachusetts Avenue. But Helen Woodring, the waitress, was not one of the Babe's light ladies. And Babe told himself that this was serious. Morning after morning he ate more breakfast then he needed to, in order to sit and make jokes or touch hands with little Helen. Then, when he realized this was no one-night affair, Babe did what all proper Boston boys had been taught to do—he asked the girl to marry him.

There must have been young men in Boston then who viewed marriage as a sort of growing into even longer long pants—a putting away of all adolescent things, such as staying up after midnight and setting out, as if it were a fellow's duty, to persuade all lithe ladies to lie themselves down. But if such there were, Babe Ruth was not among them. He was glad to be married, glad to have his plump little prize to serve breakfast to himself alone, but damned if he was going to submit to any hitching that would narrow his range or curb his appetites. When reminded of his duties, Babe never wanted to admit that he was not what he was supposed to be, for he did yearn—as he had since he was a small, reckless boy in the industrial school—for the approval of those in authority. But once he had expressed his repentance, his sins were washed away like sand in a shower bath and Babe was ready for whatever deviltry the day, or the night, might offer.

Babe probably would have denied that he had no intent of raising a family, or that he was too devil-may-care to make any child a proper father. But it was whispered that when Helen showed up pregnant one morning he helped arrange an abortion—not a really difficult business even in that day, despite all the Catholic Church and all the Watch and Ward Society and all the Commonwealth's men could muster to root the practice out. Later, Babe adopted a child, a girl about one year old. But when some of his teammates saw that cute little moonface and turned-up Babe Ruth nose, and discovered that the child even toddled in Babe's characteristically pigeon-toed manner, they evolved a theory that may very well have been the truth: Babe's Helen had had a premature baby that had been kept in an incubator for months, and Babe, feeling perhaps that there was something unmanly about fathering anything so puny, had kept the birth a secret until little Dorothy was on her feet. Then there was nothing for it but to pretend he had found her that size. Could it have been so? There are some old men alive who insist it was.

In the locker room, Babe was still the overgrown prankster who spent part of his spare time cooking up crude practical jokes, not all of which brought laughs from the victims. Ballplayers, at that time, turned their uniform pants inside out before they put them on, laying them on the floor in front of their feet, then rolling stockings and pants on together, so that a rubber garter could be snapped on, hitching pants down and stockings up at the same point. Babe, always one of the earliest dressed, used to watch an opportunity as other men studiously adjusted their pants. He would stand close to one player, and as that man finally got his pants turned right side out but before he got them buttoned, Babe would drop a lighted cigar butt inside one pants leg. Often the player would be out in the dugout before he became aware that his left pants leg was smoldering. Then he would be hard put to pull the clothes off fast enough to keep the fire from spreading.

Babe also delighted to find bits of inedible material, a small piece of flannel, a scrap of blotting paper, or a scorecard, to slip into a teammate's pregame sandwich. The sight of the man as he disgustedly tried to untangle the food from the flannel or the paper would bring bellows of laughter from Ruth, who would then, like as not, have to duck as the remains of the sandwich came flying his way. Once, in Hot Springs, Arkansas, where Babe did some preseason training, he persuaded his wife to take a ride alone on the Ferris wheel. She climbed aboard, against her better judgment, then cried in dismay when the wheel stopped with her on the very top. Babe had bribed the operator to stop the wheel, while Babe stood below and shook the contraption, bringing shrieks of terror from Helen and yelps of joy from the Babe.

Going to the locker room in those days, one member of the Red Sox said, was like running down to the zoo to watch your favorite gorilla at play. No one ever could divine what big Jidge would turn to next. When Joe Bush joined the club, he invented a little song: "Big Babe Ruth was picking his tooth/With the limb of a coconut tree!" It would drive Babe into a frenzy.

Boston fans and writers of that day took no deep interest in the private lives of professional athletes. Or if writers did, they took care always to present the athlete as an example to the young, it being generally agreed that all whose job it was to speak out loud in the presence of the immature should utter only matter that would win them to ways of righteousness. When Cy Young was interviewed in public, he humbly acknowledged that he was indeed a man who lived a life of strict self-denial. After the interview Cy no doubt repaired to his room at the Putnam and poured himself his standard restorative of a half tumbler of Cascade whiskey, unpolluted by water, soda, or ice. Babe Ruth likewise remained in the eyes of the Boston baseball fancy a clean-limbed and clean-living youngster who shunned alcohol, strong language, and lewd company. Come to

13

think of it, had anyone asked Babe if he also eschewed tobacco, he'd have told them: "Hell, yes! All the time!"

Hypocrisy had long been Boston's most important product, at least in those circles where dwelt the folk who owned the city and made up the face it showed to the world. No child in a "decent" neighborhood ever saw a pregnant woman in the streets. The Watch and Ward Society pounced on every issue of the *Police Gazette* and saw that it was not permitted to circulate where innocent eyes might fall upon it. The society even undertook to have removed from the outer walls of the Opera House posters that showed ballet dancers in tutus, lest Boston youth be tempted to seek out what fleshly secrets lay hidden beyond the tutu's edge.

This is not to say that there was no wickedness in Boston or its immediate suburbs. Despite all the efforts of the better folk to set proper standards of behavior and to see that stage and screen were permitted to offer only representations of upright life and virtue rewarded, there were undisciplined folk in growing numbers who persisted in disturbing the calm of the streets.

In Malden one day a tall-helmeted policeman came upon one Israel Kroner taking his ease in a chair set on the sidewalk before the Kroner fruit store. The policeman urged Kroner to remove himself, so that the public way would stand unobstructed. Kroner allowed that, having sat here every fine day since he had opened the store, he was not about to be deprived of the privilege. The officer thereupon laid a rude hand upon him and threatened arrest for obstructing traffic. Kroner promptly rose up and removed the chair. But he used it to beat Patrolman Long over the head. Kroner's brother Joseph then left his post inside the store and set out to support Israel by lambasting Patrolman Long about the neck and ears with a barrel stave. Mrs. I. Kroner too rushed out and employed both hands in clawing at the officer. By this time most of the Kroners' neighbors had swarmed about the policeman and quickly wrested his billy-club away, then began haphazardly to dismember him. Someone sent a youngster scurrying for aid and soon a horse-drawn patrol wagon clattered up, bringing eight fresh cops for company. The sight of this lot, all with clubs in their hands, caused the attackers to fall back and allow the police to drag the Kroner family off to the station house. After the affray, Patrolman Long ruefully noted that he had lost every single brass button from his coat.

Policemen in those times were not given to shooting at people who threatened them or tried to elude them, not even when they had more heinous crimes to deal with than obstructing foot passage on the sidewalk. When two brawny young men from South Boston, Dennis McGrath and John Donovan by name, were discovered helping themselves to bundles from the back of a Boston Parcel Delivery wagon behind the Plaza Hotel on Columbus Avenue one afternoon, someone called the cops. The police arrived in time to surprise the young men in *flagrante delicto*. But the boys picked up rocks and flung them with such effect that the law was set back a yard or two. With the enemy in disarray, McGrath and Donovan scampered up Tremont Street, as cries of "Stop thief!" drew a swelling crowd of pursuers. The cops, taking up the chase, fired their revolvers in the air but made no effort to gun down the fugitives, even when they had clear targets. They finally cornered the thieves on Dartmouth Street and subdued them hand to hand.

It was always the Irish who were getting into scrapes like this, the proper people in town would tell you. But it was the Irish who supplied most of the police of the town too, and if anyone should drive up in a hack and ask you, they were doing it at damn small wages, and only one day off in fifteen. They were also supplying the bulk of the politicians, including, be it said, a prickly character named James Michael Curley who had got himself elected mayor, and a fellow named David Ignatius Walsh who had been made governor, despite the stories some did tell about his being more taken with (God save us from all harm!) handsome lads than pretty ladies.

Of course a fair share of the ballplayers were Irish too, although there was still some anti-Catholic feeling in the ranks, reflecting the attitude of the self-styled better people, who still nursed in their hearts much of the old anti-Pope prejudice that had inflamed the Massachusetts colony since mothers had first repeated to their children the doings of Bloody Mary Tudor. Babe Ruth was a German, on his father's side at least; still, he was also a Catholic. And he was more like an Irishman in the way he had of taking his fun wherever he found it.

Even the Irish were paying more heed in that day to what was said and done at City Hall and thereabouts than to what went on at the ball park. For this man Curley was a fellow who would speak out on any topic, God knows, and deliver himself of opinions that were calculated to curl the hair of the bloody Protestants who owned the town. There was the hell of a stink in that day about Votes for

Women, and most of the pinch-nosed folk in the neighborhood would have none of the subject except to name its proponents a parcel of silly females who aspired to wear pants. When the suffrage ladies, ten thousand strong, with their yellow ribbons and their yellow roses, staged a parade up Beacon Street, down School, along Washington, and back on Tremont, the opposition ladies, representing some of the fattest fortunes in the state, hired children to give out red roses in opposition. But the yellow roses won, because most of the working people of the town, and their young, stood up for equal suffrage, no matter that the rich ladies named it the Enemy of the American Home.

And the baseball players, who were largely a product of homes where mothers swept and scrubbed and cooked and washed and sewed and mended and shooed the chickens off the porch and wiped the tears away—they were all for Maggie Foley's cause too, Maggie Foley being the doughty lady who led the fight for equal suffrage in that end of the land. When the Boston Braves of the National League hit home runs, which was seldom enough, God knows, they called each one a "Maggie Foley."

As for Mayor Curley, he stood right up in public when the parade was done—and when other politicians were allowing cautiously that this would "surely attract deep consideration to the problem"—and said out loud that it was the greatest parade he had ever seen in his life. Like Secretary of State William Jennings Bryan, Curley wanted no rights his wife could not share. "Why," said he, "back in 1902, when it was sacrilege to vote for the cause, I cast my vote for Equal Suffrage."

And later on, when local Irishmen gathered by the thousands to protest the execution by the British of the leaders of the 1916 Easter Rising in Ireland, Curley spoke out of turn again. Here in Boston, he recalled, "we commemorate the spot where the blood of the black man ran red with the blood of the white Irishman, Patrick Carr, at the birth of American Liberty." He was talking of course about the Boston Massacre, where the black mob leader, Crispus Attucks, was shot dead on the snowy square before the Custom House. But then, whatever else he may have been, James M. Curley was a man who never looked down on any human as a lesser being than himself, and who was ready to grant that a black man might just be an Irishman turned inside out.

As for Babe Ruth, he went on in those years before America entered the First World War to win baseball games for Boston, despite a cracked ankle and a few days off as a result of a horrid sunburn he contracted while snoozing on a beach at Wollaston. And he played his part in bringing the Red Sox into the 1915 World Series. The fact there was hell to pay across the seas at this time just made life seem more blessed on the days when the sun shone bright and all the little birds in the world seemed to be singing along the Fenway, while the stately swan boats, laden with small boys and girls, swam gently in the shallow pools of the Public Gardens.

Hardly any note was made, except in the sports pages, of the fact that Babe Ruth in 1915 hit his first major-league home run. This came on a long, long drive into the upper right field stands at the Polo Grounds in New York (where the Yankees as well as the Giants played) off a Yankee pitcher named Jack Warhop. Babe, who was pitching that day, lost the game to the Yankees, but a New York writer said he was "all a pitcher should be, and more. . . . First up in the third, with no apparent effort, he slammed a home run into the stands."

Ruth's effort may not have been apparent but it was nonetheless real. He did everything with all his might. The bat he used weighed about three pounds, more than a pound heavier than the ones today's mighty hitters use. It was said to be the heaviest bat in the majors. (It was not, because Hack Miller of the Cubs swung a bat that weighed just over four pounds.) Babe used to hold this deadly mace down at the very end, with his little finger curled under the knob. He squeezed it so tight his hands wore calluses like a hard-rock miner's and he swung the bat so fiercely he would turn himself almost completely around on his follow-through. He hit only four home runs in 1915. But he hit one in St. Louis that startled everyone who saw it; it cleared the right-field bleachers and landed in the brewery district well beyond, the longest blow ever recorded at Sportsman's Park. Babe not only won eighteen games as a pitcher that season but was sent to bat ten times as a pinch hitter, he being the ablest hitter of all the pitchers on the club, with a seasonal average of .315. Even so, when there was a left-hander throwing for the opposing team, Manager Carrigan often used a pinch hitter for Ruth.

Babe increased his effectiveness in 1915 by learning finally not to stick his tongue out as he prepared to throw a curve. Many young pitchers habitually betray in some such manner the special effort they must exert in throwing "number two." They will bite the lower lip, look down at the ball as they fix it deep in the hand, shorten their windup, even hunch their shoulders. And enemy coaches, always seeking such signals, will quickly pass the word to the batter that a curve is coming.

According to Babe's own reckoning, he had already grown to manhood and so free of parole in 1915, but actually he did not reach twenty-one until February of 1916, the year he became the best left-handed pitcher in the American League with twenty-three wins and only twelve losses. (Harry Coveleski of Detroit, another left-hander, beat Ruth in winning percentage, but he won only twenty-two games and did not quite equal Ruth's amazing earned-run average of 1.75.) Ruth led the club to the pennant that year and attained his immediate goal, the right to start a World Series game. The previous year he had squirmed and cursed and growled on the bench as he watched his teammates beat the Phillies. Babe, with his eighteen victories, could see no sound reason why he did not own as much right to start a game as did Dutch Leonard, who had won only fourteen. But Bill Carrigan carried more pitchers than he needed in the 1915 series. He let Babe hit for Ernie Shore in the first game and poor Babe grounded out in the ninth. After that, Shore and Rube Foster and Leonard among them won four games in a row. In his start, Leonard gave the Phillies only three hits and struck out six. Had a sixth game been needed, Babe might have started it.

In 1916, however, there was no keeping him off the mound, for Babe was the best the Red Sox owned. The World Series that year, the Boston end of it, was played in Braves Field, a new park on Commonwealth Avenue that the Braves themselves could never fill. The games there drew the greatest crowds that had ever paid to see a World Series. When Babe faced the Brooklyn Dodgers (then called the Robins, after their plump and sportive manager, Wilbert Robinson) he was grim as a gunman, determined to annihilate this crew of outlanders from the enemy league. (Ruth, in his younger days, long before there was any hint that he might wind up in the National League himself, carried his hatred of the "curve-ball league" off the field as well as on, and would have no truck with National League ballplayers if he could avoid it.) And Babe very nearly kept the whole Brooklyn club out of scoring territory for the whole fourteen innings he pitched. Brooklyn made one run in the first inning, when Hy Myers, the Brooklyn outfielder, drove a ball out toward Tilly Walker, the center fielder who was feebly endeavoring to fill Tris Speaker's spot. The ball struck some hard spot in the turf and took a wild bounce over Tilly's head, then bounded away, away, away, across the impossibly wide reaches of the Braves' outfield. By the time Tilly caught up with it, he was too late to stop Myers from running all the way home. Babe was disgusted.

"That only ought to have been a single!" he snarled.

After that, Babe allowed no runs at all through thirteen full innings, and got back the one run himself by driving in a Boston run with a ground ball to the infield. The game went on until it grew so dark that Bill Klem, the great National League umpire, sitting in the stands that day, said that if he'd been in charge, he'd have called the thing off. Instead, Boston pinch hitter Del Gainer called it off by driving a ball far out into the dusk to where the fans could no longer follow it. It brought in pinch runner Mike McNally with the winning run. So Babe Ruth had his first World Series victory and started his string of scoreless World Series Innings. He eventually ran his string of zeros to 29 and a fraction, setting a record that stood until 1960.

Thanks to their use of Braves Field, and despite the work of the genius who scheduled one game for Yom Kippur, this Series brought the richest payday ever to the ballplayers and it sent Babe home with his wallet bulging and his head full of schemes for getting rid of his money.

Whether Babe ever knew the value of a dollar is a question. He paid a high price for one of the first dollar bills he ever had the spending of, for he stole it from the till in his father's saloon and used it to buy ice cream for every kid on his street. When he had to confess to his father where the money came from, he took a horsewhipping for it. Then he went back and stole another.

But Babe was not stealing any more dollar bills now. Still just a winning pitcher for the Red Sox, young Babe gave due thought, between sallies into offhand sin, to the need to settle into the image of a proper young man of substance. Duly married (after "running away" in accepted style to get married in Maryland, where there was no waiting period between licenses and ceremony), Babe bought a new Packard of his very own, for there would be (he must have told himself) no more lady friends to borrow automobiles from. He did not, however, learn to drive any less rashly. Every day in the locker room he had reports to offer of hills he had made without shifting into second, of speeds he had reached on the open highway, of live-stock he had scattered and cops he had outrun. Inevitably he hit someone. Driving at higher than moderate speed through the streets of Cambridge one day, he knocked down an old man who had stepped unwarily off the curb—as people in that era often did, not having grown up in the habit of looking for sudden death from ei-ther direction on a city street. Tearful and contrite, as he invariably became when he saw he had done wrong, Babe bundled the old man into his car and took him off to the Cambridge Relief Hospital, where the poor fellow eventually recovered.

But neither the bliss of marital union nor any dread of bowling over the innocent could turn young George Ruth from a boisterous, rough-talking, come-day-go-day, merry young delinquent into a tamed and halter-broke Bostonian.

There were two wholly different ways of life in Boston then, and it often seemed as if they might never acknowledge each other. Some proper men and women knew of course that there was another world where bad-mannered people indulged their appetites in un-seemly ways. But the Watch and Ward Society was always on hand to curb the too frequent outcroppings of the forces that might goad good Christians into Sin. They ferreted out gamblers, set watch on houses of ill fame, snipped bad words out of books and magazines, and reported on the illicit sale of drink. And men in public pulpits kept the purveyors of entertainment in line by denouncing all films that dealt in the violation of women. (The Watch and Ward Society coped so tenderly with the innocence of the populace under its care that it sequestered the reports of its own operatives, lest the offen-sive words one must perforce employ to detail their sordid discover-ies persist in print to sully some immaculate mind.)

But there was one famous and unquestionably scandalous picture that came to Boston in these days that the various watchers and warders made no move to suppress, even though it dealt openly in the violation of women and stirred more ugly passions than any two dozen representations of licentious living. That was David Wark Grif-fith's *The Birth of a Nation* which memorialized the manner in which the gallant night riders of the South preserved Christian morals by hanging black men from trees in the dark. Boston's youth went panting after this picture and came out convinced that the conquered Confederacy had been alive with bands of black satyrs whom only the force of arms could stay from wholesale indecent assaults upon shrinking white maidenhood. Black men and women in Boston made spasmodic and vain efforts to halt the broadcast of this libel, while many of the city's most honored minds hailed the film as a triumphant marriage of history and art.

The Reverend Dr. Charles H. Parkhurst, one of the nation's leading thinkers-out-loud, offered the picture his "unqualified approval." "A boy can learn more true history," the erudite doctor declared, "and get more of the atmosphere of the period by sitting back for three hours before this film than by weeks and months of study in the classroom."

It was true, as many Boston boys and a few ballplayers were ready to testify, that nothing this hairy had ever been offered in a local classroom. Nor was there a school text in town to document a basic theory of the picture: that a rape victim would hold on the retina of her dead eye the image of her attacker. Dr. Parkhurst hastened to mitigate black indignation by explaining that the film "represents the Negro, not as he is now but as he was when he had just had the chains broken from him and when he was rioting in the deliciousness of liberty."

The black citizens of Boston, who found their current lot something less than delicious, were not to be diverted. A few of them took seats in the theater and cried their protests aloud. Three black ladies even undertook to bring the showing to a close by shrieking steadily at the top of their lungs. And ultimately a mass meeting was held at Tremont Temple, with mostly blacks in attendance, to hear Charles W. Eliot, president emeritus of Harvard, declare that the picture preached false doctrine.

One reverend and righteous gentleman who stayed home from the meeting was E. A. E. Palmquist, minister of the North Avenue Baptist Church. "If you want to know how to raise children," Palmquist said, "ask an old maid. If you want to know about handling the Negro, ask the people of New England. Colored people are merely children and to allow them to close *Birth of a Nation* will be sowing the seed that will bring forth a harvest similar to the harvest in the South at the close of the Civil War."

So the picture continued to offer its own harvest of private excitement to grown-ups and children alike, even to old maids, promising "18,000 people! 3,000 horses!" It was indeed, as the posters proclaimed, "a Gigantic Spectacle!" But it was also, according to J. Noble Pierce, minister of the Second Congregational Church in Dorchester, "a damnable lie!" Its being so magnificent, he averred, made it "all the more damnable a lie!"

But far more damnable an entertainment, in many lofty eyes of that day, was a dramatic offering called *Within the Law,* which seemed to traduce, not lowly and childlike blacks, but many of the town's most solidly upholstered citizens, its department-store merchants. The play had come to Boston after a riotous run in Chicago, where it was credited with having brought about the passage of an ordinance setting a minimum wage in department stores. But it would wreak no such havoc in business circles in Boston, the local merchants vowed.

"Why," a spokesman for the assembled department-store owners declared, "we lose $60,000 a year in thefts, mostly by employees! And we don't even prosecute them. At least not usually. A minimum wage is like unionizing! It will destroy efficiency! A lazy girl would get as much as a hard worker! It would destroy ambition! We hire a girl to begin at $5 a week. After a while she asks for a raise. If her sales book shows she deserves it, she gets it. Why, the head of one department gets $5,000 and she began as a cash girl! You see, employes get a percentage of sales as well as salary. If we gave raises to $6 or $8, we could not afford the percentage."

Reminded that it had been determined a girl could barely keep herself alive in Chicago at $5 a week, the spokesman, who was shy of seeing his name in print, pointed out that it was much more expensive to live in Chicago.

"Don't you see," he elucidated, "the environment of Boston is much better? Suburbs are not far away where board and room are very reasonable. We have social clubs in our stores. And we let our employees buy goods at *less than retail price!"* (And, he might have emphasized, we never, or hardly ever, prosecute them for stealing the goods.)

It may well have been that the living was easy in the Boston suburbs in this era. But it was not always tranquil. In Weston about this time, a naked man kept popping out of the woods at unseemly hours to attack lone females. Police who sought him found, near his discarded clothing, a number of empty beer bottles, so they concluded he had been inflamed by drink into indulging his sex appetites wantonly. Heretofore he had been content merely to expose himself to unescorted ladies. The local police, despite their following the prints of his naked feet some distance over the forest floor, never did discover him. He must have been, they averred, "a sort of crank."

And in Malden, where authorities staged a parade to celebrate Cleanup Week and to encourage the lowly to pick up after themselves, with five hundred neatly dressed boys and girls in the line of march, rowdies along the route showered stones on the participants. The police contingent that led the parade never noticed what havoc was being wrought behind them until Samuel Miller of the Board of Health, along with the truant officer, and the superintendent of schools had all been felled by rocks and were stumbling along, disheveled, spattered with blood and mud, and ready for a thorough cleanup themselves. One battered marcher staggered in, clutching a soiled banner that inquired plaintively, "Is Your Cellar Clean?"

But spectacular drama and random violence were not the concern of the professional keepers of the public conscience. (Boston from its very birth had kept tithesmen who made it their business to see that the citizenry did not give over their idle time to wantonness. Mere lolling on a riverbank on the Sabbath, when a man should have been home digesting or discussing the sermon of the day, could cost a citizen of seventeenth-century Boston a handful of shillings or even a spell in the stocks.) Much of the watchers' and warders' time was devoted to investigating the hidey-holes where gambling flourished and where Vice—the name then used for unchurched sexual intercourse—might be savored. They discovered, for instance, that baseball pools were flourishing right inside the Boston Post Office, and they wrung from the authorities assurance that this villainy would be scotched forthwith by condign punishment of the clerks involved or even by outright discharge.

Ferrets of the Watch and Ward Society were prepared to make any sacrifice to build cases against transgressors. One day J. Frank Chase, secretary of the society, admitted to Judge Dowd in Municipal Court that he and a certain Miss Sterrett had, for a fact, registered as man and wife two weeks earlier at a Tremont Street hotel. Yes, he conceded, they had partaken of spirituous liquors at the Grotto of the Revere House and had then spent twenty minutes together in the room assigned to them. But all this was in line with

23

his duty "as a detective"—one, that is, who had undertaken to detect where sin was condoned and how it was purveyed. The directors of the society, he vowed, were all thoroughly conversant with the circumstances and the purpose of this masquerade, although not perhaps with all its intricacies. As for his having attacked, in the hotel lobby, the attorney who discovered him there, no such thing, Chase declared. He was not the sort to strike a man who stood with his hands in his pockets, as certain obviously biased witnesses had testified. Attorney John J. Cronin had pushed him and Chase had promptly and justifiably pushed back.

Sometimes it seemed there was simply too much ribaldry, revelry, and rowdyism in the secret places of the city for a handful of dedicated people to deal with. Nearly three centuries earlier an unregenerate and libidinous lot of young bonded servants had refused to follow Captain Wollaston to Virginia and chose to remain with one of Wollaston's lieutenants, Thomas Morton, to found their own community at a spot still named Wollaston. They called it Merry Mount, for they had vowed that there would be nothing but merriment in their lives for as long as the world should stand. They set up an eighty-foot maypole, shared strong drink with the red Indians, and (God grant them all forgiveness!) pranced about the maypole with their smallclothes untrussed in company with lewd Indian maidens. The whole convocation had been captured, fettered, and hauled off in irons by stern Miles Standish's armed minions and made to do penance past recollection. But surely some of their spawn must have persisted to infect the colony, for, throughout this end of the Commonwealth, and despite the vigilance of those whom the Lord had appointed to set their steps aright, young men like Babe Ruth could still be found who seemed bound to lend all their lives to merriment.

Babe moved through his own idle hours as if there was never any need to concern himself with more than lay within immediate reach of his arm. He felt no compulsion to learn anyone's name, for one companion was as good as the next as long as he belonged to the same club. "Kid," usually pronounced "keed," was his universal nickname for all who remained within his orbit. Some he might call "Doc." His steady playmates he eventually took to calling "Stud." He honored the bosses by addressing them by some sort of name, not always the one they would have chosen. General Manager Ed Barrow, whom most everybody called Simon (after Simon Legree), was Eddie or Manager to Babe. And there were all sorts of names for Babe, not all of which he delighted in.

One drizzly day as Babe was tooling his shiny Packard down Washington Street, he was hailed by a teammate who addressed him thus: "Hey! Two-head!"

Even though Babe did own a head about twice the size of a normal man's, he did not accept this name as a term of endearment. Without bothering to pull his car to the curb, Babe halted it right in the middle of the way, where it would tangle traffic in both directions, peeled a rubber off his shoe, leapt to the sidewalk, and went roaring down the crowded walk in close pursuit of his tormentor, waving the rubber aloft.

Babe's antics in Boston were not just the pranks of a rambunctious boy. As his income increased he began to widen his range, looking for girls and good times wherever they might be offered and scorning to waste his time on nickel-and-dime card games or on fishing trips into the harbor, pastimes that many of his teammates favored. Babe was not much of a man for fishing anyway, for he had a deathly fear of angleworms, or any wriggly thing, be it eel, leech, or caterpillar. One of Babe's teammates delighted to torture him by picking a fat night crawler off the outfield sod and dangling it in his face, then pursuing poor Babe all over the park, threatening to touch him with it. Nor were Babe's obscene howls of fear and anger mere playacting. He was scared nearly out of his shoes.

Now the top pitcher on the team, Babe still loved to hit the ball. Although pitchers traditionally were not supposed to clutter up batting practice for more than a few feeble swings, Babe used to stand in there, studiously fashioning his swing after that of Shoeless Joe Jackson, the Chicago outfielder. Joe's batting swing, Babe always held, was "the perfectest." So Babe would aim his right shoulder at the pitcher, haul his bat back and squeeze it tight, and work out different ways of getting his whole strength into his swing. Joe Jackson spread his feet wide but Babe found he liked better to keep his feet closer together, even to edge his right toe a little closer to the plate than the left one. Starting from this position, he could put just about the final ounce of his weight and strength into a full pivot of his body.

Babe's teammates did not approve of his crowding into their hitting time when nobody expected him to hit anyway. In his first seasons with the club, Babe more than once came back to the locker

25

room to find his bats had been sawed in half. But that just struck Babe as great sport and he diligently sawed all the other men's bats in half when he saw the opportunity.

Babe was no rube, to be cowed by petty hazing. He was tough and street-smart, quick to take up his own cause in any conflict. When the great Tris Speaker, during Babe's first full season with the club, undertook to put Babe in his place, Babe unleashed on Speaker a long list of obscene epithets, reflecting on his ancestry, sexual habits, and probable pastimes. Even tough Tris was shocked into silence and for many years he avoided exchanging much more than a grunt with Babe Ruth.

Babe was a city creature by nature, who took to crowds, noise, bright lights and late parties—all reminiscent of the Baltimore saloon where he had long dwelt so his father could "keep an eye on him." Early-morning bird songs along the Fenway were of less note to young Jidge Ruth than the rusty cries of the seagulls above the waterfront. No matter that many an impecunious Boston youth took his girl of an evening into the dark brush of the Fenway, Babe preferred a hot bed and lights and mirrors and noise and plenty of cold drink, and to hell with what it cost. He and his Packard were ready to rocket off in any direction in hopes of excitement.

The better Bostonians, old and young, some of whom would seldom wander more than a few hundred gentle paces beyond Louisburg Square, knew nothing at all of the Boston that Babe Ruth enjoyed. They made their annual gifts to the churches and the tight-buttoned charities and to the organized sin-fighters so that all flagrant naughtiness might be kept snug beneath the rug. Even the grown-ups of that day were as wide-eyed as children when they took note of the wickedness men were capable of. A few years earlier the papers had been filled with the details of the plot to do away with a New York gambler named Herman Rosenthal, and the names of the sinister characters hired to perform the deed had been on every child's tongue: Gyp the Blood, Dago Frank, Lefty Louie, and Whitey Lewis. These were more fearsome figures even than the whiskered bad men of the West and they exercised as deep a fascination. After the killers had been convicted and executed, a convocation of Congregational ministers in Boston invited the chief state witness, one Bald Jack Rose, a "reformed gangster," to come titillate their fancies with tales of that nether world where the Enemy held sway. Bald Jack urged them all to help improve the lot of men like himself by

26

making their religion "more human." Ministers generally, he observed, "are not, as we say in the underworld, 'good mixers.' " This firsthand savoring of the very jargon of the creatures who peopled the precincts of Sin sent most of the holy gentlemen home with their breaths still bated. And some of them may even have determined to walk down among the lost souls in Scollay Square—where sailors with empty purses and open hearts mingled with the men and women whose business was the leading of youth astray, and where, by dropping a penny in a slot and slowly turning a crank, a fellow could relish "moving pictures" of girls with hardly any clothes on.

But larger troubles were brewing than suggestive pictures or wicked books in lending libraries. The country, which had been flirting with war since early 1916 when it sent men down to Mexico under General John J. Pershing to deal with "bandit raids" (with siege guns? Carranza inquired) was girding itself now to cope with the mightiest military power in the world—the Austro-German alliance that had threatened to turn its submarine navy loose on any ship that dared carry supplies to the enemy. The declaration of war, long panted after by professional patriots like Teddy Roosevelt, seemed to unite proper and improper Boston in a common surge of devotion to the country's flag.

There had been an apparent eruption of fervid patriotism in 1916 when the Mexican expedition offered young men their first opportunity to bleed for their country since the bloody "pacification" of the Philippines. Sturdy ladies in low-heeled shoes had publicly offered their services then to help persuade the young to go riding off into the sands of Mexico. One wealthy lady had even led a small motor caravan all about Boston and environs beating the drums in a call to arms. While she drew a crowd wherever she stopped, there had been precious few of military age who had stepped forward to take Uncle Sam's shilling. (In another Mexican conflict, now long forgotten, Boston men who volunteered to go fight a feeble adversary to grab land we did not want had stones thrown at them by their neighbors.)

In 1916, there had even been a number of public voices who dared urge young men to stay home and not take part in the invasion of a ragged neighbor. Mayor Curley, shouting his message in a voice that would carry clear to the top of Beacon Hill, vowed that he himself would take up arms only if a few others went ahead of him.

"If there must be war," said Curley, "the Guggenheims, the Rockefellers, and the Weekses [of the Boston brokers Hornblower & Weeks] should be placed in the front row so that men who place a personal interest above patriotism will not be missed when bullets are flying. And when they are in the front rank, I will be willing to march in the second rank. Our duty is to remain true to the teachings of our fathers and keep the flag unsullied by dishonorable invasion." Anyway, Curley wondered out loud, how did we know this so-called bandit Pancho Villa was not in the pay of some United States citizens to whom war would mean increased dividends?

There was no dishonorable invasion in the offing in the 1917 war. And the plain people of Boston (except for those recalcitrant Irish patriots who would always think of England as an enemy rather than an ally) had become sufficiently incensed over the "inhumanity" of the Germans (now universally identified as "Huns") as to burst into wild cheers when the ringing of bells indicated that President Wilson had finally acknowledged a state of war between the United States and Germany. Young men of draft age, however, nursed many private misgivings. Not all thirsted to have at the Hun, and a good number, including many baseball players, hastened to find jobs in "essential industry" where they could ride out the war without danger of having their precious hides punctured. One young Bostonian, whose peaceable nature had persuaded him that there was no cause worth murdering people to sustain, applied for deferment on the grounds that he practiced an essential profession, that of poet. And it was as a poet that Conrad Aiken, rather to his own surprise, was declared safe from the draft.

Babe Ruth, being married, was counted ineligible for service too, although not all draft boards agreed that married men without children should stay home just to keep their brides company. Babe, for whom the world began afresh each morning, bore no grudges against Huns or Hungarians, or even Austrians. He did not know how to spell "Kaiser," had not read anything about the *Lusitania,* and could not have told you who was on which side in the war anyway. Although, like most healthy young delinquents, Babe was always quick to offer a man who offended him a punch in the nose, especially if the man were not quite so big as Babe, he was basically peaceable, good-natured, and deeply immersed in his own affairs. Bombs bursting in foreign air made no more impression on him than the signs in the subway. And organized baseball, in our first year of the war, seemed hardly affected. The players, carrying their bats like rifles, each had a drill sergeant to teach them squads east and west, but then so did the boys in all the grammar schools thereabouts. A few baseball stars volunteered for military service. And Babe Ruth, like other married men, joined the Home Guard and wore a soldier suit for a while. But generally the clubs played on undisturbed for that first full summer.

Babe Ruth was earning $5,000 a year now, which made him, he thought, a rich man. Who but the rich ever earned a hundred bucks a week? There were days when he could hardly believe his good fortune or contain his delight at finding himself in possession of all the dollar bills in the world. He bought whatever he wanted, traveled wherever he pleased, and stayed out all night sometimes just trying to spend what he had in his pocket. Meanwhile he was leading the Red Sox in a vain struggle for another pennant, by his hitting as well as his pitching. He won twenty-four games, best on the club, but he could not match Eddie Cicotte of the Chicago White Sox, who won twenty-eight. Ruth did hit .325, however, the best average of his career so far.

There were many in Boston, as all over the land, who had been calling for war ever since the *Lusitania* had been torpedoed two years earlier by a German submarine, just as she had apparently found shelter under the outreaching arm of the Royal Navy, almost within sight of the Irish coast. Hardly anyone noted, or even believed, that according to her manifest the British ship had been carrying 5,471 cases of ammunition and 280,000 pounds of brass and copper wire, along with another $66,000 worth of military goods, which made her fair game, regardless of how many innocents had paid passage on her. The German embassy indeed had warned passengers before sailing that the ship was sure to be attacked and Captain Fritz von Papen, military attaché to the Embassy, declared that it was absolutely criminal for the Cunard Line to carry neutral passengers on a ship loaded with munitions of war.

But editorial writers in Boston as well as New York ridiculed such warnings, as did Captain W. T. Turner, master of the *Lusitania,* and several of the famous passengers, most of whom received personal telegrams urging them to cancel passage. Alfred Gwynne Vanderbilt, discussing his telegram, had flung it back over his shoulder, saying it did not frighten him in the least. Elbert Hubbard, then the favorite sage of middle-aged schoolteachers, "self-made" businessmen, and Boy Scout leaders in Boston, had had to secure a Presidential pardon to permit him to travel abroad. (He had pleaded guilty to using the mails to defraud and had lost his citizenship thereby.) But now that he had the pardon and a passport, he was not to be deterred. "Another of the Kaiser's little jokes," said he, as he flung his telegram aside. And Captain Turner laughed aloud. "I wonder what the Germans will do next," he said. "It doesn't look as if they had scared many people . . ."

They certainly had not scared Charles Klein, a wealthy American playwright, who was off to London on the *Lusitania*. "I'll spend my time on the ship thinking about my new play *Potash and Perlmutter in Society*," Klein vowed. "I haven't time to worry about trifles."

Besides, everyone had been assured, the *Lusitania* could outrun any submarine in the world and would be protected by the all-seeing eyes and all-encompassing arms of the Royal Navy, ruler of the seas for more than two centuries past. But the great ship alas could not outrun a torpedo. She was making twenty-one knots when the first one struck her. With a heavy list to starboard she plowed on through the seas. A boat filled with women and children was lowered on the port side and was immediately smashed against the hull, dumping all it carried into the sea. Still there were those on board who could not believe so swift and stable and solidly appointed a vessel could ever go down. It would be like seeing a skyscraper crumble when hit by a stray bullet. Passengers who had gathered along the port rail to watch the second lifeboat launched—successfully this time—accepted the reassurance of a ship's officer that the *Lusitania* would soon right herself; of *course* her builders would have given her watertight compartments that would work to correct the list. A few of the passengers started to make their way over the steeply slanted deck toward some sort of shelter. Then, within seconds after that reassurance, the ship rolled on to her side like a murdered whale and started her final plunge, nose first, into the deep. Hundreds of passengers, some already in the sea, were pulled down with her. Many popped quickly to the surface after she had gone, and held themselves afloat by grabbing life rings, oars, bits of splintered plank, and all the buoyant odds and ends that had broken free from the decks.

But Vanderbilt and Klein and Hubbard and the theatrical manager Charles Frohman and more than a thousand others were lost. The outrage in New York and Boston and the other Eastern cities seemed likely to bring on war at once. A few young men, impatient with the government's failure to seek immediate revenge, promptly volunteered to fight in the Canadian or the British Army. Billy Sunday could express himself only in language he had forsworn. "It's damnable! Damnable!" he cried. "Hellish!" Billy was even saddened by the loss of Elbert Hubbard, a man he had listed as one of the country's "famous infidels." "Too bad! Too bad!" Billy exclaimed. "He's been fighting me. But I hate to think of him out on the cold cold ocean!" Others in high places named this killing of unarmed civilians "war by assassination!" It was impossible for decent people, many proper Bostonians held, to think of the Germans as civilized at all after this. No Christian surely could ever condone the firing of torpedoes on men, women, and children who had no means of defending themselves.

But the world then was so full of a number of other things that most of the citizenry through the next two years settled for acts of "preparedness" like recruiting "civilian soldiers" to go take military training at Plattsburg, New York, and sending our armed troops into Mexico to make sure no man was made president there who was inclined to render "insults" to our flag.

The reversion to the public use of strong language was not confined to Billy Sunday alone. One of the first effects of the war upon the good people of Boston was the sudden relaxation of certain moral standards such as the rule against printing or uttering words like "hell" and "damn" where they might assail the eyes and ears of women and children. When war came, a motion picture dared flaunt on its marquee the title of a new film called *To Hell With the Kaiser!* Even decent people in Boston hastened to view it and solemnly endorse its sentiments. This was war, after all.

The old ladies in black gowns who had just a year earlier visited Boston schools to give out little buttons with Liberty Bells on them and sign boys and girls to a pledge to avoid tobacco in all forms and especially to grind beneath their heels any cigarettes they might find lying unattended—they were shoved aside and forgotten as proper mothers actually urged their little ones to contribute to funds that would supply to Our Boys the Sweet Caporals, Perfections, Camels, and Fatimas they craved. (The WCTU did rather feebly urge that books be substituted for tobacco in soldiers' "comfort kits.") Just a short time before, when children in all the schools were singing "Pack Up Your Troubles in Your Old Kit Bag," they had not been

31

allowed to learn the original line "While you've a lucifer to light your fag." Instead it was rendered in Boston and environs, where it could never be granted that a cigarette fiend could be a hero: "While the Stars and Stripes are waving o'er your head!"

Males who were subject to the draft, and who could not find openings in the shipyards or other exempt industries, stampeded to the Navy recruiting stations. One of Babe Ruth's teammates sought help everywhere in landing "a yeoman deal" in the Navy, where he might sail the bounding main with a fountain pen in his hand or a typewriter in his lap, and never a chance that a hot shell might come bearing his name. The Navy, however, after recruiting several good baseball clubs to build morale in the naval bases, shut off recruiting and left thousands of would-be sailors out in the draft.

But draftees, according to Brigadier General John A. Johnston, were volunteers in spirit. There had been some talk at first that the drafted boys might have to wear blue shirts to distinguish them from the khaki-shirted volunteers. General Johnston assured Boston parents that there would be no such discrimination.

Pacifists were damned throughout the city as traitors and friends of Kaiser Bill. The Reverend Edward T. Sullivan, rector of Trinity Church, Newton Centre, declared that if the pacifist idea of Christianity were true, "then it is a poor religion for a red-blooded people! The Old Testament is full of wars. The way in which Christ spoke of soldiers showed the respect He had for their calling. War may be evil, but it is also a remedy . . ."

People with yards big enough were urged to plant vegetable gardens; public land was plowed up so food might be grown to feed the hungry armies that would soon be advancing our flag over the face of Europe. A clutch of teen-agers caught throwing stones at passing trains in Somerville were sentenced, with the consent of their parents, to pulling weeds in the Somerville Disciplinary War Gardens. British "kilties"—who were known by the Germans, the newspaper legend had it, as "Ladies from Hell"—were called in to recruit soldiers on Boston Common. (They collected 1,353 men, and rejected 261 as medically unfit.) And Harry Kaizer of Boston received the court's permission to change his name forthwith to Harry King.

Speaking of names, there was some shaking of heads in South Boston, Roxbury, and other parts of the city when it was learned, in July 1917, that the Sullivans, for the first time since one man had mentioned the matter to another, were outnumbered in the Boston city directory by the Smiths. And the Murphys, God help us, were dropped now to third, with the Browns and the Joneses close up and the Cohens, of all people, not far behind.

Bostonians generally made every uniformed man welcome, no matter what name he bore, counting any man a hero who wore his country's blue or khaki. But it was not all beer and skittles for a soldier or a sailor there. It was not beer at all, for that matter. Saloons were forbidden to serve strong drink to any man in uniform, no matter what his rank, so thirsty sailors and some soldiers roamed the midtown and Back Bay streets like castoffs on an island beach. One soldier from Brookline, Francis Connolly by name, grew so dry that he could no longer refrain from bursting straight into a Tremont Street café to demand a drink. When a bartender refused him, young Frank walked himself over to a nearby table where a young lady was drinking a Schlitz beer out of a brown bottle, took up her glass, and drained it before she could say him nay. When a waiter tried to shoo him off, Connolly drew his revolver and vowed he would blow a hole in the waiter's head. Then, holding the entire café at bay, Connolly backed out of the door in the style of William S. Hart escaping from a den of bad guys. But Connolly found that the few gulps of beer he had commandeered were not going to slake a thirst that had been so long abuilding, and in a few minutes he came back to the saloon and looked about for another prospect. The management, however, had already called the police and the law was there to lay an arm on Connolly and haul him off to the Roxbury Crossing station house, where he was laid away to be turned over betimes to the military police.

In general the war, in 1917, seemed great fun to the residents of Boston. There was the constant thrill of new flags flying day and night from every flagstaff. There were contingents of soldiery in exotic uniforms on the streets almost every week as fighting men came from France and England to stir the populace to buy Liberty Bonds. Every fence and every show window wore posters of Uncle Sam pointing a finger, or woebegone victims of aerial bombing begging for help, or even a statuesque and embattled Liberty in a clinging gown, summoning us all to cross the Atlantic and join the fray. That was the trouble with being all charged up with patriotism: there was simply no enemy at hand to vent it on. And there was even talk that the war might end before we ever got our licks in.

Corporal Henry Coombes of Dorchester wrote home from France

that the fighting would surely end by December. "We understand Edison has some wonderful inventions and Pershing is coming to try them out," Henry reported. Rumors of this sort lifted many hearts and set others wildly beating with impatience to strike a blow. Twenty-eight girls from the Shepard-Norwell stores, trimly turned out in khaki skirts and jackets, drilled every week with regular military rifles and no one to shoot them at. Roughnecks on the Common stood near the recruiting tent and accosted anyone of fighting age who failed to respond to the recruiting sergeant's call. One day such a commotion arose there that three hundred people gathered to discover what was to pay, or to lend a foot or fist to the ritual. What had occurred, the papers reported, was that two men, "a Syrian and a Socialist," had given the wrong answer when asked why they had failed to join the colors. Both were badly beaten and had to be rescued by the police. The Syrian, witnesses vowed, "had put one hand on his hip and threatened to shoot." As for the Socialist, he had started to "propound his doctrines" and had, so declared the young hoodlums who had attacked him, actually called out, "To hell with the flag!"

Insults to the flag were relatively easy to discover, particularly in the neighborhoods where men and women of German descent abounded. German barbers were all careful to wear small American flags in their lapels. And the hearty young men who just a few months earlier had been singing songs to the fatherland at Turn Hall, wearing "Kaiser flowers" (blue cornflowers) on their lapels, and solemnly proclaiming that the United States was being misled by British perfidy, were now earnestly declaring their own loyalty to the red, white, and blue and even kissing the flag when urged to do so by a crowd of self-appointed spy hunters. It was generally believed, at least among the youth of Boston, that a spy would never bring himself to kiss the flag, so saturated would his soul be with hatred for the symbol of the land he meant to destroy.

Baseball games looked tame indeed alongside encounters with enemies who could be not simply outscored but physically punished for daring to be what they were. And in the summer of 1917 there did come at last a chance for the youth of the city to strike blow after blow against a whole collection of live bodies who bore flags and signs that most men agreed were pro-German, or certainly anti-American.

On Sunday, July 1, the Socialist Party had scheduled a "great peace parade and demonstration" against the Conscription Act, to be held on Boston Common under a permit granted by Mayor Curley. The participants gathered in Park Square in front of the party headquarters, carrying banners and posters that declared among other things that "The Government Has Ordered 200,000 Coffins for American Boys" and inquiring, "A Six-Hour Day in Socialist Russia. Why Not Here?," or "If This Is a Popular War, Then Why Conscription?," and even suggesting that "War Is Hell. Jingo Capitalists Should Go to War." These obviously pro-German slogans enraged the uniformed soldiers and sailors who had coincidentally all gathered there at once, without a commissioned officer among them. The soldiers and sailors lined up across the square in company-front formation and a private led them in counting off. According to the newspaper reporter, whose own blood was obviously aboil with patriotism of purest ray, the men in uniform were calling out, in unpolluted Bostonese, "We will not let them cast dirt on the uniform of the United States!"

But Police Sergeant King of Station 4 pointed out to the servicemen that they had no parade permit and so must needs disperse. Disperse they did, trotting at double time past the assembled Socialists to the rear of the Hotel Thorndike, where the private in command had them all count off anew and led them in promising that they would halt the Socialists on Tremont Street. Said the private, according to the reporter, "Pull down all red flags. And be careful of women in line." (Among the demonstrators were 150 members of the United Mothers' League of Massachusetts.) But his orders must have got mistranslated along the way, for when the two groups ran into each other, the soldiers and sailors began clouting every jaw they could reach and even beating marchers over the head with the flagpoles they had wrenched from their hands. The small contingent of police "held manfully to their places," which were well in the rear of the marching Socialists.

Also on the scene were fifty agents of the Department of Justice led by Special Agent F. D. Schmidt. He had come, he announced, "to note any utterance against enlisting or in any way to be considered treasonable." And he did not observe, in all the fracas, anything to warrant immediate arrest for violation of a Federal statute. So the gallant young men dealt out punches right and left, and even pursued some Socialists and, after beating them bloody, forced them to come back, kneel down, and kiss the American flag, under which many of them had been born. As the row spilled into the Common, several of the British kilties—on hand to help drum up trade at the recruiting tent—joined in the fun and managed to discover a number of unprotected faces to punch. The police meanwhile, according to a reporter for the Boston *Herald,* who apparently owned a gift for divining motives, "seemed to regard the series of exciting events in the radiant light of patriotic principle, irresponsible but not particularly harmful."

The police did persuade the scheduled speakers of the day, James Maurer and James O'Neal, who had been waiting at the Parkman bandstand on the Common, to ask their followers to go home. Most of them did so immediately, but the servicemen and a horde of civilian volunteers were not ready to give over the joy of winning the war without danger of being shot at, so they pursued a number of stragglers across the Common and took turns knocking them to and fro.

Then the uniformed men formed a parade of their own, featuring the American flags they had ripped out of the hands of the Socialists. With several hundred civilians in their ranks and a scattering of small boys in their wake, they marched up Tremont Street, shouting to all who stood by, "Hats off to the American flag!" Any who failed to obey promptly enough had their hats grabbed off and thrown to the ground. Those few who resented this treatment, the *Herald* man proudly reported, "quickly gave in when two or three husky soldiers and sailors came running up." With patriotism thus deeply implanted in all hearts along the public way, the parade returned to Park Square, seeking whom else it might devour. There was one moment of dismay when the loud gong of a motorized patrol wagon sounded in the rear. A few civilians promptly ducked for doorways. But the police merely grinned at the marchers, who opened ranks and cheered as the Black Maria rolled through. Flushed with victory and righteousness, the paraders halted in front of the Socialist headquarters and responded to the call for "Three cheers for the United States and the Allies!" ("Allies" had become by this time a word signifying the fellows in the white hats; there was even a series of juvenile books starting in 1915 entitled "The Boy Allies.")

After the cheers had been duly offered, one of the parade leaders carried an American flag up on the statue of Abraham Lincoln and fastened the banner to Abe's skull. Then, inspired perhaps by the tableau that usually ended the show at B. F. Keith's, four men in uniform (the newspapers, using a fatuous nickname that never caught on with anybody, called them "four Sammies") took positions part way up the statue, clinging to Abe's arms and knees, and posed there, with right hands at salute, while the square gave out a roar of approval. But while this bit of theatrics held the attention of most of the crowd, there were a fervent few who had discovered heartier work to be done. Spying Louis Henderson, a Socialist leader, calmly surveying the mob from the open window in the third-floor headquarters and wearing a red tie, a number of patriots took instant offense. One of them hurled a splintered chunk of a flagpole at the window. It struck the lower sash within inches of Henderson's face and flew into the room, almost impaling another Socialist, John J. McGittrick. This was all the signal the uniformed crowd required to send them pell-mell up the stairs. Their first move was to thrust an American flag out a big center window, pushing it through the wire screening that partly protected the glass. Unable to get the flag unfurled, they drew it back and systematically knocked out all the screening. Other hands tore out any remaining screens and scaled them down into the square, where they threatened instant decapitation to any who failed to dodge. After the screens came fat bound copies of the Socialist paper, fluttering like tattered suicides to the paved street. Then armloads of pennant canes were flung out and after them the pennants they had been meant to hold, about three hundred triangular red flags. The soldiers and sailors grabbed frantically for anything that would come loose—metal music stands, leaflets, placards, books. One lad climbed to the windowsill and used the butt of a flagstaff to pry loose the sign that marked the place as the Socialist headquarters and to send it plunging to the sidewalk. One of the musicians who had been recruited to play at the Socialist meetings was laid hold of then and held up at the window, like an offering.

"My God!" someone screamed. "They're going to throw him out!"

There were howls of hungry approval mingled with the shrieks of dismay. But the poor man was merely required to set his cornet to his lips and play "The Star-Spangled Banner," which he did with great spirit, while the festering mob three stories below bellowed out the lyrics.

In the square, soldiers and sailors gathered up all the debris flung out of the Socialist headquarters and made a bonfire. The flames soon set fire to the oil-soaked wooden blocks with which the square was paved, and thick coils of black smoke fed into the open windows of the nearby Hotel Georgian. A Patrolman Hartigan, delighted to find some honorable work he could set his hand to without risk of having his flesh separated into bite-sized pieces, promptly pulled the fire alarm. A chemical wagon bulled its way into the square and put the fire out. After that the anti-Socialist army and navy withdrew from the field.

Before the square grew dark, however, the soldiers and sailors were back, bringing a hundred or so civilian assistants, in search of more sport. There was little left to do at Socialist headquarters except to smash the furniture and toss it out the rear windows, and throw down the back stairs a few Socialists who had come to measure the disaster. Then they took all the leaflets that were left in the offices and dumped them by the armful into the air until they had nearly carpeted the half-empty plaza.

By this time the police had run out of either patience or patriotic principle. A dozen helmeted cops, led by Sergeant King, trotted into the square and sent the soldiers and sailors flying. They flew, however, only as far as the Common, where to their ineffable delight they found a few Socialists still remaining, some with red neckties on, some with badges, and a few with red flags on their lapels. These they caught up one by one and dragged back to kneel and kiss the flag in public. One man who resisted, Morris Gilbert of Chambers Street, was hustled off by a squadron of patriots, shoved out of sight in the doorway of the Little Building, and beaten until he was nearly senseless. One or two others were taken off to one side and imbued with patriotism in like manner. Then the sailors and soldiers drifted off, with mess call on their minds, and let their victims crawl homeward or to a hospital, as they chose.

Park Square meanwhile had grown peaceful, with only an aimless throng of civilians wandering about to marvel at the mess that had been created. Nevertheless, about 6 P.M. a provost guard of thirty sailors, led by three commissioned officers and one petty officer and armed with rifles, bayonets, and rattling handcuffs, marched into the square, ready to put down a riot, protect all government property in sight, shoot down the massed enemy, stand guard over a pack of prisoners, or arrest a drunken sailor. But all they found that they could set their hands to was ridding the area of civilians, all of whom seemed merely idling there, offering no threat to the nation at all.

Nevertheless, the provost guard, rifles athwart their bodies, undertook to clear the streets of people, to what end not even history will ever recall. There was no disturbance, or any sign of one, until the armed sailors arrived, and then there were merely the outraged protests of the onlookers who were being herded out of the square. Newspaper reporters who hastened to the scene were themselves hustled out of the cleared area, where the sailors stood, with a medical officer in the center, flanked by two armed orderlies, apparently embattled and preparing to stand off a cavalry charge. "Is this martial law?" inquired one reporter. "And isn't that officer one of those ninety-day-wonders?"

The officer, a medical man named Duff, who had indeed been only three months in the service, threatened the reporter's arrest. A uniformed sailor leapt forward and dealt the reporter a wallop between the eyes, sending the man staggering. ("I thought he was a Socialist agitator," the sailor explained.) The newsmen then repaired to police headquarters to learn if the Navy had indeed taken over the policing of the town. But when they came back, armed with authority to stay within police lines, the provost guard had all marched back again to Commonwealth Pier, and the battle of Park Square was over.

Afterward, everybody in authority or partial authority had something to say on the subject. The commander of the Department of the Northeast, Brigadier General J. Clarence Edwards, contemplated no action until he was "further acquainted with the facts." Anyway, he volunteered, it was his understanding that the uniformed men had been National Guardsmen, not yet mustered into federal service. The Reverend A. Z. Conrad, of the Park Street Baptist Church, gave over his evening sermon to an appraisal of the conflict.

"God bless the soldier and sailor boys," he intoned, "who had the patriotism and courage to tear to shreds and make bonfires of the foreign and hostile flags carried in a parade through the streets of our city this afternoon. They did the right thing. They have the real fighting blood, and with such spirit as that they'll win the war in less time than it takes to tell about it."

But Mayor Curley, as was his wont, found ground of his own to stand on. He said the rioting seemed to have been "timed and planned" and had followed, with a closeness worth noting, a protest made to the mayor against the Socialists by a "State Street banker." The mayor himself had been away for the day, and in his stead Acting Mayor James J. Storrow had conferred with the police superintendent and had, Curley hinted, asked that the parade be stopped, even though Curley had issued a permit for the meeting on the Common.

In view of what had happened, would the mayor issue another permit to the Socialists? "I certainly would," said Curley. "I do not believe in stifling free speech." And to show how much he meant it, Curley promptly issued permits to the Socialists to hold meetings every Sunday throughout the year. "When free speech that is truth becomes treason," said Curley, "then this country will no longer be a republic."

Storrow vowed that he too loved free speech with all his heart, perhaps even more than the mayor did. But he had never, he declared, talked about Socialism to the mayor or to the superintendent of police or to anybody, for that matter. He had never even heard about the parade. All he ever did was tell the superintendent of police to arrest any man in the parade—if there should happen to be a parade, that is—who spoke out against recruiting.

Well, Curley elaborated, all he knew was that a certain rich man did pay him a visit and urge that all carrying of red flags and demonstrations by Socialists be stopped. "And I told him," said Curley, "that I was by no means in sympathy with the Socialists, that they talked against my religion, against me, and against the government, but I did not feel justified in suppressing free speech." The mayor added that he thought federal troops had been at fault. Oh, no! General Edwards insisted. They were all in camp, or else at the East Armory bidding farewell to friends. As for him, he would not tolerate any interference with the legitimate expression of public opinion.

And neither would John F. ("Honey Fitz") Fitzgerald, who had been defeated for re-election as mayor by Curley in the last election and thought he saw a hope of turning the tables next time around. Curley, said Fitz, in reasoned tones, is guilty of treason. If *he* were mayor, although he yielded to no one in his devotion to free speech, he would never permit a Socialist parade.

"Would it not gladden the heart of Emperor Wilhelm," Fitz inquired of the open air, "to know that his friend, Mayor Curley at City Hall, Boston, was going to permit again such a parade as we had

40

Sunday? When I was mayor a permit was taken away from a man who insulted the American flag!"

German spies, Fitz expounded, were to be found everywhere. They had even sent him threatening letters. "But that will not deter me," bold Fitz assured his audience, "in my effort to insure that America will remain unconquered!"

The ringing echoes of this pledge were still echoing over the Common when Curley hurried back to the batter's box.

"The only individual anxious to suppress the truth or restrict free speech," said Jim, "is one whose acts, public and private, will not permit of thorough scrutiny. . . . The frothing of a certain person on Boston Common last evening was not directed at me personally . . . but with a view to stifling free speech in general as a measure of protection from the truth. . . ."

His Honor, who had beaten Fitz in the previous election partly through judicious exposure of Fitz's relations with a bounteously endowed young lady named Toodles, as well as his recounting of the padding of the city payrolls with friends and relatives of the Fitzgerald clan, then swung for the seats.

"I am preparing," he went on, as a grin began to grow on his face, "three addresses which, if a certain individual had the right to restrain free speech, I would not be permitted to deliver. One of these addresses is entitled 'Graft, Ancient and Modern.' Another, 'Great Lovers, from Cleopatra to Toodles.' And last, but by no means least interesting, 'Libertines, from Henry the Eighth to the Present Day.' "

Poor Honey Fitz was reduced to spluttering: "I do not see how anyone can expect me to answer such a wild, crazy, irresponsible statement!"

All this—riots, arguments, wars and rumors of wars—was just so much wind in the willows to Babe Ruth. Babe saluted the flag and vowed that, despite his ancestry, there was not a pro-German corpuscle in his veins. He was winning baseball games and hitting the ball more often. ("I may be a pitcher," he told a fan, "but I'm more of a hitter.") He was also suffering from an injured foot, and every time he thought of how he injured it, he let out a long list of his favorite expletives, none of which would ever be found in a Boston dictionary.

It had happened when he was visiting, in company with teammate Hal Janvrin, the country estate of a wealthy fan who liked to gather up ballplayers. Janvrin, poking through the gentleman's barn, had come upon a top hat which he plopped upon his head, found it fitted, and kept it there. This irritated Babe beyond all reason. "Take that goddam thing off!" he told Janvrin. It may be that Babe, in his new role as a baseball hero, felt that a childish caper of this sort belittled him. Janvrin, hopping just out of Ruth's reach, kept the hat firmly on his head. Babe then started after him in earnest, while Janvrin, who had the speed of an antelope, fled across the cow pasture. Babe, soon far behind, kept calling out threats to demolish Janvrin and hat together. Then Hal, having got momentarily out of sight in a hollow, spied a rock small enough for the hat to cover. He set it there and waited nearby for Babe to catch up. Babe, plunging along like a bull, spied the hat and put his full strength into a mighty kick meant to drive it out of bounds. The howl when Babe's toe hit the rock caused cattle to lift their heads in the next county. It was several days before Babe could walk without limping.

The Chicago White Sox won the American League pennant that year of 1917, so there was no World Series in Boston. There was talk for a while of a "city series" between the Braves and the Red Sox, but no public clamor developed to urge this and the rival managers just tossed the decision back and forth until it was too late to play baseball. Once the season was over, baseball players began to yield to the draft or to patriotic urgings, or even to the popular disdain for "slackers," and pledge their lives to the service of Uncle Sam. Babe watched many of his teammates take up arms or at least associate themselves with rifles and cannon. Dick Hoblitzel, the first baseman; Jack Barry, the manager and second baseman; Herb Pennock and Ernie Shore, the pitchers; Duffy Lewis, the left fielder; utility man Del Gainer; Chick Shorten, the substitute outfielder; and Pinch Thomas, the second-string catcher, were all in uniform before another season could begin, while Larry Gardner, the third baseman, had been traded off to Philadelphia along with center fielder Tilly Walker. It hardly seemed the same club. Yet Babe, who probably could not have told you the names of all those who had left, felt no pangs. None of his girls had been traded off, nor had any of his favorite sporting houses closed down for the duration. Jack Barry had simply switched to running a ball club at a nearby naval base and no teammate had yet faced hot gunfire.

The war, however, had begun to lose some of its glitter, at least to Boston's poor families and to those whose sons had landed in

France. The first "engagement" of the American Expeditionary Force was a baseball game on French soil. But after that the troops moved into the trenches, to sample the mud, the body lice, the deadly boredom, and the occasional blind terror of modern warfare, which offered no cavalry charges, no ringing trumpets, no glorious planting of the flag on enemy ramparts, no flashing uniforms, no heroic tableaux. And the people at home began to feel the icy edges of one of the most bitter winters in memory, when coal was hard to come by, when more than one poor family tried to suck heat out of burning bundled newspapers, when good white bread was gone, and the black victory bread had to be smeared with margarine that was largely suet, colored at home to look like butter by kneading in a small capsule of coloring matter enclosed in the package.

The sight of healthy young men drawing inflated wages in shipyards while playing baseball much of the time, and of various sons of riches putting overalls on to play the part of laborers in essential industry, prompted some random gripes. Edward F. McGrady of the Lynn Central Labor Union told his members angrily that "rich slackers are flocking to the shipyards!" Men of wealth and political influence, he complained, were finding exempt jobs for their sons while skilled shipwrights were turned away from the job lines. But hardly anyone had time to cultivate any indignation on that score. The better folk of Boston were more impressed by the news that J. G. Phelps Stokes had given up his trifling ways—had resigned from the Socialist Party—because of the party's refusal to take a stand for democracy and against autocracy, a stand, that is, in favor of the war.

The shortage of men to fill menial jobs, the steady upsurge in prices of everything from straw hats to beefsteak, had made for a general uneasiness among some sections of the laboring classes. The waiters in Boston, timing their move to coincide with a convention of the Benevolent and Protective Order of Elks, walked suddenly out on strike, demanding one day off in seven—a bit of heresy in the hotel and food trades, where it was generally agreed that inasmuch as meals had to be served every day regardless, only the boss could take time away from the job. But the waiters quickly won their strike, there being no pool of jobless to dip into to find strikebreakers. And Local 34 of the Waiters Union, flaunting their new contract that guaranteed them thirty-five dollars a week in wages, plus a day off every week (which was more than a policeman had), celebrated their victory and consolidated their strength by voting to admit black waiters to full membership, to work under exactly the same conditions.

In most areas of Boston life, black men were usually patronized as being either childlike or too happy-go-lucky to deserve a full place in the ranks of the town's solid citizens. They were expected meekly to accept epithets like "darky" or "coon," although the favorite sidewalk term for black men and women among the middle and poorer classes in Boston then was "dinge." By whatever name they might be designated, it was always a term that clearly implied their position a step or two down the ladder of social position, of intelligence, of education, and of abilities. No one in authority would have dreamed of suggesting that blacks be offered equal status in the Army or the Navy or even in the shipyards. Their lot was to fill the service jobs, to do the distasteful labor, or to provide amusement to the better folk.

There was not an amusement park or a circus in that era that did not feature an "African Dodger," who would poke his head through a sheet of canvas so that white men might shy baseballs at him—not solid regulation baseballs, of course, which cost a dollar and a quarter each, but the "nickel rocks" that were available at every five-and-dime. Hardly anyone ever protested the degradation and cruelty of this amusement: It seemed the natural lot of a race that most people agreed owned harder heads than other men and had been put on earth to serve the whites. In this late summer of 1917, an African Dodger was arrested on a drunkenness charge at Revere Beach, where he was employed. He was so far gone in drink that the police could not coax a name out of him. But they recognized him as one who was so adept at ducking thrown baseballs he was known as "Last Possible Chance." Local ballplayers had often used him as a target in showing off the accuracy of their arms. Naturally he was jailed for his overindulgence, then handed back to the amusement park when he was sober.

Nothing, however, took place in Boston to equal the contemporary horrors in St. Louis, where white men and women turned on the local blacks like enraged animals, yanking black women and children off trolley cars to beat them in the street, grabbing black males in broad daylight and hanging them from lampposts while the police stood safely out of sight. One black man, begging for his life, was hoisted to a lamppost on a flimsy rope, which promptly broke, dumping him in the gutter. His captors then simply pumped him full of revolver bullets as he lay there, then hurried off seeking fresh game.

The motive for all this was supposed to have been, originally, resentment on the part of local white laborers over the importation of black workmen from the South; unions generally were blamed for the horror. Indeed, at a labor meeting in New York, Teddy Roosevelt shook his fist in the face of Samuel Gompers, then head of the American Federation of Labor, and warned him that "we must first cast the beam of racial violence out of our own eye."

The black people insisted however that they had not come North on the lure of steady work but to escape the lynchings, which the war spirit had seemed to inflame. And union leaders generally disowned the rioters, who were indeed somewhat less concerned with attacking "cheap labor" than simply terrorizing all blacks to make certain they would never forget "their place."

Mob violence in the South, as in Boston, was not reserved for blacks. One man who, having already donated to the Red Cross solicitor in the hotel lobby, turned down a Red Cross solicitor in the hotel restaurant, was set upon as he walked to the street, beaten, trussed, soaked in tar and feathers, tied to a fence rail, and paraded out to the city limits.

Babe Ruth had grown up with the same prejudices as practically all white working-class males in Baltimore. But, because he had supposedly come out of an orphan asylum and never bragged about any earthly parents, a legend was established that he was illegitimate. It followed logically that his wide-nostriled face would earn a suspicion that there might have trickled a trace of African blood in his ancestry. Enemy ballplayers soon discovered that Babe deeply resented any such imputation, it being generally agreed that any man guilty of owning black forebears was unfit company for decent people. So certain opponents, bent on upsetting him, took to calling Babe "nigger" on the field. This drove him once to the point of invading an enemy locker room seeking vengeance. He desisted only when he was accused of staging the whole show for the benefit of the sportswriters. Inasmuch as the part of a "showboat" was equally demeaning, Babe earnestly begged the writers, whose presence he really had not noticed, to keep the whole affair out of print. Then, his anger cooled, he plaintively granted the opponents the right to call him all kinds of a bastard, son of a bitch, and more obscene epithets—as long as they did not become "personal."

The language of the locker room in World War I days lacked the ingenuity and the breathtaking obscenity of that exchanged in to-day's baseball clubhouses. But even in Puritan Boston the ball-players, out of the hearing of the female and the young, larded their discourse with phrases as ripe as any then current in the trenches. A man who had got himself into an incurable fix was casually diag-nosed as "up shit creek"; and a whole generation before the acro-nyms SNAFU and JANFU had been conceived, a ballplayer whose head was in a whirl might be described as "all fucked up and bewil-dered." A coward was freely characterized as having "shit in his neck."

The pastimes of the Boston locker room were relatively tame, however, largely because alcoholic beverages were forbidden. But at least one poker game grew too hairy for Manager Bill Carrigan. It started on a rainy afternoon when the players were waiting for the skies to clear and it went on and on through the night and into the next day, with left fielder Duffy Lewis winding up "losies" by $4,000—far more than he ever could or would pay. Carrigan there-upon set a twenty-five-cent limit on future stakes and outlawed all the debts.

It was Babe's misfortune that his appetite for strong drink had just begun to flower when wartime prohibition made all but thin beer dif-ficult to come by. But ballplayers, like everyone else with a thirst, soon discovered ways of supplying themselves with spirits. In the beginning, it was just a matter of getting at the tremendous stores of good whiskey and gin that lay under bond in the warehouses. With a quart of good whiskey in hand and a supply of "neutral spirits" such as were sold to druggists and others who had need to concoct various elixirs, a man could make himself at least a full gallon of passable whiskey to be sold by the pint. John F. Fitzgerald's older brother Tom, who operated a drugstore on Atlantic Avenue, used to employ young men to go to doctors seeking prescriptions for whis-key to deal with a common cold or a cough. For each pint prescrip-tion he put in his file, he could legitimately remove a pint of the whiskey he was permitted to keep on hand. He would take that down cellar and, with neutral spirits, distilled water, and perhaps a few drops of glycerin or other "beading mixture," would soon concoct a half gallon of potable and intoxicating beverage that could still be sold as whiskey, at a breathtaking markup. Brother Tom soon presided over one of the busiest drugstores in town.

Soon after the baseball season was done, the war began to bite deep into the lives of most people in Boston. Rationing added gloom to nearly every life, as bacon, sugar, butter, white bread, lard, and even beef and pork began to diminish in supply. Carpers were told that all these good things were being reserved for "the boys in France." But the boys in France received precious little of the stores of such stuff that were being laid away in the States. Instead many staples were simply held off the market by the sort of men that old Bostonians used to call "forestallers"—people who bought up goods and held them off the market to drive the prices up. In colonial days they had been scorned by decent folk as men who never did a day's honest work and were even haled before a court and fined. In World War I they became known as "profiteers"—as were all those who jacked up the prices of the goods they manufactured or the services they performed—and they lived out their days, after the war was safely over, in comfort and ease, despite the fact that Senator Charles S. Thomas of Colorado had urged that food speculators, at least, should be lynched.

Prices of all things edged slowly upward as the war grew older. Even the trolley fare was raised from a nickel to six cents. Chicken had jumped to thirty-five cents a pound, so Boston restaurants began to ring in "bob veal" (calves slaughtered too young) to cut up into salads and call it chicken. Sugar was selling at eight cents a pound, more than double what New England housewives were used to paying. Citizens were urged to keep their furnaces cold until November to conserve fuel. Many poor families had no choice, for what coal could be bought by the bagful was usually pea coal, too small to use in a furnace.

But Mayor Curley was able to arrange a bonanza for all the plain people of Boston when he discovered that the United Fruit Company was about to dump at sea a whole shipload of bananas that had ripened too fast because of faulty refrigeration. Food Administrator Herbert Hoover, warned by Curley of the company's plan, ordered the fruit distributed to the needy. The company thereupon called on everyone in town to come to its pier and carry away all the bananas they could lug. Every soldier at Camp Devens, in Ayer, was awarded a dozen. Boston citizens swarmed to the pier with baskets, pushcarts, wagons, suitcases, and burlap bags. A few even drove buggies in to fill them full. After almost everyone in the city had taken his share, there were still tons of bananas left over. The government chemist ordered that they be taken out and dumped in the sea for the fish to grow fat on, for they were fast growing into an offense to the public nostrils. This time Jim Curley let them go.

It would have taken more than a few tons of bananas to lift the gloom the winter cast over Boston. What with crowding the whole family into the kitchen to use the stove for warmth, riding in heatless trolleys to work on the Blue Mondays decreed by the government, using molasses (which turned coffee green) as the only breakfast sweetener, and trying to pretend that the "victory bread," which tasted like dried grain middlings mixed with clay, was wholesome and good, it was hard to find cheer in talk of glorious victories ahead.

The war news was gloomy anyway, for the German armies had begun to push closer and closer to Paris. Men and women everywhere might interrupt their work to study war maps that showed how the bulging German "salient" had edged even closer to its goal. Still, no one talked of defeat, for the United States had *never* been defeated, and to utter defeatist thoughts aloud would have been pro-German in the extreme. Indeed, even to talk of peace was counted treasonous. An essay by Hermann Hagedorn suggesting that there were kindly people in Germany who also wanted peace was suppressed in a Boston school. There was even a sort of grim pleasure in making the sacrifices, in bearing the bitter cold and the tasteless meals for the sake of victory, and to ensure that the gallant boys who carried our flag might experience no lack of good things to eat.

The better (i.e., the richer) people of the town, who suffered hardly at all from scarcities, found many less weighty matters to divert their minds than a shortage of flour. (Julius H. Barnes, head of the grain corporation of the Food Administration, declared there was "no shortage" but "plenty of flour for all!" He had hardly uttered the statement when the mills in Minneapolis began to close for lack of wheat.) In Boston, there was much concern over the establishment of a shoeshine parlor run by girls, who dressed in Turkish costume of short jacket and billowing trousers. Mayor John F. Fitzgerald, who had indeed beaten Curley by dwelling on his rival's "friendship for Kaiser Bill," urged the city council to close the place. It was demeaning to women, he said, to engage in such duties, and a man who would let a woman shine his shoes should be ashamed. The ladies of Beacon Hill, however, who had long been distressed at their maids' refusal to black boots for house guests, thought it might set a useful example, and in any event it was no more denigrating than the sight of women in overalls working the farms while the harvest hands were off to war.

When spring came in 1918, the poor people of Boston had begun to learn at firsthand something of the hunger and personal tragedy that wars traditionally bequeathed to those who fought them. The glorious victory of Belleau Wood in June, where American Marines had lost the battle yet won the ground, was in fact a slaughter, so hideous that even German machine gunners had held back for a time, unwilling to cut down more ranks of men so foolhardy as to walk erect into point-blank fire. It was here that Americans discovered they could no longer march into battle in company front, with flag-bearers going on ahead, but must needs burrow into the ground and crawl and leap and scamper in open order from shelter to shelter. And it was here that some of the first Boston boys fell dead. As the summer grew older, boys were also shot dead or mangled by shellfire or had their lungs seared by poison gas in such strange places as Montdidier and Saint-Mihiel and the Argonne Forest, where Allied and German generals flung their troops at one another by the hundreds of thousands to gain or regain title to a few thousand yards of devastated ground.

Throughout the tightly settled parts of Boston, in Allston and Roxbury and South Boston and Mattapan, where tottering frame houses were often bolstered by brick tenements or three-decker wooden apartments, there were gold stars in many windows, and there would be many more before the leaves began to turn. Still the war seemed glorious and full of gallantry to those who merely read about it or heard the speeches that were made to encourage men and women and children at home to put their money into Liberty Bonds, or buy thrift stamps and War Savings Stamps at school.

The "Work or Fight" orders that were issued by General Alvin T. Crowder, who had charge of manpower, made it seem doubtful that baseball would be played at all. Even Ty Cobb, who had just signed a lucrative contract with a St. Louis brewer to sell some type of "soft drink" in the South, felt constrained to accept a commission in the Chemical Warfare service after vain efforts to land a job in a munitions factory in Connecticut. He left for France convinced he would never play baseball again, if indeed there was any game to play after this long, long war was over.

Baseball did continue through most of the summer of 1918, however. General Crowder allowed it to go on provided the season was ended on Labor Day. This short season was the best Babe Ruth had so far enjoyed, for he led the Sox to another pennant and, when he was not pitching, was allowed to play left field or first base, and so swing his bat at all sorts of thrown balls. He had a new manager this year, for Jack Barry, who had taken Bill Carrigan's place for just one season, had joined the Navy. Edward Barrow, who took over for Barry, was a man with an eye for a good hitter and a determination to get as much power into the outfield as he could, even if it meant overworking the club's best left-handed pitcher. But Babe did not count batting as work. He relished the chance to make believe he was Shoeless Joe Jackson at the plate and to drive baseballs as far as they would go. He was particularly happy at batting high in the order—fourth, fifth, or sixth, where he would usually come to bat more often.

For the first time, that year, Babe Ruth became the most famous ballplayer in town. He won 13 games as a pitcher, out of 20 that he worked in. But he did his best work as a hitter. In 317 times at the plate, Babe made 95 hits for an average of an even .300. He made 26 doubles, 11 triples, and 11 home runs. His home-run total equaled that of Tilly Walker, his former teammate who had been traded to Philadelphia. Together they led the league in homers. It was Babe's first time on top in that department. There were eleven seasons to come when he would lead the league in home runs all by himself.

There was much restlessness that wartime summer among the men who worked for wages. Profits of the steel manufacturers, the shipbuilders, and the makers of shoes and uniforms mushroomed so suddenly that even the owners of the businesses were taken unawares and often found themselves hard put to find hiding places for all the cash. Cost-plus contracts in certain industries enabled men to find jobs that had hardly any work to them, just the task of staying out of the foreman's sight during the day and showing up on time in the morning. But generally, working people were urged to make sacrifices, to match those required of the men in the services. Working families forgot the taste of butter. New York milk dealers threatened that if they were not permitted to charge twenty-five cents a quart for milk, they would send their cows to the slaughter-house. So milk too was often denied the poor.

When the time came for the World Series to begin in 1918, the Boston ballplayers were already fretful, not merely at the manner in which the cost of living had left their paychecks behind but also over a new scheme for dividing up the players' share of the gate receipts. This season, for the first time, part of the players' pool was to be shared out among the members of the clubs in both leagues that had finished in the first division—second, third, and fourth place, that is. In addition, the players, before they had time to assess the meagerness of the receipts, had agreed to donate 10 percent of their take to war charities.

The Series was scheduled to be played in two sections—three games in Chicago and three in Boston, to save using the trains more than necessary. Rain held up the beginning of the Series, and when it did begin, hardly anyone in Chicago seemed to care if their Cubs beat Boston or not. In anticipation of a large crowd, the Cubs' owner had moved the Series from his own little park (capacity 20,000) to big Comiskey Park. But on the first day, fewer than 20,000 showed up. In only one game out of the three played in Chicago did the crowd exceed that figure.

The players took out their gripes on each other for a time, bumping the enemy on the baselines, coming up from slides with fists pumping, aiming baseballs at each other's heads. But by the time the clubs had returned to Boston and the Red Sox had a 2–1 lead in games, the players were seething at the owners. They had been growling all the way to Boston on the train on Sunday. Why the hell, they wondered aloud, couldn't the clubs have scheduled a game for Sunday in Chicago, where Sunday ball was permitted, and where a decent crowd might have turned out?

After the Red Sox had won the first game in Boston, before another medium-sized audience, the players decided to turn against the common enemy. In a long conference preceding the fifth game, the players of the two clubs agreed to ask two things of the National Commission, which ran the Series. Either the plan of cutting the first-division clubs into the players' pool should be postponed until after the war or the players should be given a flat guarantee—$1,500 for the winners and $1,000 for the losers. If the commission would not agree, the players would not take the field. Two of the commissioners, August Herrmann and John Heydler, listened glumly to the players' complaints as presented by Harry Hooper of the Red Sox and Leslie Mann of the Cubs. But they could not, they insisted, make a move without consulting the third commissioner, Byron Bancroft ("Ban") Johnson, president of the American League.

On getting word of a players' strike, the Boston police chief sent in a call for reserves. "Strike" and "riot" seemed like synonyms to Boston minds in that period, and so more than a hundred uniformed police were soon on hand to "keep order." There was plenty of order but just no baseball. The crowd of nearly twenty-five thousand began to stir and grumble and ask each other questions. But no fists were raised nor bruising objects thrown.

Mayor Fitzgerald, always quick to put himself into a position to get his picture taken or his name in the papers, entered the clubhouse and set out to persuade Hooper and Mann to lead the players on to the field. But the players would not move until Johnson appeared.

Johnson had been delayed at the Copley Plaza Hotel, where he and two friends had uncovered a store of contraband whiskey. Ban had taken aboard a good deal more of the stuff than his friends had, and when he came at last to the dressing room he had a tight grip on the shoulders of the two men with him. Otherwise he surely would have fallen down.

Without an ounce of comprehension, Ban listened to Hooper and Mann. Hooper made a new offer from the players—let everybody, including the owners, give up *all* receipts from the Series and turn the entire pool over to the Red Cross. Heydler and Herrmann must have turned white at that suggestion. Their take had been cut down enough, they felt, when they failed to raise the price of admission for the Series. To give *all* that nice fresh money away! It was atheistic!

Then as now, it was always the working athlete who was deemed to have "an obligation to the fans," and Honey Fitz urged this consideration upon Hooper and Mann—but not upon Herrmann and Heydler. One doubts that, had Curley still been on the job, he would have neglected to point out the inequity of asking professional ballplayers to work for cut wages while the owners' percentage was undisturbed.

Hooper and Mann were steadfast against the honeyed talk of Honey Fitz. But they did not know how to deal with Ban Johnson. He lurched toward them and got both arms around Harry Hooper, as much out of a need to steady himself as out of affection. "Harry, old boy, old boy," he babbled. "Whyn't you stop all this and play ball? Huh?" He went on about his deep love for them all and how wonderful they all were and how wonderful were all those wonderful fans. When Hooper tried to repeat the players' proposals, Ban would have none of them. It was all just noise to him as he recounted again his unplumbed devotion to good old Harry and everybody else in the room.

Hooper looked helplessly at Mann. Mann shrugged. How the hell were they going to talk sense to this guy? So they gave it up and went out to play. And Honey Fitz strutted out to home plate (amid a small scattering of boos) and announced, just as if he had done it all himself, that the players had agreed to play, largely for the sake of the wounded soldiers in the stands. (No one had mentioned them before.) This brought cheers and handclapping and the game began an hour after the scheduled time.

The Cubs won the game and then the Red Sox won the championship on the day after. There was really not much stir in Boston at this event. Many fans were in France or in the military camps, and most of the people left behind had their minds elsewhere than Fenway Park. Babe Ruth's winner's share of $1,018 did not overload his pockets. But he had less to gripe about than some of his teammates. He had been paid $7,000 for the short season, more than he had ever earned before in his life. He had a new contract coming up and he was dreaming already of salaries with five numbers in them. And the thought of being able to bat every day instead of every fourth or fifth day filled his soul with delight. He had also begun to savor for the first time the inexpressible joy of being young, rich, famous, and free of all the restraints that circumscribe the celebrations of common folk. He frequently stayed out all night, ate and drank as much as his appetite told him he could hold, and set out often to help himself to almost any qualified female who came within his reach. He never knew a hangover, never felt sick, and arose each forenoon as fresh and full of vigor as he had been the day before.

In November, after the World Series was long forgotten, the war was over. The plain people of Boston had not been privy to the maneuvering that brought on the armistice, had seen the surrender of Bulgaria on September 29 as but the first step in a long road of conquest, and had indeed, some of them, even looked forward to a triumphal march across Germany, to bring the horrors of war to the

Hun, to capture vast stretches of enemy acreage so that the salients on the map would dig into Germany rather than France, and to corner the Kaiser and the weak-chinned Crown Prince and hang them both to a tree. So the armistice burst on them like an explosion in a silent church. In response the citizenry exploded too, in such a wild tumult as the city had never known in all its history.

All the church bells rang, yet hardly anyone could hear them, so deafening was the uproar from the streets. Whole families, on hearing the news shouted by newsboys or by passersby, hastened to load themselves into trolleys and gather at the Common to give themselves to unrestrained rejoicing. There were horns and whistles for sale at every corner, yet the buyer of a whistle could set it to his lips and blow and not know at all if it was even making a noise, for the screaming, the hornblowing, the sounding of klaxons, the twirling of rattles, the beating of tin pans together so submerged all individual sounds that there was no picking out any single strand of noise. People who stood next to each other for a moment must needs shout into each other's ear. Sailors on shore leave flocked more plentifully than the pigeons to the Common, where it soon became the sport of the day to come up behind a sailor unawares and send his round hat flying off his head, so that it would roll like a barrel hoop on the pavement. In response the sailors set out to grab all pretty girls and kiss them. And some girls grabbed sailors and kissed them back. "The war is over!" strangers screamed into strange faces, and the strange faces would scream it back until it blended into the wordless racket all around: "The WAR is over! The WAR is OVER!! The God damn War is OVER!!"

But the war was not really over, for there was still a bitter reckoning. The influx of ships and men and goods from foreign soil had brought along—whether first to the west coast or to the east, who could say?—the germs of the Spanish influenza that spread through the big cities as swiftly and insidiously as an underground flame. Boston had known epidemics before. (A little more than a year earlier, hundreds of children had died or been crippled when infantile paralysis swept the state.) But there was something especially treacherous about this new disease. For one thing, it would seem hardly worth taking seriously at the start, just a form of cold in the head that set one's eyes to watering and nose to running, with an accompanying small fever that would cause ringing in the ears. Many victims tried to keep working while they were ill, dosing themselves with sugared whiskey, cough drops, or carbolated Vaseline. So death came quickly to many who had hardly had time to count themselves sick, and who indeed had barely taken to their beds. Families found themselves one day catering to Mama's cold and the very next day standing stunned around her deathbed.

The crowded Army camps, filled with young men just awaiting demobilization, offered the ripest fodder to the plague. In them, young men who had blessed God for sparing them died every day, with no trumpets blown or shots fired, and their bodies had to wait their turn for the caskets that were in such short supply.

For the civilians there were hardly any doctors left to deal with the disease. Those whom the war had left at home were soon half distracted from working through the day and night. There was not much they could do for the victims but to cope with the symptoms, try to keep the fever from raging too high, try to restrain patients in their delirium, try to force fluids down gasping throats. In the poor neighborhoods women who stayed well would adopt all the neighboring families and go from house to house, to keep sickrooms clean and babies dry, to make meals and put the garbage out.

There were not nearly hospital rooms enough to house all the hundreds whom the disease had struck, so barracks-like buildings were erected in open spaces all in and around the city, manned by volunteer nurses and attendants, who would hasten up and down the bare corridors in gauze masks, like creatures in a horror movie. Out in the streets and on the streetcars too, men and women wore gauze masks over mouth and nose, in hopes of filtering out whatever animalcules there were that could bring humans down in this manner.

More people put their faith in horse chestnuts, which they pierced and hung about their necks on string as a talisman to ward off the plague. Others, who scorned such superstitions, still wore small camphor bags about their necks to cleanse the air before they breathed it.

But nothing availed. The Spanish influenza seized all it could lay hold of and killed a large share of those. Then it petered out like a rainstorm and left the city to count its dead.

But the end of the flu epidemic brought little surcease to the sidewalks of Boston or other great cities. Prices crawled upward day by day, as the speculators held tight to all the good things they had been able to get hold of. Sugar became rarer than good whiskey, something to be kept under the counter and provided only to favored customers. (This practice was outlawed by the authorities but it proved impossible to police.) Families that had been wont to buy sugar in ten-pound sacks or even in barrels found themselves begging to get hold of a small paper bag holding one pound. Clerks who measured the sugar out were required to do so while holding each bag over the barrel, lest even half an ounce escape. Before the war was forgotten, sugar would reach twenty-seven cents a pound, and a few men would grow indecently rich from having had the foresight to hoard the stuff.

Popular songs after the war dealt with hard times. "Bring back the milk without the water!" one song prayed. "Bring back the dinners for a quarter!" And a favorite everywhere was, "Not much money,/Oh but honey,/Ain't we got fun!"

There were no hard times for Babe Ruth, however. Having won two World Series games in addition to leading the American League in home runs, Babe in 1919 decided he was ready for the big time. And that meant $10,000 a year, a figure that would have spelled success in those days even to a college man bent on forging ahead in business. Owner Harry Frazee of the Red Sox, whose chief interest was the theater, vowed that no ballplayer alive would ever get that kind of money from *him*. Why, he wouldn't give that even to the finest actor in his whole troupe! But Babe held out that spring and seemed likely to sit all of 1919 out before he'd play for less. Finally Frazee offered him $9,000 and Babe accepted it. He could always pick up a few thousand more on "endorsements." (Before the season was over, and while Babe was hitting home runs at a rate unprecedented in professional baseball, Frazee gave him a new three-year contract at $10,000 a year.)

Even actors began to grow restless at the speed with which living costs were causing their supposedly lavish salaries to shrink. (Sirloin steak, which had sold for thirty-five cents a pound before the war, now brought seventy-five cents, while rump steak cost eighty. The Boston *Herald* suggested that such prices were the fault of soldiers who had learned to "spend money like water overseas.")

In September an actors' strike closed all the Boston theaters. It had begun when a representative of Actors Equity had come to the Tremont Theater just a few minutes before the curtain was to rise on *See-Saw,* and talked a seventeen-year-old chorus girl named Kathleen Carroll into walking off the stage. The refusal of one actor to report for work gave legal justification, under their contract, for the stagehands to walk off too.

But the veteran producer Henry W. Savage, who was putting on the show, was damned if he would allow this. When Kathleen told him she was walking out, he first argued with her, then followed her on to the stage-door alley and called a cop.

"Arrest this girl!" he shouted.

The policeman, seeing young Kathleen standing all peaceful and polite and pretty, wondered what on earth the charge might be.

"She's walking out of my show!" Savage explained.

Well, the policeman offered, there was nothing much he could do about that. She was a big girl, and she could walk where she wanted to. So off she walked and the entire complement of stagehands soon followed. Before the week was a day older, the stagehands everywhere were out and actors had joined them. The theater managers filed suit for $150,000 against Actors Equity. The truck drivers then refused to haul the property of the shows that were leaving town. Thereupon the theater managers gave in and actors and stagehands celebrated a victory.

This minor triumph may have helped persuade the policemen of Boston, who had been quietly forming themselves into a union, that the temper of the times was favorable to their cause. Working conditions for the police in 1919 were almost antediluvian. Men who manned patrol wagons put in fourteen hours a day seven days a week. No policeman, according to the rules, had more than one day off in fifteen. Night men worked eighty-three hours a week and day men did seventy-three hours. Actually their hours at the station house were often even longer. Men would report there at 6 P.M. and remain "off duty" in the guardroom until 9 P.M., when they were supposed to go to sleep. At 12:30 A.M. they went out on street duty and stayed there throughout the night.

But the cops had more gripes than merely long hours. They could see no call for putting ten to fifteen officers on duty at a band concert in the Common. Least of all did they see any need for using uniformed officers as newsboys. Yet a number of captains sent patrolmen every day to go gather seven or eight copies of each newspaper from the newspaper offices as they came off the press and then go deliver them to the captain's friends, including former Police Superintendent W. H. Pierce.

Police pay did not compare with a ballplayer's, nor even to a bookkeeper's. A patrolman started at $21.09 a week and after six years he could attain $30.68. The cost of his uniform and equipment ($207.25) came out of his pay. Living conditions in the station house were no better than those in the city jail, and perhaps worse. In five station houses, where 125 men worked, there were four toilets and one bathtub to serve them all. Mice in the station houses ate the leather off policemen's helmets. Bedbugs and cockroaches were so abundant that the policemen often brought home live samples in their trouser cuffs. On their one day off, policemen were not allowed to leave the city limits without the superintendent's permission. And if they had gripes, they had best not offer them in too loud a voice. They did have the right to elect in each station a "grievance officer." But the captain always counted the written ballots in secret and gave out the result himself. The cops were never surprised when the man "elected" was one that none of them had voted for.

Their only recognized organization had been a "social club" that was allowed to approach the commissioner within arm's length at least. But after thirteen years of dealings between social club and commissioner, there was not a cop alive who could recall that any good came of it. So they had turned at last to unionization, with Patrolman John F. McInnes the head of the union and a sort of hope that they might connect themselves some day with the American Federation of Labor.

But Police Commissioner Edwin Curtis vowed he would have no truck with any union of cops; indeed he would get rid of the whole lot of them if they had the face to come to him with any "demands." If a patrolman had a gripe of some sort, he could open his mouth and say so. But there'd be none of this union stuff as long as *he* was commissioner.

After a few angry statements back and forth, Curtis declared a truce of sorts to last over Labor Day. But there'd be no giving in. The police, who had been asking improved working conditions and recognition of the union, never mentioned more money. But they did, almost in one voice, promise that if, after the truce was over, a single union leader was "even reprimanded" they would walk out on strike.

So, once the truce period was over, Commissioner Curtis suspended every last mother's son who had named himself any sort of leader in the Police Union. And the policemen, steamed up by this time into a sort of fury, all began at once to pack up their duds and carry them out of the station house. The strike vote was 1,134 to 2.

Former Superintendent of Police W. H. Pierce, the very man who had had his morning and evening papers carried to him by trained policemen, had been recruiting a force of volunteer police to go on duty in the event of a strike. But when the strike came there were not volunteers enough to man a lifeboat. The Boy Scouts did help out in directing traffic. And one fourteen-year-old with a white handkerchief tied about his arm won cheers for his work in keeping traffic moving at State and Devonshire streets.

But traffic was the least of it. Once it was certain the cops had gone off the street, boys and young men, bent merely on raising hell, formed into a sort of parade, along with a crowd of sailors, and began to march up and down Tremont Street, between Boylston and School streets, brushing aside the few park department police who had volunteered to keep order, yelling and gathering up bricks and stones. Before long they began to shy a brick or two through shop windows, to see what might come of it. One man fired a revolver into the air. When the Devil failed to pop out from under a rock and snatch them all away, the mob grew bolder. Once a window had been smashed, they piled in to grab all the goods within reach. They paraded down to Washington Street and found a richer harvest. But at Hanover Street two police sergeants carrying revolvers drove them back and sent them scattering. They reassembled, with a hundred new recruits, in Haymarket Square and continued to smash any window that looked inviting. The United Cigar Store at Washington and Friend streets was cleaned out of cigars, cigarettes, pipe tobacco, plug tobacco, and the previous day's receipts.

Elsewhere in the city, other small mobs, often including sailors—who of all servicemen were the most short of cash—invaded shops one after another. The stores on Court Street were not only stripped bare of goods but completely wrecked inside and out. A new march began in Scollay Square, where every window was broken that held a display of goods. This crowd, again with a heavy sprinkling of uniformed sailors, flowed down Hanover Street like kids celebrating a football victory. A few pedestrians who happened to stand in the way were knocked down and roughed up. At Devonshire Street the crowd spied a fruit stand and they made for it with howls of delight. But a few dozen stout Italian neighbors armed with broomsticks and God knows what stood them off. So they contented themselves with breaking all the windows in the shop of Arthur E. Dorr, a meat wholesaler, where a night watchman carrying a gun kept them from getting inside.

Nearby was another cigar store. This they smashed into and looted of tobacco and cash. They visited the Puritan Clothing Company, bursting through broken windows and smashed doors to outfit themselves helter-skelter with suits, hats, shoes, neckties, shirts, and underwear. Many marchers, loaded with loot, quit the party right there and hurried home to revel in their new wardrobes.

At this point, six police sergeants in a motor patrol climbed out with drawn revolvers to face the crowd. The marchers were momentarily halted but they did not disperse until Superintendent Michael H. Crowley and a parcel of uniformed inspectors reinforced the sergeants and indicated their resolve by firing six revolver shots into the air. With that, the youths all fled in a body, breaking windows even as they ran and taking a few moments now and then to snatch a fur coat or a necklace or half a dozen watches out of a show window.

It was going-home time for office and shopworkers now, from those shops that had dared remain open. The crowd, broken into roving bands, took to laying hold of random pedestrians, backing them against walls and rifling their pockets. All along Washington Street men stood helplessly against the buildings while two or more thieves lifted their watches, wallets, and stickpins.

As dusk came, a group of sailors undertook to complete the work that had been begun in Scollay Square. Moving gaily yet methodically from door to door, they smashed every unbroken pane of glass. This sport soon attracted a crowd of more than a thousand, who thundered along the midtown streets at a dogtrot, tossing bricks and occasionally cleaning out a partially looted window. (The next day, one clothing store posted a sign urging those who had taken any clothing to bring it back and exchange it for the right size. No one accepted the invitation.)

In South Boston, the whole area seemed to boil over as soon as evening came close. Men and boys, gathering from every alley and side street, rallied together as they had not done since young roughnecks, in 1770, ran through snow-covered Boston streets at dusk, calling "Town-born, turn out!" This time, instead of mobilizing to take vengeance on arrogant British lobsterbacks, the mob was bent on squaring the score with the strutting bluecoats who had been wont to keep order by batting wrongdoers in the face with their fists. They gathered outside the police headquarters to watch the cops walk out on strike and they yelled repeatedly for Patrolman Florence O'Brien, who had taken punches at many a citizen, to show himself and take his chances without his gun and club.

But Patrolman O'Brien was off on vacation and all the game they could find was one Patrolman Downey, who came out of the station burdened down with a pasteboard box full of his extra clothing. He had hardly set one foot on the sidewalk when a stone knocked his helmet off and sent it bouncing along the street. Downey promptly set his box down and made ready to fight off the whole lot, but before a blow could be struck, a squad of cops rushed out and helped Downey push his way to the streetcar stop. A Patrolman Eaton came out alone soon after and got himself a handful of fresh mud in the face. He had no more than wiped that off when a new lot struck in the same spot.

With the cops gone out of the station house, the mob looked for new sport. They began to throw stones at passing trolley cars that bore folk off to the fancier sections of town, and then to yank the trolleys off the wires to halt the cars altogether. The frightened passengers piled out and scurried off this way and that, with no one offering to halt them. A few police sergeants appeared now and commanded the peace, but the front rank of the mob promptly pulled the spare tires off an automobile and scaled them at the cops. A delivery wagon carrying fresh oranges and apples and other goodies was hailed like a long-awaited ship and quickly relieved of all its cargo, while the driver ran off and left his poor horse to tend for himself.

In those days it was a simple matter to make off with an automobile, for many of them had merely to be cranked up to get them started and those that had self-starters had only a little metal key that was usually left in place to turn on either battery or magneto. So the South Boston boys made off with some twenty standing vehicles and no one ever did find what had become of them. Fire alarms were pulled so often that the fire bells were sounding without letup, yet nary a flame was found. The South Boston crowd just stormed about the neighborhood, yelling, throwing random rocks, and occasionally breaking a window or pushing down a fence.

Next day, what the young men of Boston seemed to want to do most was play dice games in the open air. Every narrow street that led off Washington presented a dice game of its own, with players and spectators jamming the way right to the building walls. A number of pedestrians who dared walk the midtown streets openly carried guns or clubs—just as citizens, during the time when King George's 29th Regiment patrolled the town, carried short clubs or swords to protect themselves from "insult." But most violent crime seemed to have subsided, with stores boarded up and laced with barbed wire, and private guards with revolvers showing themselves in many doorways.

One man who stopped at a guarded cigar store to get a cigar, leaving his panting new Buick at the curb, came back with his cigar and found he no longer had a Buick. And a few shots were fired, with no injury done, by store guards warning "suspects" off. Federal property was all guarded by armed soldiers or sailors, who had orders to shoot anyone who made as if to trespass. More volunteer police appeared on the streets, and were quick to brandish their guns at any who failed to give way. But most of the "crime" now consisted of the dice games. Still, no one was inclined to open his store up in these circumstances, and not many women, nor many men, dared walk the streets unarmed. The park police and the volunteers, added to the sergeants and inspectors, made hardly a patch on the body politic, and, to hear the rumors that ran about the city, there were thugs from everywhere racing by train and motorcar to come help pick the city clean.

Ex-Mayor Curley showed up on the second day and stopped his car at the corner of Washington and Bromfield streets to address a crowd of nervous citizens. The city had a new mayor now, named Andrew Peters, but he had been off taking his ease somewhere when the cops had been negotiating with the city. Any man, said Curley, who was collecting the sort of salary Peters was getting ought to stay on the job and earn it. With that, Jim Curley jumped back in his car and sped off, going the wrong way on a one-way street.

Peters was on the job now, at any rate, and he was not letting any moss gather on *his* shoes. Ultimately, Governor Calvin Coolidge would get the credit, and the political advantage, for calling out the troops to save the city. But it was really Mayor Peters who did it first, and Coolidge who pushed the mayor aside and took over. First, Peters called Assistant Secretary of the Navy Franklin D. Roosevelt to see if there was not some pretext under which a provost guard from the Navy yard could be called out to patrol the streets. But Roosevelt, in a ten-minute discussion, could come up with no solution. Then Peters, acting, he said, under Section 6, Chapter 323, of the Acts of 1885, took over the Police Department, superseding Commissioner Edwin Curtis. He promptly called out the 10th Regiment of the State Guard—the Boston regiment—and called on Governor Coolidge to send in more troops. Coolidge, who had made a speech at Plymouth on Labor Day to the effect that the property-owning class and the wage-earning class were one and the same, and that "all of us must work and there must be no interruption," made himself "unavailable" for forty-eight hours, no doubt biting his knuckles as he tried to decide if he dared leave the Boston property owners to the mercy of the wage earners. He soon made up his mind that it was he and not Peters who should be playing the part of strong man. He ordered out the 11th, 12th, and 15th Regiments, along with the 14th Machine Gun Company. All evening long, men in civilian dress gathered at the armories to be mustered in, while crowds of young men pelted them with rocks and trash. Then, within minutes, they came out again as troops, all uniformed with bayonets fixed, and the crowds scattered.

At this juncture, Coolidge superseded the mayor as head of the police department and, as commander in chief of the State Guard, took over all law-enforcement authority in the city. Commissioner Curtis, who had threatened to resign when Peters superseded *him,* now declared he would stay. And Peters angrily charged that Coolidge had been blaming *him,* the mayor, for the violence. I never said any such thing, Coolidge responded. But Peters would not believe him. And more than one person insisted that if the damned commissioner hadn't been so stiff-necked in negotiations, if he had yielded even half an inch, the walkout could have been avoided altogether.

Now there was talk that the men of the Boston El, who operated trolleys on the streets and in the subway as well as the elevated trains, might walk out in support of the police. And the Central Labor Union was still muttering about closing the whole city down. But the state troops were busy now striking terror into the hearts of all the local rowdies. Their first act was to fire into a disorderly crowd in South Boston, killing a sixteen-year-old boy and a twenty-four-year-old man and wounding nine others. State cavalrymen with drawn sabers charged into the crowd at Scollay Square, sending them all scrambling and hacking wildly at any heads within reach. They managed to kill one man in the melee.

After this, the state troops turned their attention to the open-air dice games, which, to tell the truth, usually drew more spectators than players. But the leaders of the State Guard vowed to wipe them all out. Two Guardsmen first attacked a giant dice game in Jamaica Plain, trotting up to it with bayonets fixed and ordering all the spectators and participants to surrender themselves. According to one newspaper, the dice players scorned this order and "put themselves in an attitude to fight." The fact is that they all ran like hell. Who but a madman would set out to "fight" with his fists a pair of armed soldiers? The two Guardsmen called on the scattering crowd once more to halt, and when they failed to do so they both fired. Four men were killed by the two shots, including teen-aged Carson McWilliams and Henry Grote. One man, who halted when told to but did not exhibit proper respect, had his jaw broken by a rifle butt.

The major dice game in town was that played on the Tremont Street mall of the Common. There must have been hundreds of males crowded around there to watch the dice roll out. The Guardsmen came upon the scene quickly, scaring off all but the tight inner core of the crowd, surrounded the game, and ordered all present to raise their hands. One man who was slow to get his hands up was belted with a rifle butt. The soldiers then arranged their captives in ranks and marched them all off. Kids who had stood in the offing immediately descended on the scene and grabbed up all the money that had been lying in the pot.

One man was killed in this engagement, an eighteen-year-old merchant sailor named Raymond Barnes. He had tried, the soldiers reported, to lead a fight to rescue one of the prisoners. One of the Guardsmen knelt down, took careful aim, and shot Barnes through the neck. He died a few moments after reaching the Relief Hospital.

In court, the soldiers were unable to identify a single prisoner as having been engaged in gambling. They had brought in forty-three men and one pair of dice. The court dismissed the charges. But one man who had simply refused to move on when the Guardsman had told him to, and who had struck back when the Guardsman hit him with his rifle, was sentenced to sixty days in jail.

In the midst of all this, the Boston Lunch Associates published a rather plaintive ad, protesting against a contemplated strike by its own workers. "Lunchroom employes," they explained, "work nine hours daily and have one day off a week." But Boston citizens soon had more on their minds than the petty woes of the men who ran the restaurants. The crap games were off the streets and back inside the private clubs and bowling alleys, where they belonged. Guardsmen in pairs, along with a scattering of volunteer police, appeared at every corner. Beer had grown thinner and thinner until it was not called beer anymore—just Bevo, or some such nickname to indicate that its alcoholic content was not worth measuring. (Former Secretary of State William Jennings Bryan, long an advocate of abstinence and promoter of grape juice as a substitute for wine, took public satisfaction in making it known that within a year, when the alcoholic content of beer would drop to less than half of 1 percent, "a man will have to drink 25 gallons of water to get enough alcohol to get drunk.")

The policemen now were talking about coming back, it having become obvious that the great majority of their neighbors blamed them for the vandalism, the thefts, and the killings. Samuel Gompers, who had stood ready to welcome them into the A.F.L. and had made as if to back their strike with sympathetic walkouts, now urged them to return and asked Coolidge to accept them. Coolidge, who personally opposed any reinstatement, told Gompers it was up to Commissioner Curtis—the man whose hard-nosed attitude had brought about the crisis in the first place. Curtis promptly declared that all the men who had held leadership positions in the union were now discharged. The police, still nursing hopes that there might be other strikes to support them, said they would come back only as a union. So they did not come back at all. And Coolidge, assured now that the electorate was at his back, sent Gompers the message that eventually was to earn him the job of President of the United States.

"There is no right," Coolidge declared in a telegram that someone wrote for him to sign (people came to recall that Coolidge had made this statement at the very moment he called up the troops), "to strike against the public safety by anyone, anywhere, at any time."

As he sent this slogan echoing down the corridors of history (where politicians in later ages would try, often disastrously, to adapt it to some confrontation of their own), he suddenly assumed the role of a strong, silent, and indomitable foe of all the hideous forces that had secretly arrayed themselves against the state. Hardly anyone ever remembered afterward that he was actually a mild, garrulous, small-minded, easygoing little sandy-haired fellow who had got ahead in the Republican Party by doing exactly as he was told. When his name was first mentioned at the 1920 Republican convention, Massachusetts newsmen laughed aloud.

But the country yearned for tough-talking leaders then. It was obvious to men in every cigar store that the real danger to the stability of the economy came from those agents of Bolshevism who were bent on luring America into the very abyss that had just swallowed the Russians up. Senator Henry L. Myers of Montana, making public note of all the talk of strikes, in steel, on the railroads, and even in the Post Office, declared that Congress had the clear duty to put a stop to the growing unrest. The Boston police strike, he warned, would, unless crushed beneath the heel, lead to a Soviet government in the United States "within two years."

And Attorney General Charles D. Newton of the state of New York interpreted the Constitution thus: "To permit foreigners or anyone else who enjoys all our privileges to stand on a street corner and indulge in disloyal utterances against our government is not free speech in the accepted sense of that term. To permit them to do this is simply to connive at treason and sedition. The framers of our constitution never contemplated tolerance of seditionists and disloyalists."

This sentiment, which might, had it been translated into Russian, have served as a toast at a birthday party for Josef Stalin, actually assumed the force of law throughout our nation in that era and for decades to come. Meanwhile the seditionists and disloyalists who had framed our Constitution slumbered on in the delusion that they had set their ideas down in language so simple and clear there would never be any disputing them.

On the fields of friendly and unfriendly strife, there were also great deeds being done in 1919. Jack Dempsey, having broken the jaw and the heart of the Texas Giant, Jess Willard, on the Fourth of July, now declared that he would take on Fred Fulton, the American challenger; the French champion, Georges Carpentier; and Joe Beckett, champion of Great Britain—all at the same time in the same ring. And Babe Ruth, going to bat in every game, was closing in on the home-run record set by Gavvy Cravath four years earlier—twenty-four in a single season.

Police strikes, Prohibition, the high cost of living—these meant nothing now to young George Ruth. He could hardly move about the streets of Boston without half a dozen admirers close on his heels. Whatever he might choose to do or wherever he might decide to leave his automobile, not even a State Guardsman would say him nay. Babe could find liquor to drink wherever he wanted it. But the fact is, he was never a confirmed boozer even in his thirsty youth. He took more to beer than he did to whiskey. And often as not he liked to combine girls with champagne.

Still, Babe's manager, Ed Barrow, could not see how any man could stay out all night and play nine innings of baseball in the afternoon. So he set out one time to lecture the whole club, in the seclusion of the locker room, on the importance of keeping regular hours. Except for Babe, there was no one on the club at the time who was abroad much past the curfew, so as Barrow went on to detail what sort of wickedness had been going on, the other players began to grin at Ruth. But Ruth was damned if anyone was going to label him a dirty stay-out-all-night. He stood right up in the meeting and told big Ed Barrow that by Jesus Christ if any of this horseshit was aimed at *him,* he'd be glad to close Ed's mouth for him by flattening his nose down over it.

The clubhouse fell silent as a schoolroom (of those days) might have done if a sixth-grader had sassed the teacher. Ed Barrow nodded. He stood up and asked quietly if all the other players would be good enough to leave the room. Then, he allowed, he would find out how close Ruth could come to shutting his mouth for him. The players scrambled for the door. And Babe, who had stood for a moment waiting for his threat to take hold, turned and scrambled with them. He was not the first man out, Ed Barrow reported, but he was not the last. Maybe about the fifth.

That was Babe all over, as the current phrase had it. He would talk as tough as any man alive, and tougher than most. But he was not a fighter. He wanted people to like him. He was truly repentant if he ever did another man an injury. And he was as reluctant as the next man to get his face dented by an angry fist. So he and Barrow promptly made peace, with Babe promising that he would stop at the hotel desk every night and leave a note marking the time when he was on his way to bed. And so he did. And Barrow, who had paid a hotel employee to report the time of Babe's return each night (on one occasion Babe came in at 6 A.M.), stopped spying on him and made believe he took Babe at his word.

By mid-September, Babe had broken Cravath's record, with twenty-five home runs. Then someone noted that Buck Freeman of Washington had made twenty-five in 1899. Babe broke that record too. Then the record readers found that Ned Williamson of the White

Sox had hit twenty-seven home runs in 1884. Actually this was not a comparable mark at all, for the game being played in the 1880s was not the modern game of baseball. There were still pitchers in 1884 who tossed the ball up underhand (even though a "shoulder-high" delivery was permitted that year). Batters could call for a high or low pitch. And it took six "wides" or "balls" to give a man first base free. (A "wide" was called when the pitcher failed to deliver the sort of ball called for.) The pitching distance was only fifty feet. And the baseballs varied widely in liveliness, there being no uniform source of supply nor any standard ball.

Still, Babe was happy to have another mark to aim at. By this time, the city fathers had decided it was time to offer some official recognition to their young Goliath, or someone in the Knights of Columbus so decided and talked the city council into it. So September 20, when there was a double-header scheduled with the Chicago White Sox, was named Babe Ruth Day and fans were urged to come out and do public honor to the man who was making Boston a byword across the nation. The fans responded in such numbers that they overflowed the stands and had to be accommodated partly in the outfield, in front of the right-field bleachers. Here they were restrained by a rope and stood guard over by a complement of State Guardsmen. And the size of the crowd, as it turned out, actually cost Babe a home run.

Babe pitched the first game and won it. During its course, with the fans beseeching him to tie Williamson's record, Babe drove a long line drive into the right-field bleachers. It struck the sunbaked boards with a ringing whack, somehow missing all the packed bodies there, and bounced back on to the playing field among the overflow crowd. By the temporary ground rules, a blow into the crowd was worth only three bases. The umpires saw only that the ball landed in the crowd, and they stopped Babe at third base. The uproar that ensued might have made men wonder if the police-strike mobs hadn't broken loose again—except that the State Guardsmen joined in the protests. Indeed, so incensed did some of the soldiers become that they passed a petition throughout the bleachers, for witnesses to sign, to the effect that they had seen the ball land in home-run territory, among the seats. The umpire urged the soldiers to go back to strikebreaking and let him decide what was right and what was wrong on the ball field.

Then, in the second game, when Babe played left field, he came to bat with the score tied in the last of the ninth. Never before in recorded history had baseball fans so loudly begged one of their heroes to deliver a home run. But Babe was up against Lefty Williams of the White Sox, as mean a pitcher as lived, and hardly the man a left-handed batter would choose to face when he wanted to hit the ball a mile. There were two out and Williams was not about to lay a pitch in there where Babe could get solid wood on it. So Williams put a pitch right in on the batter's fists, where no hitter in the world could get any power behind it. Or no one could before Babe Ruth tried it. Babe not only hit the ball, he hit it to the "wrong" field—left field—and he hit it over the tence. Williams was really shaken at the sight. Even the enemy players joined in expressions of amazement. And Fenway Park rattled as it had never rattled before, with fans stamping, roaring, clapping, whistling, and jumping up and down.

Afterward, in the locker room, all the White Sox players, including Lefty Williams, came in to tell young George what a mighty deed he had done—driving a pitch from a *left*-handed pitcher over the left-field fence! But Babe, that spring, had performed what his manager thought was a mightier deed. In an exhibition game against the New York Giants in Tampa, he had driven a ball far far out over the head of Giant center fielder Ross Youngs. A Boston newspaperman had measured it and found that it had traveled 579 feet on the fly! Manager Ed Barrow always declared that *that* was the most miraculous blow Ruth ever struck.

Babe Ruth went on to beat Ned Williamson's mark with a home run in the Polo Grounds, New York, four days later. Again he did it in the ninth inning but this time with hostile fans daring him to try to hit another. Up to that point Bob Shawkey of the Yankees had not allowed a run. And no reformed pitcher from Beantown was going to make one now, the fans were confident. But Babe, who eventually made a habit of producing a long blow when it was most desperately needed, then hit one of the longest home runs of his career. There was a handy right-field stand at the Polo Grounds where, if a man could drive a ball close to the foul line it might pop into the stands on the fly, without much effort required. But the stands themselves were skyscraper-high and faded quickly backward from the plate. Shoeless Joe Jackson had once hit a baseball hard enough to land it on the roof of that stand, and fans had talked about that for months. But Babe drove the ball high over the top of the stand and it bounced free in a field across the street.

Now he owned the record for the most home runs *ever* hit in a full season in the major leagues. And he still had a few games to go. The Red Sox were not going to make it into the World Series. (The White Sox did and became the Black Sox when they took money for losing the Series on purpose.) But in the days remaining in the season, Babe found time to add another home run, to make it twenty-nine, a mark all knowledgeable fans agreed would probably never be equaled, not even by Babe himself.

Babe was in love with Boston now. He could not walk through a restaurant door without having total strangers hail him. The new crop of policemen—mostly war veterans, younger, leaner, and more alert than the potbellied crew who had walked out on strike—were every bit as inclined to bend the city statutes in Babe Ruth's favor as the old-timers had been. The supply of willing young ladies, despite the sudden replenishment of the store of young males as the soldiers returned from France, gave no sign of diminution. So nearly every day Babe had new tales to tell to his enraptured teammates.

"Boy!" Babe was heard to exclaim as he recounted a previous night's adventure. "Was she beautiful! Not a blemish on her body!"

But Babe, despite his shining Packard and his newly fattened wallet, still comported himself like the bartender's son from Baltimore. His trousers were often unpressed and his cap visor bent. And his ties seemed to have been selected by a paperhanger. He smoked a pipe continually and often showed up in a sweater. But he was comfortable, happy, rich and beloved. There was no other place he wanted to be but right here in Boston.

So when word in early 1920 came that he had been sold to the New York Yankees, Babe was dismayed. Oh no, he assured his wife and friends and manager, I won't go down there! Never for the smallest part of a minute had he even considered that he might be sold away—especially if he didn't want to go. He had seen New York, had timidly sampled some of its excitements, and had not been tempted to immerse himself any more deeply. For one thing, everything *cost* so goddam much! It was not that Babe ever counted over the price of what he reached for. It was just that he still carried the poor boy's superstitious awe of rich men's price tags. A dollar and a *half* to ride in a taxi! *Five dollars* for a show! Goddamit, I just couldn't afford to *live* there, Babe complained. At least not live the way he wanted to, without bothering to add up totals or dicker for bargains.

But Babe had made extra money in exhibition games about New England in the fall and soon had an extra $6,000 from appearing in twelve games. He invested this bankroll in a cigar factory that turned out handmade cigars wearing paper bands that carried his own moonface in full color and his name in ornate lettering. He had acquired a business manager by this time—a fellow named John Igoe, whose job it was to collect Babe's fees, arrange appearances, make his hotel and train reservations, and, rumors had it, even hone the big man's bats. Babe was the only major-league baseball player in the nation at that time to have a business manager all his own.

Igoe signed Babe up for a series of exhibition games on the Pacific Coast with a club organized by Buck Weaver, the Chicago White Sox infielder who had, although the world had not learned it yet, just completed his part in throwing the 1919 World Series to the Cincinnati Reds. Babe bought himself, for a thousand dollars, a new leather overcoat that caused even people who did not know him to stop and stare when he walked by. He packed the coat and his wife aboard a Pullman for the long, long ride to the coast.

In San Francisco and thereabouts the Babe was welcomed by worshipful fans. The big, black-haired, round-faced, everlastingly cheerful twenty-three-year-old was greeted first in San Francisco by a pretty young lady in a Red Cross outfit, who pinned a button on his coat in return for a generous donation. The picture of the two handsome young people beaming upon each other made hearts glad all over town.

Ruth had been booked to pitch a Sunday game against Dutch Ruether, the leading pitcher in the National League and star of the 1919 World Series. He agreed to go to bat before the game and hit pitched balls for five minutes. But this part of the exhibition ended ahead of schedule. Promoter Gene Doyle, who had signed the Babe for those appearances, had brought only six two-dollar baseballs along and Babe knocked all six over the fence before more than thirty fans had arrived to marvel. Buck Weaver had served the balls up to Ruth, who knocked pitches 1 and 2 beyond the fence in right field. Pitch No. 3 came in just about the height of the lowest button on Babe's shirt. "Now!" Babe yelled as he stepped into it. He drove the ball high over the center-field fence and struck a house nearby. Then he put the next three pitches over the shorter right-field fence.

As one sportswriter observed, the whole San Francisco ball club and its opponents together, in batting practice or in games, had not knocked six balls out of the park all season.

In a game the following week against Captain Tim Harrington's "Quartermasters," Ruth played first base, while a lithe young left-hander named Lefty O'Doul pitched for the Quartermasters. These Quartermasters were a squinty-eyed bunch of sailors, not too strong for ballplayers who had fought the war from the safety of a shipyard or a Home Guard assignment. So when O'Doul struck the great hero out on his first two trips to the plate, there was much disgusted spitting of tobacco juice and loud complaints against the press agent who had sold this bundle of soiled laundry. But on his third visit to the plate, Babe met a pitch squarely with his enormous bat and sent it streaking so fast and so far that even the enemy ballplayers yelled. The goddam bat, said somebody, looked like a full-grown tree. On his fourth trip Babe took another good pitch fair in the middle and knocked it over the fence. But the bemused umpire called it foul—not because it went over the fence on the wrong side of the marker but because it *landed* foul beyond the fence. How the hell did *he* know? the fans demanded. The goddam ball didn't come down at all!

So Babe went on to Oakland and Sacramento, and converted the heathen there, as much by his happy grin and merry manner as by the wondrous workings of his outsize bat. In Oakland someone offered Babe an airplane ride and he chivalrously urged his wife to try it first. When she returned to earth white and shaken, Babe decided he had better stay downstairs. He was never a man to go out of his way to find trouble.

There were of course matters of greater moment than baseball games to occupy the hearts and minds of the citizenry of California—where citizenry, in that day too, wore its head sometimes rather more askew than did the rest of the nation. The city council of Oakland, during Babe Ruth's visit, met in special session to deal with the alarming upsurge of anarchism, whose minions, along with every other sort of Bolshevik, had been preaching un-Americanism right and left at East Bay. At the request of Commissioner E. F. Morse, the council passed a set of resolutions designed to choke off all radical assemblages. East Bay, the commissioner declared, is for Americans only! And no American, one knew, could stand up and speak out for any kind of "ism."

Babe Ruth went back to Boston determined to ask for $20,000 a year. Buck Weaver told him he was worth it, and his accomplishments on the coast, where he earned $500 a game, persuaded Babe that Buck was right. Not that he wouldn't have settled for something less. He had all he needed now to live like a king in Boston, what with this exhibition money and the cigar factory. And there were a dozen or more young ladies in town who would open their doors for him whenever he might choose to knock. How could he afford to reproduce arrangements like that in New York, where even ice-cream sodas cost twice what they did here?

Then, of a sudden, when 1920 had hardly begun, he learned he *could* afford it. For the New York Yankees had doubled his salary without a murmur. Twenty thousand dollars! With that kind of money a man could live in Palm Beach.

PART II

New York

SO Babe moved his small family to New York, not without some uneasiness, and took a flat in one of the residential hotels on the West Side, the Ansonia. He began at once to try to improve his dress and his ways, to fit the image of a prosperous New Yorker. Men in New York wore felt hats and derbies in the winter, and were not seen sporting sweaters in the public streets. So Babe put aside his beaten cap and looked for fedoras big enough to fit him. He wore them about for a while too, although he could never get rid of the feeling that he looked damn silly with a felt contraption perched on top of his enormous head.

When the warm weather began, Babe took to going about without any hat at all—a striking social lapse in that day, when a hatless man would either be a thief on the dead run or a shop clerk who had just popped outdoors to show a customer what a suit looked like in the daylight. Eventually a Philadelphia hatter, distressed that Babe might teach boys everywhere to start walking hatless into the weather, sent Babe about a ten years' supply of headgear, including a panama and a brown derby.

On the baseball field, Babe began his New York career as if he were fresh up from the minors and still shaking from the size of the crowds that surrounded him. In his very first game as a Yankee, played before a vast crowd in Philadelphia, Babe dropped an easy fly ball in the eighth inning, allowing Philadelphia runners to score two runs, just enough to lose the game for the Yankees. Next day, in the same park, he struck out three times, one right after another. O God, he must have told himself, to be back in Boston!

But in May, when the Red Sox, carrying his old playmates, came to New York for the first time that season, Babe responded to their presence by driving a ball high over the roof of the right-field stands at the Polo Grounds. He had done this once before, the previous season, when he wore the Boston uniform. Only he and Joe Jackson had ever managed such blows in that park.

From then on, Babe began to hit home runs so often that it seemed like a disease. Newspapers began to feature his wondrous deeds on the front pages, and men and women who could not have told you what league he played in still were tempted to come out to view this freak of nature—a man who hit round balls out of the playing field at five times the rate of the great men of other years. Late in May, a warm Sunday saw 38,600 people in the Polo Grounds when Babe was there—the largest crowd ever to fill the field. And all over the circuit, crowds of like dimension rushed the turnstiles when Babe Ruth came to town. Babe now began to understand, for the first time, what the life of a hero was like. It was not just people hailing you in the street, or knowing you the moment you walked into a restaurant. It was a mob blocking your way as you tried to walk out to the street from the ball park. It was a crowd surrounding your table in the hotel dining room, until you could hardly find time to raise your fork to your lips. It was your telephone persistently calling you back after you had just finished putting off some anonymous admirer. It was the mailman carrying in forty and fifty letters with your name on them. It was policemen stopping your car, not to arrest you for speeding but to shake your hand. It was a lady halting you in the street to beg you to help her pay her family's rent. It was grinning and hearty men insisting they had chosen you, of all the men in the world, to share in the millions their investments were about to bring them. It was pretty girls proposing marriage—or less formal arrangements. It was total strangers grabbing your hands and insisting you must remember them from Boston. It was little boys seeking only to stand near you and goggle into your face, and grown men and women reaching out just to touch your garments. The autograph madness had hardly begun in that era. But handshakes were sought after as if they were treasures to be carried home and displayed to the neighbors.

Babe finally had to stop eating in hotel dining rooms, even at home. His fame had burst open with the suddenness of the recent armistice, and he had not made preparations for it. Even rival ballplayers gaped at him now as if he had suddenly grown twelve inches taller, and they would pause in whatever they were doing to watch Babe in batting practice drive baseballs farther than any living human had ever driven them before.

Ty Cobb's fame, which still flourished, began to pale beside Babe Ruth's, for Babe seemed twice the batter Ty had been. When Cobb, in Cleveland, drove a ball out of the park and it hit the wall of a house across the street, the local newspapers had printed pictures of the house as if it were a historical monument. But when Babe Ruth knocked a home run over the same wall, it carried clean *over* the same house to land in the yard beyond. And so certain was everyone that Babe would hit a home run in every game that hardly any notice of the length of this one was offered in the press.

By the middle of July, Babe had already hit twenty-nine home runs—as many as he had hit in his previous record-breaking season. He was obviously on the way to turning baseball upside down. There seemed hardly an arena in the whole world large enough to hold all the people who wanted to catch Babe Ruth. The Yankee owners, Colonels Jacob Ruppert and Tillinghast L'Hommedieu Huston, began to talk about a new baseball park for New York, right in the middle of town, where everyone in the city could reach it. The site they first selected was Broadway and Eighth Street, handy to all streetcar, subway, and elevated lines, with plenty of curb space for those dandies who insisted on bringing their motorcars.

It mattered not to Babe Ruth where he played; he was as famous in one city as the next, with crowds pressing close to him whenever he showed his face in public. He wore silk shirts now of every hue, paying more for each one than he had been used to paying for a suit of clothes. He smoked imported cigars of unusual virulence (he still puffed his big pipe at home). He bought a new maroon Packard roadster, and very soon lost the radiator cap, so that he sent it whistling up the avenues like a slavering dragon, with spume flying.

He signed to act in a motion picture (and was felled by an insect bite when he went to Haverstraw, New York, to make the first scenes). He invited the band from St. Mary's Industrial School to accompany the Yankees on road trips, so they could give concerts everywhere to raise money to rebuild a part of the school that had been destroyed by fire. He left his door open at the Ansonia, for friends, acquaintances, and total strangers to walk in and out, and to share in the Babe's bounty as borne in by a parade of room-service waiters.

The citizens of New York in that day, like the citizens of most major cities, were fighting a rear-guard action against Prohibition. The state assembly had voted in the spring to investigate the Anti-Saloon League, which was busy lobbying in Washington for stricter enforcement of the new Volstead Act that was to put Prohibition into practice. In New Jersey the legislature had authorized a 3.5 alcoholic content for beer, inasmuch as that could not be deemed "intoxicating." Federal law would soon set the legal alcohol content at one half of 1 percent, so even this tiny trickle of relief was quickly shut off. Six men in Brooklyn sought more direct relief by entering a grocery store and demanding at gunpoint a supply of wine.

"We know you have it!" the leader of the group told Mr. Oliva, the store owner, "so bring it out." Oliva insisted he had none, so the leader shot him twice, then took $1,800 and a gold watch out of Oliva's pockets and marched off with his squadron of followers to see if perhaps they could not *buy* a bottle.

They might have bought whiskey in the New York theater district, where it was said a man who called himself United States Marshal McCarthy busily distributed the stuff in pint bottles through a horde of deputies.

There were still echoes of the war, indeed there was still war going on, for American soldiers were being killed in such places as Kovno, Lithuania, where they were helping to suppress an "army mutiny." And Grover Cleveland Bergdoll, the most famous and the wealthiest of the draft dodgers in the land, had won a habeas corpus writ on the grounds that, having never been in the Army, he could not be tried by court-martial. (It was charged meanwhile that his mother, through the Burns Detective Agency, had tried to corrupt government witnesses.)

The conscientious objectors who had been jailed wholesale in such places as Alcatraz, Fort Leavenworth, and Fort Douglas, Utah, were still being denied their freedom. They hadn't cleaned their cells or made their beds, the authorities explained. No such thing, said a spokesman for the American Civil Liberties Union. Secretary of War Newton. D. Baker was just trying to force them to recant as a price for setting them free.

At the Hippodrome in New York, General Pershing told five thousand listeners that the soldiers in the American Expeditionary Force had made a "record of morality never made by any other army at any other time." The soldiers, he said, had been prompted to enter the service by a "deep religious note" (from the draft board?) and thereby had acquired a moral tone that prompted them to lead moral lives. (According to figures in the *Literary Digest,* the chief physical ailment uncovered in the army was heart disease—except of course for "blood taint," known in vulgar circles as venereal disease, and no decent person talked about that.)

The railroads had been turned back in good order to private ownership (but with too many employees, some investors griped), and freight cars rolled into yards everywhere bearing slogans chalked by returning soldiers—chief of which was a cry that had been chanted in a hundred cities when the returning heroes had been unloaded. "No beer! No work!"

New York in that day was a restless place, frantically trying to adjust itself to burgeoning traffic and a swollen populace. Soldiers without pay in their pockets sought excitement wherever it might blossom. Saloons still stood open in some corners of town, reluctant to admit that there would never be any more beer. Prices crept upward. The fare on the Hudson Tubes rose from a nickel to eight cents. Sugar remained more precious than whiskey. And criminals, inspired perhaps by the talk of millions and billions that had been borrowed to sustain the war, had begun to dream of operations that would reach far outside the old neighborhood and into the realms where money grew on trees. Jules W. ("Nicky") Arnstein, an elusive and articulate crook whose name was connected with all sorts of enterprises in which he probably had no part at all, was supposed to have been one of the brains that organized a ring of Wall Street messengers who had managed to steal more than five million dollars in securities.

Prices of theater tickets in New York startled the outlanders who had been brought up on five-cent picture shows or thirty-cent vaudeville theaters. Why, it cost $3.30 to see a first-run musical com-

edy from a decent seat! (The extra thirty cents was "war tax"—
which everyone assumed would soon be dropped.) And on top of
that, some ticket brokers had the gall to double the prices on all the
hits. When Detective Michael Kelly, on his night off, took some
friends to see *The Gold-Diggers* at the Lyceum Theater, Lee Newman, a ticket broker at 1482 Broadway, tried to hold him up for $6
each for $3 tickets. "Twenty-four bucks for four seats!" Kelly roared.
"That's against the law!" But he laid down his twenty-four dollars
and laid his badge right down beside them.

"You're under arrest," said Kelly. "The law says you can only
charge fifty cents."

"No I'm not," said Newman. "A judge just said that law is uncon-
stitutional."

"It's still the law," said Kelly, "until somebody higher up decides
it. Give me them tickets!"

Newman quickly slipped the tickets to a counter clerk beside him
and as Kelly moved down the counter, grabbing for the tickets, the
clerks passed them from hand to hand and kept them one jump
ahead of Kelly. But at the end of the line, Kelly snatched up the evidence, then he snatched Newman and started to march him outside.

"Help!" Newman screamed. "Murder!" And he fought to break out
of Kelly's tight-clamped fist. Jack Cohen, who lived on West 106th
Street and soon wished he had stayed there, leapt out of the crowd
to rescue Newman and in a moment or two he was in handcuffs himself and carried off to night court with Newman. Newman, when his
case was heard, was promptly discharged. Cohen was paroled in his
own custody for a hearing later on. Kelly and his friends went home
without seeing the show.

"Gold-diggers" was a brand-new pejorative then used to identify
those young ladies who seemed bent on going out with men not for
romance and caresses but for costly meals and front-row theater
tickets and rides in limousines. This behavior was deemed just one
more evidence of the general breakdown in morals that the war had
prompted. There were new and admittedly indecent dances, notably
the shimmy, that scandalized chaperones even at high-school so-
cials. And one weekly supplement featured a leering report of how
girls actually checked their corsets along with their coats before
going out on the dance floor.

It was possible now to buy a man's suit that offered, as a complement, a pair of matching golf knickers; golf had begun to grow into

the major weekend preoccupation for businessmen. Most of the players still wore white flannels on the course, as Babe Ruth did, along with a silk shirt, when he took up the game in Florida. But there was no one in the land who walloped a golf ball with the heartiness of the Babe, who attacked it as if it were a thrown baseball. On one of his first appearances on a Florida course, he drove ball and driver-head into the distant water together, having swung hard enough to rip the head right off the club.

War's alarms began to quiet a little, as the wily Bolsheviks started a "peace offensive" designed to diminish the brandishing of arms along their borders. (Walter Duranty, in the New York *Times,* warned against our being taken in by these proffers of peace that were being sent by wireless to all nations, great and small. But he granted that the temptation to make peace was strong, what with the mountains of raw materials the Russians could offer to British and American industry. Then there *was* the fact that the anti-Bolshevik forces in Russia were a notably noisome lot. "Rotters and blackguards," the British had called them.)

Bolshevism in New York and environs, no matter what its disguise, was being rooted out by competent authority, so the common people might sleep serenely of nights. The controller of New York City, Charles L. Craig, discovered disaffection right in the city council, where a plump, raucous young man named La Guardia had the impudence to question the manner in which sites for storing snow equipment was being handled. Said young Fiorello: "If the Controller would use the same scrutiny and care in assigning city-owned property to city departments as he does in assigning city property to close personal and political friends, the city would be better off."

That, the controller replied, "is the wildest kind of radical, socialistic, *black*guardia statement!" And there were many who agreed with him.

It was a political year, of course, with most of the excitement as usual attending the Democratic convention, where it seemed certain that William Gibbs McAdoo, President Wilson's Secretary of the Treasury and son-in-law, would receive the nomination. (There were unpleasant whispers, however, that California businessmen had set up a slush fund of several thousand dollars to finance the McAdoo campaign.) Al Smith, the New York governor and an earnest advocate of a "wet" plank in the platform, was the local favorite.

But how could any politician draw attention from Babe Ruth, who was hitting home runs at a rate no man had ever dreamed about before? By midsummer, when the Democratic convention was hogging the headlines, Ruth looked likely to double his twenty-nine homers of the year before, to put the home-run mark far out of reach of any human competitor, living or yet unborn.

More than one observer took note of the fact that, while the crowds who gathered to watch the news unfold on the lighted bulletin in Times Square stood nearly mute at every report from the convention, they broke into wild cheers when Babe Ruth's name was flashed, to report his hitting another home run or his just missing one. The Knights of Columbus scheduled a special day for Ruth at Yankee Stadium, July 9, when they gave him a watch fob studded with large diamonds in the shape of the K of C emblem. Ruth thereupon hit a home run, and the stands at the Polo Grounds, according to a newspaper report, became a "field of waving straw hats." So spectacular was the sight that the newsreel cameras all focused on the spectators rather than on Ruth, who was trotting in his oddly pigeon-toed manner, with tiny steps, from base to base.

(Babe and the team took off then on a road trip and Babe left the priceless fob behind in a Detroit hotel, where it was discovered by a chambermaid and forwarded to the frantic Babe at once. Babe promptly wired the chambermaid a hundred-dollar tip—his standard fee for favors of any sort.)

Automobile prices, like prices of nearly everything, had climbed to unheard-of heights by this time. Even a six-cylinder car might set a man back over $2000 and it was possible to sink $5000 into a Pierce-Arrow. Babe, who never let price deter him, and had bought himself a new $10,000 Packard roadster in June, ran it into a tree in Wama, Pennsylvania, on the Fourth of July, while speeding from Washington to Philadelphia in the dark. Babe, traveling with his patient wife and three other ballplayers, had tried to make a right turn at high speed and wound up in the woods. As often happened in those pre-radio days when famous men had accidents, Ruth was immediately reported dead. But no one had been hurt at all and Babe was ready to play ball the next afternoon.

There just had never been a baseball player in all history who drew the attention Babe did. When he traveled by train, station agents along the line would tap out the word that Babe was coming, and regardless of the hour there would be section hands or car-tinks (journal-box inspectors) or just plain passengers gathered in small knots to yell for him whenever the train stopped. This sort of thing never annoyed Babe Ruth. He reveled in the existence of so many who loved him and he would beam on them all. He took special pains to respond to the admiration of small boys, with the instinct of a poor boy who, by his size and his strength, had often been King of the Kids at home or along his street. Once, at the Polo Grounds, a boy carrying a small camera approached Babe and asked if he might take his hero's picture. Babe happily posed, then called teammate Derrill Pratt over, gave Pratt the camera, and told *him* to snap the picture while Babe stood with an arm around the boy's shoulders.

Toward his own teammates, however, Babe began to take a slightly more lordly attitude. Not that he really pulled rank on anyone or lost his temper if a man played a joke on him. He played jokes on everyone himself, be he friend or foe. (He once chased Brooklyn first baseman Jacques Fournier down a railroad-station platform, waving a jointed wooden snake that Jacques thought was real.) But he knew he was the big man on the team, the head of the gang, and he wanted his mates to consult him if they contemplated any move out of the ordinary. He went for months without speaking to one team-mate who left the team in Washington to return to New York, with the manager's permission, but without telling Babe—who often liked to take this particular pal with him on his nightly rounds.

Still, from the moment he showed up at the Yankee training camp, puffing his brand new twelve-dollar meerschaum pipe and extending an open box of Babe Ruth cigars, Babe was beloved by the Yankees as he had been by the Red Sox. Indeed, Babe hardly ever had any real enemies among baseball players—except Ty Cobb, whom he long despised, and Leo Durocher, whom he once accused of stealing his watch.

In that sense, at least, Babe, who in many ways epitomized the Roaring Twenties, was out of tune with the times, for it was fast becoming fashionable to spurn all outsiders—all the nonrich, non-elect, and nonfamous. Babe himself had helped make it clear to a whole generation that success—that goal of every decently raised American—could be attained in one mighty stroke of the bat and that fame, which was the banner of success, was within reach of any who could do one thing better than all his fellows. Babe never did learn to hold himself aloof (as later athletic heroes did) from the pests—noisy kids, bush leaguers, breathless fans, strangers seeking favors—who cluttered the pathways of all the great. He smiled at everyone, exhibited sincere repentance if he was told he had hurt someone's feelings, and visited sick kids in hospitals with the devotion of a priest, and without publicity.

That was not the way of the true insider of that day. Throughout this era of Normalcy, when the Democrats stumbled to defeat while trying to preach further involvement in the keeping of peace in the world, distaste grew for all things alien and hard to pronounce. There was not much stomach in the land for the further sacrifices Democratic campaign talk seemed to promise. The Republican candidate, Warren G. Harding, scattered gentle platitudes from his front porch in Marion, Ohio. Eugene V. Debs, the Socialist candidate, conducted a "front cell" campaign from his place in Federal prison (from which President Wilson refused to free him). But most of the electorate stayed home on election day to further their own affairs, while the self-elected "better" people voted overwhelmingly for the man who seemed to symbolize soft speech, gentle manners, good food, well-pressed clothes, Protestantism, temperance, and the quiet enjoyment of wealth.

These were Ku Klux Klan days, when even the Northern cities were alive with "Klaverns" where young men solemnly vowed to extirpate from their blessed land all Romanism, Zionism, Alienism, and people who wore unfashionably pigmented skin. It had always seemed plain as meat and potatoes to such folk that practically all the ills the common man was heir to in this country were the work of hairy agitators, conniving Jewish moneylenders, hook-nosed spies, atheistic promoters of race mingling, and upstart niggers who would work for nickels and dimes. While anti-Negro and anti-Semitic ranting would outrage most sensibilities in the upper reaches of society in that day, the theories themselves, with their hair combed and their clothes cleaned up, found harbor in practically all the better homes. College fraternities everywhere frankly excluded Jews and Catholics—and did not even need to mention blacks, who were expected to "know their place" without being reminded of it. Resort hotels did not hesitate to invite a "strictly Christian clientele," and even National Guard companies invited only "fine Christian fellows" to join up. "Gentile"—which Babe Ruth probably would have deemed a dirty name—was accepted everywhere as the proper tag to pin on all who were white, polite, Protestant, and of Anglo-Saxon or some other obviously North European lineage. "Darky" jokes, blackface comedy, minstrel shows, and comic fiction about "nigger society" were flaunted as unashamedly as had been the anti-Hibernian jokes and vaudeville skits of an earlier day, when even Cap Anson, the leading ballplayer in the land, took part in a skit in which he wore green whiskers and sang a song naming himself and his fellows as "Ten Chubelin [shoveling] Tipperary Turks."

The most common put-down word in colleges then was "wet"—which undoubtedly derived from the phrase "wet behind the ears"—and was meant to designate any who were revoltingly naïve, given to childish enthusiasms, dressed unfashionably, were bereft of sophistication in all social intercourse, lacked what was known to the elect of that era as "smoothness," or in some other manner betrayed the fact that they were ineligible for membership in the circle of the socially adept and worldly wise.

Of course, wealth and fame, such as Babe Ruth owned, rendered a man immune from most of the exclusionary unwritten social bylaws of the day. Indeed, all successful athletes, stage and motion-picture stars, or any others who by calling lent themselves to brightening the idle hours of the well-to-do were exempt from most (but not all) of the restrictive private covenants. A Jewish performer might be made welcome under many a Gentile roof, but his son would no sooner have made it into New York's College of Physicians and Surgeons than he could have enrolled in the Ancient Order of Hibernians.

So gradually that hardly anyone seemed to notice it, the ideal image of a foursquare American had changed from the two-fisted, morally pure, physically vigorous, fearless, chivalrous, spiritually exalted Teddy Roosevelt version of Sir Galahad to the slick-haired and sexually indomitable Valentino "sheik" and then to the completely imperturbable smoothy, who could hold his liquor without vomiting or staggering, could cast an eye both cynical and "sincere" on the world around him, could take up ladies or cast them aside as the mood struck him, spent his money freely, spurned the company of the unfashionable and the indiscreet, spoke in deep, well-modulated tones, and was generally a prince of good fellows when there was fun to be had. Old-fashioned virtues, such as honesty and truthfulness, were much honored in other people, especially when applied to the stealing of money by the poor or the concealment of some dereliction by an employee. Industrial bribery, cheating on college exams, deceptive advertising, and payoffs to police, politicians, and judges were accepted as everyday social and business practices, to be deplored only when they were laid out before the eyes of the unwashed.

The truly adept, while acknowledging that such deeds were "wrong," forgave them freely on the grounds that "everybody" engaged in them. All businesses in New York, large, small, or medium, were built on pyramids of petty corruption. Even the apartment-house superintendent took payoffs from the paper boy, the milkman, and any others who required his assistance in maintaining a minor monopoly. Restaurants who tried to buy from the "wrong" iceman soon discovered they were getting no ice at all. The old lady who tried to cross the street while the traffic cop was busy keeping the crossing open for the stream of trucks from the newspaper plant that financed his family's vacation might as well have sought help from the lamppost. Newspaper reporters kept themselves supplied with free hats, free meals, and free suits of clothes by working the names of selected shops into their news stories. Even the lowly makeup man, who positioned the "run-of-paper" advertising, would find boxes of goodies awaiting him at home as a reward for keeping the proper ad next to reading matter at the top of a right-hand page.

The municipal clerk who performed the "free" marriage ceremony always kept his cashbox open on his desk so the happy couple might be saved the embarrassment of asking where to drop their donation. Parking places along the midtown streets and avenues could be rented from the cop on the beat. Christmastide saw uniformed policemen ambling from door to door, in office buildings or along rows of shops, carrying, as postmen always did, lists of the officers to be "remembered." When the proprietor of some exclusive "restaurant" (where guests had to make themselves known through a slot in the door before entering) paid a social visit to City Hall, he always carried in an inner pocket a long white envelope fattened by a packet of brand-new hundred-dollar bills and looked for an open desk drawer to lay it in. Whorehouses as well as speakeasies received lists of payoff recipients, along with suggested weekly amounts. Detectives could quote an exact price for squaring even a homicide rap.

Of course the kickback, a method of keeping the wheels of industry properly greased and turning, had been invented deep in the dark backward and abysm of time by some anonymous purchasing agent. Even household cooks had taken presents or percentages from purveyors since the lord of the manor had first delegated the

This clumsily retouched photo of Babe and his bride, Helen, was presented to his in-laws by Babe right after the wedding. (*Wide World*)

When Babe came to Boston, good little boys and girls were thrilled by riding twice around the pond in the Public Gardens in a swan boat. (*Culver*)

Boston looked like this when Babe was there. This is Back Bay. Trinity Church and the Public Library face each other across Copley Square. The Copley Square Hotel is a block south of the square. The Putnam Hotel, where Babe first lived, was still farther south on Huntington Avenue, the street on the right. (*U.P.I.*)

The Clown of God, Billy Sunday, strikes one of his standard revival meeting poses while his manager, who arranged for the picture, smiles upon the effort. (*Wide World*)

Billy Sunday, in his youth, was a Mercury-footed outfielder for the Chicago White Stockings. (*Wide World*)

The *Lusitania* starts on its final voyage, to meet a German torpedo off the coast of Ireland. (*Wide World*)

John F. (Honey Fitz) Fitzgerald was mayor of Boston when he rode this horse in a 1913 parade. Next year, Jim Curley defeated him. (*Wide World*)

When Babe Ruth was new to the Yankees he still liked to borrow bicycles. This picture was taken by a fan when Babe was barnstorming in Vermont about 1920.

By 1928 Jim Curley and aging Honey Fitz were friends again. They both supported Al Smith.   (*Wide World*)

The New York Armistice Day parade in 1918 stopped to have its picture taken. The celebration in Boston was even wilder. (*Wide World*)

New-fangled motor buses in the New York Armistice parade. (*Wide World*)

Boston businessmen, after their stores had been looted during the police strike, knew how to take a joke. (*Culver*)

When Babe moved to New York the moving men were on strike. *(Culver)*

Massachusetts State militia rounded up these "criminals" on Boston Common during the 1919 police strike. One of them was later shot dead. (*Culver*)

The Brooklyn transit employees were on strike, too, and commuters had to find new ways to travel. (*Culver*)

Miners in Pennsylvania who had been evicted for "contract-breaking" (joining a union) lived in tent cities like this, supported by the union. *(Culver)*

When the dynamite went off on Wall Street in 1920, it left this wreckage on Broad Street, in front of J. P. Morgan's door. Subtreasury building in right background. *(Culver)*

After the explosion.　(*Culver*)

After the explosion. (*Culver*)

Searching for clues in the wreckage near J. P. Morgan's. (*Culver*)

A New York jitney bus in World War I days. (*Culver*)

Kids during New York streetcar strike. (*Culver*)

BABE
RUTH

job of buying at the market. But in New York, in the 1920s, it had grown into a structure so complex, yet so standardized, that it was often accepted as a vital part of the machine. And often enough, God knows, it was so polite, so clothed in professional jargon, and so blatant withal that to this day there are men and women who can see no immorality in it.

Such was the Morgan "preferred list" of the 1920s, which purported to offer to "preferred" customers, supposedly those longest on the books or fathering the largest accounts, an opportunity to buy, at the issuing price, certain stocks the house was handling. In practice, however, the customers on the list, without ever investing more than the price of the telephone call, could accept the offer, then promptly "sell" the stocks at the price at which the stock had opened when tossed on the market. In the boom days that was *always* several points higher than the price arbitrarily set before issue, so the customer, buying and selling within the space of a few breaths, would have himself a "profit" of five or six dollars multiplied by the hundreds of thousands of shares he had elected to buy. Some ill-mannered investigators of a latter day named that profit a present. And so it was, as surely as the recipient of some of this largesse was the President of the United States.

It may have been that baseball grew great in these years, not just because of Babe Ruth and the throng of his imitators but because it was one game that one knew could not be fixed—where the race went to the swift and the battle to the strong, even though bread was not always bountifully awarded to the wise. But even in baseball there were the grifters and grafters. The ushers at Ebbets Field, Brooklyn, were happy, in exchange for a quarter, to lead a bleacher-seat customer to a reserved seat. Rube Marquard, the great Brooklyn pitcher, was arrested for trying to sell World Series tickets worth $52.80 for $350. (He was given a severe talking-to by a judge and fined a dollar.) But some people did say that half the Brooklyn team was busy scalping Series tickets. And one club executive was detained by Federal authorities for handing out test tubes filled with illicit whiskey. Once during the 1920 season in Brooklyn, a bleacher fan flung a bottle at outfielder Bernie Neis of the Dodgers and just missed his head. Another time, angry Brooklyn bleacher bugs swarmed on to the field in such numbers that the umpire had to forfeit the game.

Of course it was in 1920 too that the truth came out about the 1919 World Series, in which gamblers from all over the nation set out to hire eight White Sox players to lose the Series to the Cincinnati Reds. And with that revelation came charges of wider and more ancient corruption throughout organized baseball. Charles Dooin, former manager of the Philadelphia Phillies, recalled that back in 1908, gamblers had offered three of his pitchers $150,000 ("laid right out on a table!") to lose an upcoming series to the New York Giants and that he himself had had $8000 thrust into his hands in the clubhouse. (He had called first baseman Kitty Bransfeld over to "throw the guy right down the clubhouse stairs.") Benny Kauff, New York outfielder, testified that his teammate Heinie Zimmerman had offered him a "big piece of jack"—something like $125—to "hit the breeze at bat" and drop flies in the outfield when they played the Chicago Cubs in 1918.

The appointment of a granite-faced (and granite-named) Federal judge, Kenesaw Mountain Landis, to see to the purity of baseball was assurance enough to the fans that the game, regardless of the past, was out of reach of the fixers. But it had fast become, and would long remain, the most important carrier of "action" for the bookmakers in all the major cities. In several parks, gamblers operated openly in the stands, using private signals such as those employed by the operators at the Curb Exchange in New York to indicate what they wanted to buy—a ten-dollar bet that the batter would hit the next pitch or that a run on base would score, or whatever. And every bookmaker in New York had a private "pad" that set forth what payments had to be met to ensure safety from interruption by the police—so much to the patrolman, so much to the sergeant, so much to the captain, and God knows what to the inspector.

For those who could not lend themselves to the transports induced by mighty deeds on the baseball diamond, the motion pictures in the twenties became the chief source of solace—the confirmation to many minds that life, besides being great fun when there was money rolling in this way, was also real, earnest, and full of meaning that could, despite all doubts, be articulated. Little girls who crowded to see Rudolph Valentino "in person" at a New York theater might have brought home only mild amazement that a *man* would wear blue suede shoes. But older ladies came away in a daze of fond conviction that some day a desert lover would burst into their tent and press his fierce kisses on them forever and ever.

Young men meanwhile hastened to mirrors to anoint their locks with Slikum and comb them back into flat shiny wedges on either side of a clean part. Even Babe Ruth learned to douse his own unruly black hair with some ointment or other to keep it tightly in place.

The motion pictures, which undertook generally to indicate that suffering followed sin and pure joy awaited repentance, were far more concerned than even the baseball-club owners of that day with presenting a clean face to the public. To that end they banished from the screen forever and ever a plump and talented comedian named Roscoe ("Fatty") Arbuckle, who had been involved in a drunken sex orgy that resulted in the death of a young woman. (She died of peritonitis, and many young people, reading that awesome name in print, assumed it was a Latin word for an unheard-of-venereal affliction.)

But the Fatty Arbuckles of business had no fear of being drummed out of the corps. The free indulgence of their sexual appetites was a major industry in New York, so important that eventually the gangsters moved in and "regulated" it by siphoning off the major share of its income and allotting territories so as to avoid wasteful competition. Crime in the 1920s had not yet ordered itself into a national syndicate to divide up the whole country into satrapies. Each major city instead was ruled by a single overlord, or by an uneasy alliance among born enemies, any one of whom could see himself as the lone leader. But gangsters all the same were part of the unacknowledged aristocracy of the nation, ruling the inner cities through control of elections and intimate association with public officials. Indeed, the hard-eyed gunman whose job it was to murder victims who had been placed on the spot by one or another of the gang chiefs became almost a folk hero, like an outlaw of the West. He too, the current legends had it, was cool under fire, fiercely loyal to his mates, reckless of danger, and chivalrous to gentle ladies. (That final fairy tale was eventually replaced by the image of a strong and angry man who did not hesitate to push a grapefruit into a lady's face it if he thought she warranted it.) Small boys, who confused gangsters with bank robbers and holdup men, played games on the New York streets in which they gave themselves names like Vanny Higgins and Vincent ("Mad Dog") Coll, two small-time gunmen who earned occasional headlines in New York. And two of Babe Ruth's teammates actually sought and, after long delays and much careful routing to the hideaway, were actually granted an audience with the most noted gangster of all—Scarface Al Capone of Chicago, the new-style gang leader, inordinately greedy, self-indulgent, breathtakingly cruel, and shrewd as a Yankee.

Standing before the great man's desk in the hotel where Capone hid himself like a medieval prince in a castle, the New York third baseman looked up and saw on the wall above Capone's head pictures of George Washington and Abraham Lincoln.

"Three great Americans!" the dazzled ballplayer exclaimed. "Lincoln, Washington, Capone."

Scarface Al's swart and fleshy face cracked wide open in a grin. "Sure! Sure!" said he. And he guaranteed the boys that they had nothing to fear from any hand in this preserve of his—not even from a creature as lowly as a Chicago cop. And in that day, you may be sure a safe-conduct from Capone was of far more worth than a proclamation by the President.

Organized gangs, when they were at peace with each other, ruled New York and other big cities more tightly and more efficiently than any elected administration ever had. Policemen in that day were far quicker to accept an order from the top gangster than from their own commissioner, who might not even stay in office if he offended the real source of power. Indeed, when it became necessary to wipe out Vincent Coll because he had made all gangdom to offend by kidnapping Big Frenchy Lelange, one of the "division" leaders during a negotiated truce, the police kept Coll on the phone until Owney Madden's men could get to him. Poor wild Vincent, disguised in dyed hair and whiskers, had been silly enough to imagine that he could turn himself in to the cops and find protection from Owney, who ruled New York then from a quiet apartment in the West Fifties. But the police had simply marked Coll's whereabouts—a midtown drugstore—and passed the word to Owney, who dispatched his own chauffeur and two or three others to the spot in a long black car. Two of the men undertook to keep customers from entering the store. ("A man is getting a treatment," they told the innocents who tried to enter.) Then one man with a submachine gun, a weapon that had come into favor in the First World War, blasted poor Vincent where he stood in the telephone booth, awaiting instructions for throwing himself into the comforting arms of the law.

Plain people were terrified by such deeds, which seemed to promise sudden death to almost anyone who stepped by mistake across an invisible line. But the businessmen of that era, counting the swollen profits that stemmed from mass production, low employment, and scanty wages, generally agreed that if "these fellows" were content just to eliminate each other as they seemed to be doing, no permanent harm need befall the state.

Certainly Babe Ruth in that day had no reason to be concerned with the intricately woven structure of business, crime, and politics that assured him of good drink when he desired it. He was moving through a poor boy's paradise, with doors opening before him almost before he could reach out his hand. Rich and famous men whose names he could never remember even sought out his company to lend some special cachet to their parties. Girls by the dozen offered themselves to his tireless embrace. One former teammate from Boston, who accepted Babe's offer of a ride (up Riverside Drive at about sixty miles an hour) to the ball park in the Packard, recalls that Babe kept pointing out windows in the high, luxurious apartments that flanked the Drive in that day.

"I've got a girl up there," Babe would say. "And there. And up there. And on the top floor there. And on that corner. And one up there. And another one where that balcony is." He went on and on, until he must have named more than twenty. And the teammate, who had known the Babe in Boston and had sometimes traveled in his wake, believed every word.

By this time it was acknowledged by everyone on the Yankees, including the upstairs brass, that Babe Ruth was a property of special worth, who could not be broken completely to harness and required a great deal of gentling. He asked for and was promptly granted a telephone in the locker room. It was also found necessary to provide a tall wire basket to hold the barrelful of mail Babe received every day. Babe seldom dug through the letters, for he did not need to. His teammates gladly sorted them out, opened them, and rejoiced in their contents, particularly when they were letters from girls who were eager to meet the young hero. The other players would divide such letters up among themselves and hasten to telephone the many lovelies who sought appointments with Babe. They would make dates for Babe in all parts of town and would sometimes go to size up the girl, all unbeknownst, and perhaps approach her themselves if she seemed desirable. Often the poor girl simply stood and stood until it became clear that no baseball hero was in the offing. Then she might go home and pen an angry or sorrowful note that Babe would never even get a chance to look at.

Letters from little boys always received Babe's attention when they were handed to him. He accepted solemnly his obligation to respond to kids, as if they were his special charges. It was almost as if he were called upon to comfort the scared and homesick little boy he himself had been, coming to the industrial home only fifteen years before. In the 1920 season, he sent out five thousand autographed pictures to small boys who had asked for them. He also made so many free appearances for charity, in cities all over the circuit, that no one could ever reckon them all up. He auctioned off autographed balls, shook countless hands, and gave remarkably articulate talks to kids and grown-ups under all types of auspices.

It never occurred to Ruth for even half a moment that his constant celebration—of his new riches and his new fame—would affect his playing. He came home to his own bed only when he ran out of other places to turn to. He was never an alcoholic, even though he would drink his share of beer as long as the tap was working. But no one ever saw Babe Ruth drunk at the ball field. He never staggered under a fly ball as the great Mike Kelly had done. He never turned up in the locker room unfit to take the field as men like Grover Cleveland Alexander and Shufflin' Phil Douglas had been known to. He never had to be hauled out of a saloon to make the train to the next town, nor did he miss games from drinking as Bugs Raymond and Louis Sockalexis often did. Three drinks of strong liquor would make Babe too dazed to enjoy life.

In fact, Babe did his damnedest not to miss any games at all. An upset stomach, such as he often began to experience from simple overeating, never caused him to beg off his turn at the plate. Sore joints, infected bug bites, swollen fingers, scraped thighs—these were just the ordinary hazards of the job and no reason to stay away from the ball park. He strained his back in his first year with the Yankees and often winced in pain as he put his uniform on that summer. He would snarl at the suggestion that he might lay off until the back stopped hurting. In 1920, of the 154 games the Yankees played, Babe appeared in 142. The bug bite that forced the abandonment of the movie was reported in the papers as a mosquito or hornet bite. But actually it was the bite of a wood tick which, improperly treated, blew up into a serious infection. It kept him out of the lineup for several games. When the season was over, and the Yankees had not made the World Series, Babe organized a team of All-Stars (including a number of nonstars) to play exhibition games throughout the East. It was typical of Babe, who tried hard to cultivate a true regard for a square deal, that he turned down a trip with the Yankees to New Haven, where, under the auspices of a young promoter named George Weiss, he could have picked up $5,500 for three games. He had already agreed to play a double-header at Dyckman Oval in uptown New York against Jeff Tesreau's Bears for a mere $1,000, and he would not crawl out of the contract. He hit three home runs in that doubleheader and struck out three times. In a game in Oneonta later on, Babe broke a small bone in his wrist while sliding into a base but went to bat all the same in the eighth inning, grimacing from pain, and hit the home run the customers had paid to see. Yet when Babe went to Cuba that winter, to earn an extra $10,000 for playing in twelve games, he took the time to write to Miller Huggins, the Yankee manager, that he was going to play "every single inning" next season "if I can even walk." He was sure, he said, that he could hit more home runs than just fifty-four.

Babe very nearly kept his word about playing. He did have to stay in the locker room one day when he became sick to his stomach. And one day he was arrested on Riverside Drive (for the twentieth time or so) for exceeding forty miles an hour in his Packard. The cops who stopped him saw to it that he was locked up for a few hours, while they stood outside the bars and made jokes with him. Finally they turned him loose and urged him to break the speed limit again so that he could get to the Polo Grounds before the game was over. Babe, who had already paid his $100 fine, missed five innings. (A plain citizen that season who was stopped for going thirty-six miles an hour on the Drive was sent to jail for ten days.)

Babe gained thirty or forty pounds in Cuba and came home bursting right out of his new silk shirts. He was persuaded that he must not grow soft in the winter, so he signed up to play basketball, a game for which he had no aptitude. He simply could not adjust to a game where you could not grab the ball and take it away from the other guy, wrestling him meanwhile to the floor. Nor could he get used to the idea that the point was not to heave the ball a hundred yards but just fling it into a silly little string basket. He missed the basket nine times in a row and committed a foul almost every time an opponent tried to get by him, for Babe's idea was to grab the man and rip the ball away. He gave up after one game, and went back to his standard pastimes, singing to the tune of his own ukulele, playing cards for money, eating every time he felt the urge, and indulging in rough games with girls. His wife soon grew weary of trying to restrain him and she sadly moved back to Boston with their daughter. Babe was sorry to see them go, but once they were out of sight he hardly missed them. He was always intent on the immediate moment; the memory of things past trickled out of his mind like signs he had seen through a train window. He almost never talked with his teammates or with anyone about his early days, and some men who knew him well were convinced he had had no childhood or any parents at all but had simply leaped out of a cloud somewhere, baseball spikes on and bat in hand, looking for a pitch to swing at.

Babe's first year with the Yankees was a parlous one for baseball and all sports, for other reasons than Babe's own stroking of home runs. It was the year Carl Mays, the Yankees' testy underhand pitcher, killed shortstop Ray Chapman of Cleveland with a pitch that struck poor Ray on the head. Mays had not been trying to hit the man at all, although he had been known to throw baseballs at people for that purpose. This time he had simply wheeled up his sizzling, deceptive pitch as close as possible to the batter's body and Chapman, misjudging the flight of the ball completely, leaned into the pitch and took it on the temple, with a crack that sounded much like the bat meeting the ball. Indeed, when the ball, bouncing off Chapman's head, rolled part way back to the mound, Mays hurried in and fielded it before he realized that Chapman lay flat in the batter's box.

Chapman, still conscious, was carried to the locker room, asking for his wife. Then he went into a coma and died in the hospital that night, while his teammates wept and Carl Mays sat pale and dismayed at the news.

This was also the spring in which the Boston Braves and the Brooklyn Dodgers, on a gloomy day when it seemed that rain at any moment might bring the game to a close, played the longest game in history—twenty-six innings to a 1-to-1 tie, which was called off "on account of darkness" although it was no darker in the twenty-sixth inning than it had been in the first. And, as has been noted, it was the year when fixing of the 1919 World Series was revealed, first of all by a Chicago sportswriter named Hugh Fullerton, who was very nearly ostracized for daring to print the rumors that had been on nearly every lip on the baseball benches. It was the year when organized baseball decided to turn its conscience over to Judge Landis—not really because of the Black Sox gambling scandal but because the "National Commission" that was supposed to be running the game could not even get the two league presidents to abide by its rulings. So they made Landis dictator and spent the next twenty-five years wishing they hadn't.

In 1920, organized baseball also ruled out all freak deliveries that required any tampering with the ball, such as bathing it in saliva. Pitchers had discovered years before that by using spit or sandpaper or grease, they could eliminate the spin on the ball that is imparted by the fingertips, so that the ball, apparently thrown with full force, would seem to float toward the plate and would drop like a stoned sparrow before the batter expected it to. By outlawing the spitball (seventeen pitchers who depended on the pitch were allowed to continue to use it), the emery ball (with one spot polished slick by emery paper), and the ball roughed up on the belt buckle or darkened with licorice, the rulemakers hoped to make life easier for the batter. (Babe Ruth was teaching them that it was batting hard and batting far and batting often that really made the mare go.) It took several years for pitchers to realize that there were other ways of robbing the ball of spin, and to learn to employ those methods in ways sufficiently devious to make it possible for umpires to overlook them.

Babe Ruth never used a spitball that anyone could recall. He had great speed and control when he was a pitcher and scorned trickery, just as he scorned as a hitter the Ty Cobb method of using an adjustable grip on the bat so as to punch the ball to different fields. Babe could bunt as well as any man alive. And under extreme circumstances, as when the enemy "overshifted" on him to get all the fielders in the path of his power, he might poke a ball into left field. But generally, when he spoke of "hitting a couple" his mates knew he meant hitting a couple out of the park. And that is where he hit most of his fifty-four in 1920. Not a single one of his home runs had anything freakish about it. Umpire Billy Evans, one of the sharpest ever to enter the profession, noted that all but two of Ruth's Polo Grounds home runs in 1920 went into the upper stands or over them. And certainly no one had built the park to Ruth's measure.

But there were rumors, stronger than ever now, that the Yankees, drawing fans by the tens of thousands as they were, would soon build a park of their own, to accommodate more people than any other baseball park in the world.

This was also the year that women, finally recognized as people, would be allowed to vote in a national election. They still could not enter the major professions with any real hope of getting through the training period alive. They could not even hold school jobs, in some communities, if they were married—for it was deemed that *two* breadwinners in any family meant that some other family was being deprived of the very little cash that was available in that day to distribute among working people. It was everywhere accepted that women's wages should be lower than men's. In department stores where male clerks would earn a princely eighteen dollars a week, girls would be hired to do the same work for twelve. Even speakeasies did not welcome unescorted women. And a lady who lighted a cigarette in a stylish restaurant would be asked to put the weed out—or even take herself out of the room. (Ladies' rooms, in those days, one imagines, were often so blue with smoke as to earn a zero visibility rating.)

To the sophisticates of the age, the notion of allowing the little darlings to have the vote—and presumably even to run for office—was a matter almost too funny to be borne. Benjamin De Casseres, called "an apocalyptic genius" by a contemporary, contributed to the *New York Times Magazine* a piece that the editor promised held a "laugh in every line." It is just possible that the editor miscounted, for a few of the lines were such as these:

"Man has become a mere remnant. We will soon be on the political bargain counter."

"We men used to vote in the open. Now we will vote from a muff and our little mental life will be rounded by ice cream."

"The inauguration address of Matriarch I will be a castigation of men from Adam to Ponzi." [Charles Ponzi was a contemporary get-rich-quick swindler, who promised to double investors' money in a week or two through some hocus-pocus with international reply coupons.]

"Her Secretary of the Treasury will demand a bank reserve in every city for extravagant shoppers."

The readers of the *Times* were perhaps able to stifle their laughter rather quickly at these observations, for the papers were filled in that time with solemn portents. The Brooklyn Rapid Transit strike had prompted rock throwing and other types of random violence, with one strikebreaking motorman knocked unconscious as he drove his train through a cut where chunks of rock were everywhere available. Three thousand moving men and a lesser number of plumbers had also gone out on strike, along with fifteen thousand painters. The painters wanted ten dollars a day instead of nine; the moving-van men wanted a forty-four-hour week instead of a fifty-hour week. And the plumbers wanted nine dollars a day, a forty-four-hour week, and a few more holidays—including May 1, International Labor Day.

Government employees in Washington also went off their jobs. They did not strike—that was illegal. But they all resigned at once and asked for a raise in pay from $1,800 a year to $3,000. Government laborers wanted a raise from $899.50 a year to $1,196.

Landlords in New York, perhaps to make ready for the surge of affluence such pay raises portended, sent out forty thousand eviction notices in a move for a general increase in rents. And in Tennessee, to add a note of utter confusion, the state House of Representatives, which had just finished voting approval of the Women's Suffrage Amendment, voted to expunge ratification from the record and withdraw their assent. The state's attorney general said this could not be done. But the lawmakers did it (twenty pro-suffrage representatives had been unable to get back in time for the vote) and urged the attorney general to put *that* in his pipe and smoke it. But this final bit of male chauvinist panache went almost unnoticed and the ladies made ready to vote—for peace, some of their leaders proclaimed.

But there was not too much peace in the land, or even overseas, where many of the Irish were in a frenzy as Terence MacSwiney, the lord mayor of Cork, drew closer to death from a hunger strike in Brixton Jail, London. Polish troops under Marshal Józef Pilsudski reported almost daily triumphs over the Bolsheviki—and yet never seemed to do them completely in. Red General Semeon M. Budenny would be in full retreat one day and next day would be back in the fight.

Strikebreakers were being brought into New York by the thousand to help break the BRT strike. When political leaders pointed out that the BRT could finance the raises the trainmen wanted for far less than it cost to import strikebreakers, the company spokesmen explained that all this was reckoned capital investment, as it was a sort of insurance against further strikes. And who was to say it was not also striking a blow against Bolshevism?

The New York State legislature struck its own blow against the plague by voting to expel all five of its Socialist members. Duly elected or not, they were obviously not "American" and so had no place in the councils of the state. So arrogant was this move, and so distant from any semblance of due process, that even the New York *Evening Post* was prompted to reprint a passage Mr. Dooley (Finley Peter Dunne) had written about the Dreyfus case:

" 'Judge,' says the attorney for the difinse, 'an gintlmen iv the jury,' he says.

" 'Ye're a liar,' says the judge."

Of course these symbolic burnings of the red flag and shakings of the fist at Bolshevism drew no blood and were of no consequence compared to the horrors of the previous season, when coal and iron "police" hired by Weirton Steel had broken the steel strike by murdering a union leader and scattering the strikers with pistol shots—after which they rounded up a hundred or more of the frightened men and made them kneel and kiss the American flag to illustrate their devotion to the nation that granted them the right to live like animals within barbed-wire enclosures. But there was still a great deal of uncharged-off patriotism bubbling in the veins of even some of those who had made it all the way to France and had been shot at. A chance to do violence to some live and acknowledged enemy was openly sought after by men both young and old in every city. This was simply one of the unreckoned costs of war—a deeply implanted conviction that it was a sweet and noble thing, not only to die for one's country, but to kill and injure people who spoke out against the sacred government. Men who sought *reasons* for fighting were recognized, even by the clergy, as mollycoddles and pantywaist pacifists. And "pacifist" in that day was another word for traitor, even when the war was two years past.

Anarchists of course were fair game for everyone. Big Bill Haywood, leader of the Industrial Workers of the World, was reckoned an anarchist, if not a Bolshevist, and so received short shrift indeed in Federal court where he was tried during the war before Judge Kenesaw Mountain Landis on a charge of violating the Espionage Act. The good judge, who would soon assume the task of purifying organized baseball and keeping it pure, made certain that no one might mistake him for a fellow who would be soft on anarchists. When the prosecution failed to make Big Bill squirm, he took over the cross-examination himself to ensure a finding of guilty. Then he sentenced Big Bill to twenty years in the jug, plus a $10,000 fine. Big Bill was mighty lucky, many upright folk agreed, not to have been awarded the electric chair.

The hunt for anarchists was given sudden horrid impetus by a fearful explosion in Wall Street on September 15 at just one minute past noon. The bell of Trinity Church had not even completed tolling twelve when there came a blue-white flash on the street in front of the Subtreasury Building, a flash as blinding as a lightning bolt. Instantly the whole area seemed split in two. Windows two blocks away were shattered to splinters. While a terrifying roar still echoed, men and women could be heard screaming all up and down the streets and roadways, where there had been swarms of office workers just turned out for lunch. In the office of J. P. Morgan & Company, just across from the Subtreasury, tall plate-glass windows were blown in and shattered glass fell like a shower of ice. William Joyce, a young clerk who was to be married in two weeks, was struck by a ragged piece of iron and killed instantly. Junius P. Morgan, son of the senior partner, received a cut on the head. But along Wall Street and Broad Street there was carnage. Mangled bodies lay where they had been hurled, twisted into heaps of bloodied clothes. A few victims tried to struggle to their feet, screaming in pain. Some, clutching their bleeding heads, staggered blindly this way and that and a few fell to the roadway again and died. Men and women ran wildly to escape the scene. Within the New York Stock Exchange, maddened traders fought with each other to escape the great lethal chunks of broken glass that tumbled from the high windows. President William Remick hurried to the balcony and rang the bell that ended trading. And outside, a boy seized a standing automobile, piled into it all the injured it would hold, and started at high speed for the hospital, the auto horn wildly squawking.

The police were soon overwhelmed with the job of trying to sort the dead from the living, stanch the wounds, and get the injured off to hospitals. Screaming women grabbed policemen and begged for word of their husbands, whom they had walked with but moments before. Friends who suddenly found each other alive, with the blast still echoing in their ears and the smoke stinging their nostrils, frantically pumped each other's hands, as if they had returned from a ten-year separation.

Finally a hundred infantrymen from Governors Island arrived by ferry to keep the crowd in order. Already scavengers had made note that there were thousands of dollars' worth of stock certificates and bonds scattered about the pavement where they had been blasted out of the hands of messengers who had been caught in the explosion. Some of them never returned to their proper owners and some were found days later in odd corners of the area, piled like trash.

Within minutes after the blast, there were "experts" on the scene to determine the cause. There was a unanimous feeling that anarchists had done the deed, in an effort of course to assassinate that archetype of capitalist exploiters—J. P. Morgan himself. But Morgan was in Europe. And reporters dwelt on the stupidity of the Reds, who had timed their explosion for the moment when the streets would be filled, not by captains of industry, their natural prey, but by mere messengers and clerks, turned loose at the workingman's lunch hour. The captains—that is, the partners of J. P. Morgan & Company, or those four who were in town, Thomas W. Lamont, Dwight W. Morrow, George Whitney, and Elliot Bacon—were all snug inside their offices behind fortresslike walls when the explosion occurred. Within an hour or so of the blast, workmen had already started to mend the dents the flying metal had made in the outer walls of the Morgan building, just a few scars where the stone had been broken away.

Some expert theorized that the driver of the wagon that carried the bomb—for bomb it surely was, all the experts agreed—may have been caught in a traffic jam and, fearing the timing device might tick its last at any second, had abandoned the wagon before he had quite reached the J. P. Morgan front door, his obvious target. There was no question about the wagon. Several witnesses recalled it—a one-horse truck, with lattice sides. Broken wagon spokes lay at the scene, where the explosion had made a hole in the pavement. And hard by lay the disemboweled and shattered horse.

Captain William J. Flynn, head of the Secret Service, hastened from Washington to take charge of the investigation. The police bomb squad came up with the names of a number of men of radical views, and were determined to run them *all* down. William J. Burns, after a thorough glance around, said flatly that it was a bomb, probably made out of TNT, encased in a box with chunks of iron window weights. Captain Flynn, after hearing witnesses who reported suspicious characters fleeing from the scene, said there was no chance at all that it had been an accident. But still the police had some doubts. *Could* it have been some dynamite or gunpowder being transported to a construction site? Not at all, said divers experts. No permits for transportation of explosives in that neighborhood had been granted. DuPont de Nemours shipping some dynamite? No, DuPont reported that there had been no such shipments—except one, and *that* truck was supposed to be far uptown. The horse's shoes were examined. They wore the marks JHU—Journeymen Horseshoers Union. Perhaps, if one could run the blacksmith to ground . . . ?

Meanwhile there were far more exciting leads to follow. There was talk of a man who had stood near the site, talking to three other men, who were *laughing*. If *he* could be found . . .

Then a gentleman of seventy-five, who had chanced into the neighborhood and had been knocked unconscious by the blast, recalled that he had seen three men, who looked like "East Side peddlers," fleeing the site just before the explosion. One, "a greasy fellow," had been standing near the wagon and had called to the other two, "Let's get out of here!" And on Nassau Street, two and a half blocks away, a letter carrier had taken out of a mailbox a handful of circulars bearing the legend "American Anarchist Fighters" that warned "Free Political Prisoners or It Will Be Death for All of You." That, said Captain Flynn, put a cap on it. It could *not* have been an accident and was surely a plot. (Only Frank Francisco, an investigator for the Department of Justice, insisted that there were "indications" that it *was* an accident.)

Another witness turned up who had seen a motor truck with the word DYNAMITE lettered on its side going down Broad Street before the blast. Another recalled seeing a one-horse truck with a wooden box in it. And still another told police he had watched three men—one "splattered with blood"—pile into an auto after the explosion and go speeding away. The police brushed that last story off. Why would the perpetrators stand around until the bomb went off? Maybe they were taking the guy to the hospital.

But those three peddler types—that was different. Police started digging after them. And of course a few still checked horseshoers, on the chance that the horse at least might have been known. They did finally uncover one James Haggerty, of Park Avenue and 102nd Street, who vowed he knew the horse well, had indeed shoed him just the other day, but could not for the life of him recall his owner or even what nationality the man had been. The police leaped on Haggerty's story at first and questioned him at length, hoping for some sort of description, however hazy. But Jim could scratch up nary a clue. He never gave a damn about the owners anyway, said he; it was the horse he dealt with. Finally the cops had to conclude that old Jim was talking through his hat.

By this time, more experts, of whom there seemed a king's bounty, had actually, from examining fragments of metal found scattered throughout nearby buildings and appraising the extent of the shock wave, come up with a detailed description of the bomb. It was, they said, shaped like an aerial torpedo, and contained thirty pounds of TNT. (But still another expert, a man named Dunn who had invented an explosive called dunnite, averred that the explosive could not possibly have been TNT, else the whole area would have been demolished.)

Now the police had suspects by the dozen to round up, including one man of vague description who had been seen "near the site" of the mailing of the anarchist circulars. (The official Anarchist party and other radical groups officially disowned the affair, but no one believed *them*.)

There was just one disquieting note, to which the Secret Service paid as little heed as possible. A man *had* appeared, just before the explosion, on the scaffolding above the sidewalk at Broad and Wall streets, where a building was being reconstructed, and had announced that he had dynamite to deliver. Told that there was no need of dynamite there and none had been ordered, he went off to telephone his office and get the right address.

Another workman at the construction site also recalled meeting a stranger on that scaffold. Asked what he was doing there, the man said, looking down at the crowded street, "I'm looking for my horse."

Within a few minutes the blast came, and no more was seen of the man, nor did any recall just what he looked like, except that he had been "well-dressed." Did this make it remotely possible that the disaster had been an accident? Not by a damn sight, said William J. Flynn, William J. Burns, the New York bomb squad, the New York *Times,* and the New York police. But if it *were* an accident, said Captain Flynn, then by God this man with the horse would find himself indicted for homicide!

There had been thirty killed outright at the scene and three hundred injured. More died every day, until finally there were thirty-eight altogether. And more suspects kept turning up. The New York police reached out to the far corners of the Bronx and brought in the man who had been seen talking with the three men who laughed. He, it was shown, was a radical for sure, in possession of radical leaflets and other evidence of alienism. Besides, he was a Russian Pole, the same as a Bolshevik. And he admitted being in Wall Street when the bomb went off and refused to name his laughing friends. The police promptly went to work on him.

The *Times* pontificated in its editorial columns that this murderous explosion was a prime example of "what mad passions are ready to be stirred by the wild and whirling words of editors and politicians!" And it urged, in wild and whirling words, that anarchists be hunted down like animals in their lairs.

The man from the Bronx was Alexander J. Brailovsky, who called himself a journalist. He had come to see a man about establishing a Russian theater in New York and also to bargain with a jeweler to whom he was trying to sell some ornate jewel cases. His story was verified at every point, despite his "extreme radical views" which had long been known to the police. His companions had not even a taint of anarchism or violence about them. There was no dynamite to be found among the whole lot, so the police were reduced at last to holding Brailovsky merely as an undesirable alien.

The three frightened peddlers turned out to be Hungarians, and they had unquestionably run like thieves from the scene of the explosion. But they had run *after* the blast, as hundreds of others had done, determined to get as far as their legs would allow from whatever deviltry was afoot.

By this time cash rewards had been offered totaling $20,500, so men and women everywhere were scrambling for suspects. There was talk now that perhaps the plotters had not been out to kill J. P. Morgan after all but to rob the Subtreasury and the Assay Office, which were together at Broad and Wall. There had been nine hundred million in gold stored in vaults there, enough to drive any man to deeds of desperation.

Two weeks or more had passed before the authorities finally laid hold of the livest suspect of the lot. He was captured in Pittsburgh by the local police, who had come warily to his hotel door, knocked, and received no answer. Whereupon they broke the door in and found their quarry sitting in his chair "reading a radical newspaper." The picture of the man's sitting calmly in a chair reading an incriminating document while his door was being splintered about his ears presented no incongruity to the panting readers of the report. Nor did it immediately strike anyone as strange that the police could identify the political slant of the paper so promptly. Well, they had said, it *was* in Russian (actually it was in Polish).

But there was a firmer basis for their suspicions than any collection of untranslatable propaganda. The man, whom they identified as Florian Zelinski, had been pointed out to them by a recent arrival in Pittsburgh who had met Zelinski on a train. The informant, a grim-faced type named Konkel, reported that Zelinski, after making friends with him, had shown him a quantity of dynamite and said: "This is for another explosion. I am taking it to New York. You saw what we did to Wall Street. Next time it will be bigger and more terrible."

The police did indeed find in Zelinski's hotel room a large quantity of dynamite, along with percussion caps. And when Mr. Z. admitted not only that he hailed from Brooklyn but had been in New York on the day of the explosion, the cops locked him up and triumphantly reported their catch to Captain Flynn of the Secret Service.

Captain Flynn and the New York police hastened to the suspect's address in Brooklyn and learned many amazing facts. In the first place, the man's name was Zelenko. A copy of *Russky Golos* (hardly a radical newspaper) was found under his bed and confiscated. In his trunk they found a large batch of papers, including a pay envelope from the Hercules Powder Company and a discharge from the United States Army. Zelenko had been excused from active service because he was not a citizen. This discovery seemed hardly enough to hang the man on, but the police learned also that there was a restaurant or club close by that was noted as a "Communist haunt."

From Pittsburgh came further word that Zelenko could not account for some missing dynamite. He said he had picked up twelve sticks on his job as a miner in West Virginia but now had only seven. Nor could he, the Pittsburgh cops reported, account for his movements on the day of the explosion. But just as the noose seemed to be tightening about poor Zelenko, it began to unravel. Konkel, it turned out, instead of being a Cincinnati man, as he told police in Pittsburgh, was himself a resident of New York, of East Fourth Street, near the Bowery. He had a reputation as a "bitter anti-

Bolshevist" and had a tendency to find Reds under every bed. (He had followed Zelenko from the train and had spotted his hotel before calling the police.) And Zelenko himself was well known in his Brooklyn neighborhood. He was a devout communicant of the Polish Catholic Church, was not known at all in the "Communist haunt," often sat on his stoop at night to talk with his neighbors, and had never been known to utter a radical word. He had worked for the Hercules Powder Company some seven years before, as a common laborer, with no chance at all to learn the technical side of working with gunpowder. Since that job he had held several others, including a hitch as a motorman on the BRT. Captain Flynn observed too that it was common practice for miners like Zelenko to carry their dynamite with them from job to job.

Captain Flynn then took Zelenko right off his list of suspects and declared Konkel's story was not worth listening to. But the Pittsburgh police were determined to hang the charges on him. They would hold him for illegal transportation of explosives and keep him in the lockup, they vowed, until he was completely cleared or else proved a dangerous man. Besides, the Pittsburgh police had received an anonymous postcard, addressed to Zelenko in their care, which hinted of a plot to blow up City Hall, the Court House, the Custom House, and the Post Office. And *that* was nothing to take lightly!

Still, there were signs everywhere that Bolshevism was breathing its last. A correspondent for the New York *Herald* brought word from Russia that the Soviets had failed and that their regime was near its end. And from Paris came word that the treacherous Lenin was now the "abject slave" of a beautiful twenty-three-year-old Russian adventuress, Olga Gorakhoff, who was said to possess mystic powers. Lenin, the unnamed observer reported, obeyed the young lady's slightest whim. And inasmuch as she was a bitter enemy of Great Britain, for some reason no one had yet fathomed, she was likely to will the entire Bolshevik Army into an attack on British interests in Persia and India. (She had already brought about the demotion of a number of Red Army officers whose "friendship" for the girl had exceeded the "limits agreeable to the chief commissioners of the Soviet government.") As for Lenin's partner, the wily Trotsky, he had succumbed in turn to a French danseuse and, it was said, gave in to her "every murmur." Whether her murmurs also ensnared any army officers, the story did not tell. But it seemed clear enough, to everybody who was addicted to this sort of gossip, that the whole Bolshevik movement was decaying from the top. Indeed, Helsingfors sources reported that an "anti-Bolshevik wave" was sweeping Russia, as it was certainly sweeping the United States. With a little more diligence, one was convinced, the police and the Secret Service might soon have the entire calendar of anarchist and Bolshevik saints behind bars—along with Gene Debs and Nicky Arnstein. (Nicky of course was no Bolshevik, just a slickster who seemed bent on living like a millionaire without working for his money. Right now he was rusticating in the Ludlow Street jail for contempt of a grand jury that had endeavored to question him about the bankruptcy of one of the firms in which he was reputed to have an interest.)

Baseball folk, although shaken, as the whole nation was, by the Wall Street explosion, were soon more involved in the 1920 World Series, which Cleveland, despite Rube Marquard and Burleigh Grimes, won from Brooklyn in seven games—five games to two. But another unsung Brooklyn pitcher, Clarence Mitchell, managed to hit into five outs in two trips to the plate in the fifth game. His first time at bat, with two men on base and the hit-and-run play on, Mitchell hit the ball hard. But he hit it straight at Cleveland second baseman Bill Wambsganss, who had started for second base as soon as he saw the runner coming down. Wambsganss met Mitchell's blow head-on, gloved it automatically, continued across the base to put out the runner who had just left it, and then reached down and tagged the runner coming in—an unassisted triple play, the very first ever in World Series. Next time up, Mitchell hit into a double play, marking the first time since the beginning of the world that any man had hit into that many outs in only two tries. (As for the triple play, John Heydler, president of the National League, who was naturally rooting for the Dodgers, saw nothing remarkable about that at all. "I could have done that *myself*," he snorted.)

When the Series was over, with Cleveland's easygoing young pitcher, Stan Coveleski, winning three games on a total of 261 pitches, scandal of one sort and another kept baseball on the front pages. When the grand-jury investigation of the great fix had begun to peter out with the disappearance of the signed confessions and their prompt retraction by most of the accused players, there was still Giants Manager John J. McGraw to read about.

John, who had been suspended once before by the Lambs Club

106

for obstreperous behavior, had got himself into another row there in which he was badly beaten by an actor named William Boyd (not the beloved cowboy but a saturnine smoothy). Then John, in turn, had rewarded one of the men who took him home by belting the poor fellow out on the sidewalk in front of John's home and fracturing his skull. And another Good Samaritan who had gone to commiserate with poor John on having been kicked out of the club for good limped away from John's sickbed with a broken ankle. There were lawsuits threatened and criminal action pending along with random recrimination whenever John or one of his victims opened his mouth.

That organized baseball in the city survived all this, on top of the endless recitals of fix and attempted fix that rolled out of the Chicago grand-jury room, was due far more to Babe Ruth than to Kenesaw Mountain Landis. When the New York Yankees traveled out of town, the crowds that came to see them—even when the championship had long been decided—were not simply a few hundred more or even a few thousand more than ordinarily. There were often two and three times the normal attendance in the park. Nor was there ever a doubt about what the new fans came to see. As soon as Babe Ruth had made his final trip to the plate, the fans would file out by the thousands. Often as many as twenty thousand out of thirty thousand fans would pick up and leave when the Babe's work at the plate was completed.

When the season opened in 1921, professional baseball entered its Golden Age. And its Golden Boy was a big good-natured rowdy from Baltimore who had always thought baseball was the most fun in the world.

PART III

A Thousand Dollars a Week

ED Barrow, the man who had changed Babe Ruth from the boot left-handed pitcher In Boston to the best outfielder in baseball, quit the Red Sox when the 1920 season was done and came to the New York Yankees, just as all good Boston boys had been doing all season long. The fact was that changing Ruth from pitcher to outfielder had not been Barrow's idea originally. He was not the sharpest appraiser of talent in the game. (In the spring of 1920 he announced that the Red Sox had a "new Babe Ruth" in Ben Paschal, a substitute out-fielder who hit twenty-four home runs in eight seasons.) But Harry Hooper, the veteran Red Sox right fielder, had persuaded Ed, against Ed's better judgment, that a bat as mighty as Babe's was worth even more than a mighty left arm.

Now Ed, called Simon Legree by everyone except Jake Ruppert, the Yankee owner (who called him Barrows), once more took on the job of keeping the frolicsome Jidge halter-broke. And Jidge, happy to be working with Simon again, celebrated by frightening American League pitchers out of their pants. On opening day, April 13, 1921, against the Philadelphia Athletics, and before the largest opening-day crowd ever to gather at the Polo Grounds, Babe hit two doubles and three singles in five times at bat, his first "five for five" since he made five hits for the Red Sox in May 1918. In the remaining two weeks of April he hit five home runs. In the first two weeks of May he hit seven more. Then in June, after he had put in those few hours behind bars for speeding, Babe hit seven home runs in five games.

Babe had started off the exhibition season with a strained wrist that kept him out of action for several days. But then, on the trip home, playing in Southern cities against the Brooklyn Dodgers, Babe had started to slug the ball again, until the crowds that piled out to see him filled the little Southern parks so full that they actually overran the playing field, and once brought the game to a close by pushing the police aside and filling up the outfield. (In Birmingham and Atlanta, in protest against being shoved here and there by police, the crowd took to heaving seat cushions onto the diamond. For a while the players tossed them back, but eventually the things just came too fast and the game was ended.)

Crowds of this sort were meat and drink to Babe. He let himself be posed and reposed and posed again by photographers in every sort of position—batting, fielding, squatting down, smoking, or standing with his arm around little Jackie Coogan, then the most famous child actor in the land. And he threw himself into every game as if it were the last he would ever play, for the championship of the Universe. He somersaulted over the sod to catch fly balls or stop long drives. He belted every good pitch as if he meant to break the ball in two. Crowds in New Orleans had cheered him wildly for driving a mighty foul ball out of the park and then lustily striking out.

The previous fall, in Middletown, Connecticut, Babe had narrowly escaped serious injury when he wrecked his gleaming Packard Twin Six roadster in a head-on meeting with a truck. But now he was back at the wheel once more, sizzling up Riverside Drive and back as if he were on a country road. The people remaining in New York who did not know Babe as the most famous hitter of baseballs in the world could still recognize him as the man who was always getting arrested for speeding.

Right from the start of the season, Babe, whose bank account always seemed bottomless, kept running out of cash. But he never suffered for need of it. When the ten- and twenty-dollar bills ran out, Babe had simply to call a teammate and seek a loan of $1,500. (That seemed to be the only amount he felt safe with.) And the teammate would tap one or two others and come up with the cash. The whole club knew who was drawing in the crowds, winning the games, and boosting the salaries. Now earning $30,000 a year, plus all his side money, Babe never felt the need to count his roll too carefully. He always paid back his loans on payday, and usually borrowed again before the next check came through. He handed out ten-dollar tips for petty attentions and hundred-dollar bills for special services. He seemed to have taken an oath never again to shave off his own whiskers. Instead he would pay the hotel barber a day's pay to come to his room to do it for him every morning. "That's what they're for, aren't they?" he would respond if anyone questioned this indulgence.

With a thousand more dishes he still had to taste and joys he had to sample, Babe greeted each new day with the fresh face and eager eyes of a boy turned loose from school. He was obedient to little Miller Huggins, the harried manager of the Yankees, who had been floored with what had looked like appendicitis in the spring but was probably just a violent attack of nerves from the continual criticism he took from Colonel Huston, one of his bosses, and his fear that Ed Barrow had been brought in to supplant him.

When Huggins asked Babe to bunt, Babe bunted. And one day when he urged Babe to push a hit to left, Babe, following orders to the letter, pushed the ball right into the left-field seats. In Detroit one day that season, when Huggins was desperately trying to spread his scanty pitching staff over a string of doubleheaders, Babe offered to pitch a game himself. He had been longing anyway to take the mound against the man he hated —Ty Cobb, player manager of the Detroit ball club. Babe walked Ty Cobb once, got him to pop an easy fly to the outfield, and then struck the great man out. Babe left the mound then and the Yankees won the game.

Cobb, who always seemed openly at war with his opponents, made a special point of tossing vituperative comments at Ruth, whom he saw as his only rival for top position in baseball. Babe was no master of repartee. His usual reply to some taunt was "Oh, yeah?" or "Is that so?" or "So's your old man!" But on the bench, his mates would pass him comments to shout to Ty or suggest gestures that would drive the great man to a frenzy. (One of Ty's least favorites was the holding of the side of the hand, salute-fashion, at the Adam's apple, which was sign language for: "You've got shit in your neck.") Ty knew that Babe would never invent any very complex insults on his own, so when Ruth offered any especially biting comment, Cobb would accuse the men on either side of Ruth of having thought it up. One day Al DeVormer, sitting at Ruth's side, while Cobb, standing by the batting cage, was exchanging bitter insults with the big man, pleaded guilty to Cobb's charge of being the real source of some new epithet. Then he stood up and ambled quietly over to look Cobb right in the eye. DeVormer, third-string catcher for the Yankees, was a ballplayer of very modest accomplishments. But he was tougher than horsemeat and almost exactly the same size as Ty Cobb.

"If you want to mix it with me, you son of a bitch," he told Cobb in a normal tone, "just say so and we'll go under the stands right now."

Cobb, despite his combativeness, was really a complete also-ran when it came to fighting with his fists: he was more of a rassle, choke, kick, and scratch type. He knew that Al was probably still in search of the guy he couldn't lick, so Ty turned his attention immediately to what was happening in the batting cage and made no answer at all. Babe roared with delight and Ty's neck began to glow like a hot stove lid.

This was probably the last year of Babe's boyhood, just as it was the first year of the New York Yankees' championship tradition. Still young enough to bounce back from bruise or hangover or lack of sleep, and still panting with a desire to keep doing better and better on the diamond, Babe loved his manager, loved all his teammates, and loved all the fans who gathered to greet him. Only his bottomless appetite gave him trouble. His stomach seemed to turn sour every day soon after breakfast and he took to cajoling it with a heaping tablespoonful of bicarbonate of soda. Eventually the spoonful of bicarbonate became a superstitious ritual, which Babe dared not disregard lest his batting eye desert him. He had other superstitions too, which he obeyed religiously. Trotting in from the outfield, he took care always to step on second base. He usually left his hotel by a side entrance. But whatever entrance he used on the day his club won a game, he would continue to patronize that one until the club lost. Any butterfly that was not colored white was a flying jinx to Ruth and he drove them off like a madwoman in a swarm of hornets.

Superstitions, in that day, were much honored everywhere by men and women who should have known better, so baseball players who cultivated such petty fears were not deemed eccentric. It had even come to be accepted as a mark of honest manliness to refuse to allow a third light from the same match. There were young men who would solemnly and ostentatiously knock down the match if it had already lit two smokes, or even tear a cigarette from a companion's mouth and crush it out if it had been lit third in line. Large hotels in New York admitted no thirteenth floor—only 12A or some such evasion. A few just skipped from twelve to fourteen. The young reporter who so far forgot himself in the press box as to mention aloud that a pitcher had not yet granted a single hit might be paralyzed by the avalanche of venom that his peers would pour upon him. He had *ruined* a no-hit game by mentioning its possibility!

Babe had no superstition about indulging his appetites. When he found himself short of eating tobacco on the field one day he asked a former Boston teammate for a chew. The enemy player gladly handed Babe a large plug of tobacco and Babe bit into it like a hungry dog.

"Jesus!" the other man exclaimed. "Give me what you bit off and keep the plug!"

Manager Huggins tried now and then to persuade Babe to devour a little less food, for his belly had begun to balloon over his belt. Babe listened to the little man solemnly and earnestly promised to try to limit his intake. He might then go a whole day, or even two, without asking for that extra pint of ice cream between meals. But he would always slip right back into living as if each moment existed for itself alone, forgetting the promise and hardly noticing that he had ever done any differently.

Babe had not yet become an important enough man in his own eyes to defy his manager. But he just never felt any urge stronger than those that bade him to get his share of everything that tasted good and to get it immediately. Perhaps, if his extra weight had kept him from hitting home runs or caused him to stumble on the base paths, or made it impossible for him to play every day, Babe might have grappled with his appetites and beat them. But he was hitting home runs at the same pace as the year before and seemed bound once gain to collect more than fifty.

Fifty had sounded like a sort of ceiling the previous year, when there was more excitement over his reaching and exceeding that "magic" number than over his breaking his earlier record. After fifty, who counted? No man alive would ever drive out home runs to that number again.

But this season was apparently going to be the greatest of Babe's career. He missed so little play that he may have been said to have contributed to every victory. For even when he was not destroying every third pitch served up to him, pitchers, afraid that he might, had begun giving him free bases on balls in order to pitch to Wally Pipp, the first baseman, who was batting very close to .300 himself. The deliberate base on balls, rare enough in earlier baseball to prompt batters and spectators to rage at pitchers who resorted to it, now became as common as the pitchout—the wide pitch thrown out of the batter's reach to trap a base runner. And stealing bases seemed hardly worth all the effort with Babe Ruth coming to bat behind you and likely to provide you with a free ride all the way home. So base running too began to decline as an art—although Babe himself was always an aggressive and swift runner of the base lines.

Babe actually stole seventeen bases in 1921. But no one ever came to the park to watch him slide into second base. And he usually hit the ball so far anyway that there were no bases for him to steal. Babe came close to winning the batting championship of the league that year, with an average of .378 (Harry Heilmann of Detroit won the title with .394 and Cobb came in next with .389.) Babe did lead the league in runs scored and runs batted in as well as in home runs. (Nearest to his mark of fifty-nine homers were his teammate Bob Meusel, with twenty-four, and Ken Williams of St. Louis with the same number.) And he led the Yankees to their first pennant since the team was invented twenty years before.

Along the way, Babe suffered a sort of personality change. It was impossible to be Babe Ruth in that era and not gradually conclude that you were not subject to the restrictions that fretted other men. Babe was as happy and outgoing as ever, as openhanded with all who served him, and as devout a competitor. But one of his bosses, Colonel Huston, had made a particular pet of him and had invited him down into rich man's country to hunt quail and God knows what else, like a millionaire. And real live millionaires panted to meet him. Even movie actors and actresses, accustomed to moving about the world like royalty, with doors opening before they could set their hands to them, with policemen making a highway for them through clamoring crowds and hired hands bowing and scurrying to do their bidding almost before it was articulated—even they found themselves competing for Babe Ruth's attention. (Babe hardly knew one of them from all the others and could not keep any of their names straight.)

On September 15, 1921, Babe broke his previous year's home-run record. With two weeks to go, he ran the total to fifty-nine and made ready to enter the World Series against the Giants. It would be the first World Series for most of his teammates. For Babe it was the fourth.

But Babe, who had been hurling his overweight body over the outfield sod and into the gravel of the base line without regard for bumps and scrapes, developed a painful elbow which grew worse as he tried to ignore it. It was a long Series—the last of the "five out of nine" World Series that would be played—but it was speeded somewhat because all the games were played in the same park, New York's Polo Grounds. Swinging his bat in constant pain, Babe hit a home run in the fourth game, and attained a batting average of .313 for the Series. But he struck out eight times and made only one appearance at bat in the last three games. The Yanks lost the Series. But Babe had no time for regrets. He had signed up for his usual barnstorming tour—a project that paid him more than the World Series—and he was about to take off for Buffalo, leading a club made up of three or four teammates, plus a collection of New York semiprofessionals.

John McGraw had been outraged at the manner in which the stepchild Yankees had been outdrawing the great New York Giants, and had consistently belittled Babe Ruth as being only a poor imitation of Rogers Hornsby, the leading batsman of the National League. (Rogers had hit twenty-one home runs that year, second to George Burns of the Giants, who hit twenty-three.) Now he felt he had demonstrated for good and all that New York belonged to the Giants. But Ruth knew that New York belonged to Babe Ruth. In fact, all baseball belonged to Babe Ruth, and not even Judge Landis could call *him* to account.

The wiry little judge, as a matter of fact, was setting out to do exactly that. There was a rule that members of the championship teams could not go barnstorming after the season was over; Judge Landis, apprised that Ruth was planning a tour with his "all-stars," tried all one day to get Ruth on the phone. Babe did not return his call until late in the evening, when the little judge was all asimmer. Landis ordered Ruth to come see him immediately. Ruth, using a line that he had always liked the sound of, explained that he could not come as he "had to see a party." Well, tomorrow morning then. Oh, no, said Babe. I'm off to Buffalo on the midnight train.

In a trembling voice, the judge told Ruth that if he persisted in taking off on his trip, he would long regret it. Then he slammed down the phone and darkened the air about him with a flood of profanity as foul as any that had ever desecrated a baseball clubhouse.

Fred Lieb, a gentle sportswriter who had come to Landis's room to be in on the showdown with Ruth, hurried to warn the Yankee owners that their darling was about to step into a deep, deep hole. The two owners, Colonel Ruppert and Colonel Huston, long at war with each other, had declared a truce to share their joy at their first championship and had celebrated together at the season's end. Then Huston and Harry Frazee, the Red Sox owner, had continued the festivities even after the Yanks had lost the Series. When Lieb found Huston at the Hotel Martinique, the good colonel, drunker than a little bear, had laid himself down to sleep fully clothed crosswise of a bed, with Frazee, almost the same as dead, beside him. It took Lieb the better part of an hour to rouse the colonel and warn him of the danger. By that time, Babe had left the Ansonia and Huston had to hasten by cab to intercept Ruth at Grand Central. There he explained, as best he could with his slightly thickened tongue, the risks Babe was running. Can't be helped, Babe told him with some logic; we already signed the contracts and we got to fill them.

So Babe went to Buffalo, where it was cold and wet and where hardly anyone came out to watch him. Dates in some other cities were called off when the big-league clubs that owned the parks dared not, for fear of little Landis, open the gates to Babe. Before half the scheduled games had been played, Babe and his friends came back to New York with somewhat less than half the money they had expected to be carrying.

Landis allowed himself to cool off a little before imposing a penalty. Then, just when Babe had begun to believe the judge would not dare try to discipline a player as valuable as himself, Landis gave out word that he was fining the players the total of the World Series shares of all those who had taken part in the barnstorming trip and was suspending Ruth and Bob Meusel and Bill Piercy, a Yankee pitcher who had been among the All-Stars, until May 20 of the following year. Babe growled at the fine and counted on his bosses to have it remitted. The suspension, being so far in the future, he did not even contemplate. The future to Babe was the next day and the day after.

His barnstorming was over, but he *could* go on the vaudeville stage, where he learned to shuffle about a little bit, to tell some rehearsed jokes, and to sing, in his really fine voice, a song written for him alone: "Little by Little and Bit by Bit, I Am Making a Vaudeville Hit!" When Babe sang this song in New York, many of his clubmates sat in the front rows to lead the applause.

As Babe hopped about close to the footlights, bending his grinning face to the audience to start his song, his teammates began to wave at him frantically. Babe acknowledged them with a glittering smile and eased into his routine. Someone up front began to laugh at him and laughter spread through the audience. Even his *pals* were laughing, fit to choke. Finally Babe, to rollicking applause, backed off into the wings. When he did, he looked down and learned what it was his mates had been trying to tell him. His trouser fly was totally unbuttoned! And for a man who never wore underwear . . . ! Jesus Christ Almighty! Babe screamed. And he turned red from his collar to his scalp.

Still, everything else was going well for Ruth. He was to sign a new contract in the spring and he already had decided what he was going to ask for—and what he felt sure he would get. He would live well enough without the World Series dough, for his stage appearances paid him much more than that brought him. He would be off to Hot Springs before winter was over to play golf, drink the supposedly healthful waters, and boil off excess weight without any regimen so unpleasant as going without his dinner. Meanwhile New York was replete with pretty girls, good food, and illicit beer.

But the fall and winter of 1921 proved to be a hard time for drinking in New York. Police Commissioner Richard Enright was charged with the job of *really* halting the flow of illegal booze. There had been just too much scandal about it, with even Mayor John F. Hylan accused of attending parties where bootleg liquor was offered. So policemen on the beat were ordered to walk into *every* bar whenever they came to it and see exactly what was being served. John McGraw of the Giants, having reported that he had drunk too much whiskey at the Lambs Club to recall what happened in his famous fight there, was himself arrested and charged, on the basis of his own words, with the possession of unchurched whiskey. The club itself was raided and an employe pinched when he was found desperately trying to find places to hide a great cellar full of bottles with gin and whiskey in them. Even at Delmonico's two men were arrested and charged with selling, to two prohibition agents, whiskey and gin at $1.75 a drink. Of course they'd have been arrested if they had charged only half a dollar, as most places did. But a dollar seventy-five! For *one* drink? They should have been charged with larceny.

Throughout the back reaches of the nation, and even in the outback of the city itself or in its early-to-bed enclaves in the corners and creases of the island, there was little of the false prosperity that the sport and entertainment world was feeding on. Mothers in country villages made bloomers out of flour sacks for their little daughters and still had to pay more for sugar than for bread, despite the fact that the wholesale price of sugar had been cut in two. Work was hard to come by in small towns and pay was scanty. House and hotel workers who made a dollar a day were among the fortunates. Railroad workers were offered wholesale wage cuts as the price of having any jobs at all. Investors in construction complained that the mere decline in prices of building equipment and the award of tax exemptions was not enough to assure dividends. There would *have* to be wage reductions. In Massachusetts, wages in the construction industry were promptly reduced by 20 percent and there were strikes in Lawrence, Worcester, and Springfield. Railroad workers were told that they would be getting about 25 percent less money—30 cents or 37½ cents an hour instead of 48½ cents for common laborers; 47 cents for skilled mechanics instead of 59½ cents. Otherwise the wheels would stop rolling altogether.

The new Secretary of the Treasury, Andrew Mellon, urged that business be "encouraged" through repeal of the ugly excess-profits tax and the substitution of a general sales tax. And the thinkers and figurers at National City Bank told the working people of the nation that they were suffering from delusions when they complained that wages were going down. Because prices were going down too, and that meant that wages were really going *up*. So why should we not all be as happy as kings, or bankers?

As a matter of fact, prices were not even going down so that anyone could notice them. Clothing cost like hell; even high-salaried businessmen began to gripe at what a man had to pay to keep himself in clean collars and fully threaded suits. And in the fall of 1921 a movement began to drive clothing prices down through wearing old clothes to work and to school. Businessmen ostentatiously put on blue work shirts and even bib overalls to travel by limousine to their offices. Young men who would have blushed scarlet to have walked into any formal affair without a jacket and tie now attended college classes in sweaters or woolen shirts. Unpressed khaki pants and shirts without even sleeve garters to adorn them became commonplace in city high schools. But, perhaps because most of the people in the nation had been wearing old clothes at all times all their lives, the movement did not actually sweep the country. It resulted merely in the wearing of informal dress for the watching and playing of games or for walking about at the beach or in the country. Throughout the nation, men and women generally still wore shoes that came over their ankles, although oxfords for men were worn by boys as soon as they were permitted to select their own clothing. "Full-bloomered" knickers, later known as plus fours, had long been familiar on golf courses and now young men began to wear them on the city streets. But anyone (except Babe Ruth) who walked outdoors without a hat could be accused of being a "goddam college boy" or an utter simpleton who had nothing to keep warm up there anyway.

The stock market and the produce markets reported lower and lower prices. Potatoes that had been bringing $10.50 a barrel wholesale the year before were now quoted at $3.50. Coffee, once twelve cents a pound, was now six cents. And meat seemed to slide downward every day. Still working people were poor, short of meat and sugar, counting chicken a delicacy, handing clothes down like heirlooms, sleeping cold at night, and doctoring their own ills with nostrums cooked up by the old lady across the way or with packaged cure-alls like Father John's Medicine, Lydia Pinkham's Vegetable Compound, Carter's Little Liver Pills, Cascarets, Doan's Kidney Pills, Nuxated Iron, and Save-the-Baby.

Babe Ruth meanwhile stuck to his bicarbonate of soda and let nothing diminish his consumption of tender steaks, foaming beer, roast chicken, lamb chops, spare ribs, ice cream, and home-fried potatoes. At Hot Springs before the 1922 season had begun and when he had still not given any thought to his upcoming suspension, he talked with Colonel Huston, his indulgent boss, merry companion, and ardent admirer. The colonel wondered if Babe had given thought to the terms of a new contract. Yes, said Babe, he had. Well, what about $40,000? No, said Babe, he had something higher than that in mind. I'll make it $50,000, said the colonel. No, said Babe. But make it fifty-two and I'll sign. Not a penny less.

All right, said the colonel, I'll not argue about $2,000. But why $52,000? Because, said Babe, I always wanted to make a thousand bucks a week.

So now he was making it and now he was certainly rich. How on earth could a man spend more than a thousand a week? Of course Babe had been living for two or three years now as if he owned all the money in the world. But he loved the sound of that salary. A thousand bucks a week!

There were portents, early in the season, that this was not going to be a blessed time, for Babe Ruth or for his club. In the preseason exhibitions, the Brooklyn Dodgers again and again beat the Yankees by handsome scores. And fans who in better days had screamed for Babe to drive every pitch out of the park booed him happily now when he struck out, and cheered when the home-town pitcher put him down. In Fort Worth, when Wilcy Moore, the pitcher for the locals, allowed Babe only to roll weak ground balls to the infield, the yells of triumph grew as loud as they had the year before when Babe Ruth belted one far away. And in Dallas there were more howls of derision when Babe managed only a one-base hit in five visits to the batter's box.

Babe had two sore knees and a wrenched muscle in his back. But he was damned if he would give in. He did get four home runs in the first five days of the tour with the Dodgers. But then he went a whole week without another and sportswriters began to wonder in print if he would ever get going again. Then on the seventh day, in Richmond, Virginia, Babe drove one of Burleigh Grimes's pitches for such a long trip that one reporter vowed that it traveled more than five hundred feet. Local writers acknowledged it was the longest home run any Virginian had ever seen. Babe apparently had not yet admitted to himself that he was not going to play ball for the first month of regular play. And New York fans had gathered up countless signatures to petition Judge Landis to let their hero come keep the Yankees in the pennant race.

The Yankees had begun by this time to growl at each other and at Manager Huggins. Babe Ruth took care to shun the company of Carl Mays. And Carl Mays, removed from the pitcher's box by the manager when the Dodgers started to hit him hard, heaved the baseball over the grandstand and stamped off the field in a pet. When Huggins declared he would fine Mays $200, Carl announced he would quit the club if the fine were levied. It was not fair to take me out in the middle of an inning, he complained. He doesn't treat the other pitchers that way! Then Carl allowed he would wait until payday and see if the fine really stood. Then he said he would put it up to Colonel Huston, who was always fair. Then he said nothing and took his turn on the mound without further complaint.

Babe at first thought he might at least be permitted to practice with the club. When Landis forbade that, Babe had to watch the games from the press box. He lent his name to a column of baseball comment during this brief sabbatical and filled up with golf, bowling, and attendance at prize fights the hours left over from his visits to the choice New York bordellos—where the best food and drink as well as sex of the finest order could be sampled. As a matter of fact, the whorehouses in all the great cities, but particularly in New York, always offered the choicest beer and the most succulent steaks. The gangsters who controlled these houses of happiness also patronized them and they took care that the provender was skimmed right off the top of the available supply. Dutch Schultz might distribute (as he did) the country's most villainously adulterated drink to the speakeasies he required to deal with him. But the sporting houses where he and his minions took their own ease always furnished bed and table alike with the best.

Also, during this laying-by time, Babe took a trip to Boston to buy a farm in nearby Sudbury. It was not that Babe had any urge to till the soil. But it was the part of a rich man, as he well knew, to own a country place where he could gather his companions about him of an autumn evening to share a steaming cup by a log fire. Babe, after paying a man with a truck ten dollars to "move out all that junky old furniture" (some of which must have cluttered the farmhouse for a century) filled the place full of Jordan Marsh's best. Then he outfitted the farm with one horse, one cow, one pig, one prize bulldog, and an indeterminate number of chickens. He made little use of the retreat after that except to bring up an occasional "hunting party" in the manner of his patron, Colonel Huston. But Babe's hunting parties were like nothing any man had ever experienced before, for they were given over to floating about a small pond in a flat-bottomed boat at night and blowing bullfrogs out of the water with a 12-gauge shotgun. Babe was devoted to frog's legs. But this system usually produced only spatterings of frog flesh that were hardly worth the patience to go gather up.

When Babe finally returned to the Yankee lineup on May 20, 1922, there was an overflow crowd at the Polo Grounds to watch him resume his battering of baseballs out to the horizon. But what the fans saw was a Yankee disaster of strange dimensions: loss of a game even though the final enemy had been called out with the Yanks one run ahead. What happened was that the call of the third out in the ninth made by one umpire was reversed by another. And the St. Louis Browns, rescued by this reprieve, then scored seven runs in their final at-bat to win the game 8 to 2.

Babe Ruth, with friendly yells ringing in his ears, struck out in his first time at bat. In his next three visits to the plate he rolled out to the infield. He played no part in the odd sequence of events that gave the Browns an extra chance to turn defeat into victory. The first two St. Louis batters in the ninth inning hit easy ground balls to Yankee second baseman Aaron Ward, who threw them out at first. Then Chick Shorten batted for St. Louis second baseman Marty Mc-Manus and hit a single to center field. Pat Collins then batted for pitcher Urban Shocker. Collins hit a ball through the shortstop position that Everett Scott was barely able to deflect with his glove and Shorten ran all the way to third base. The next batter was right fielder Jack Tobin, who hit a ground ball to Wally Pipp, the Yankees' first baseman (and their home-run star before Babe Ruth joined the club). Pipp gathered the ball up easily and tossed it underhand to pitcher Sad Sam Jones, who had run over to cover the base. The umpire, Oliver Chill, promptly signaled that Tobin was out. The Yankees ran out across the field toward the clubhouse. Fans, seeking shortcuts to the gates, paraded out over the diamond. But Lee Fohl, the St. Louis manager, who had been coaching at first base, observed that Jones did not glove Wally Pipp's toss immediately. Instead, the ball had bounced off his glove before Sam finally closed his hand on it and the ball was actually in the air when Tobin crossed the bag.

Fohl appealed to Brick Owens (called Brick because a fan had once hit him with one), who was umpiring behind the plate. Owens agreed with Fohl, and Tobin was declared safe. As Shorten had crossed the plate on the play, his run counted and the score was 2 to 2.

It took fifteen minutes for the special police detail to persuade the fans to get back into their seats. They had *seen* the man called out, for God's sake! It took just as long to talk the half-dressed Yankee players into getting back into their uniforms. Sam Jones came back to the mound distraught and angry at himself for not squeezing the ball. He pitched with only half his heart and the mighty St. Louis hitters—Wally Gerber, George Sisler, Ken Williams, and Baby Doll Jacobson—unnerved him still further. He walked Sisler on purpose. (George hit .420 that year, a league mark that will probably stand forever.) Then he passed Ken Williams without wanting to, and an extra run was forced over the plate. Baby Doll Jacobson (who was neither a baby nor a doll but a homely, tough lad with a lot of power) then drove everybody in with a home run.

This loss completely stunned Manager Huggins, who sat motionless before his locker and could not speak. Babe Ruth spoke for both of them, pacing the locker room, waving his fists and bellowing phrases that editors even in this day would think twice about committing to print. That was the beginning of a ten-game losing streak for the Yankees, and the beginning of one of Babe Ruth's worst seasons.

Babe, with his thousand-a-week salary, now began to act the part of the big man on the team. He talked back to his manager, shoved him around, called him names, refused to follow his advice.

"If you don't want to play ball, why don't you go home?" Huggins would ask him.

"*You* go home," Ruth would reply. "If you don't like the way I play why don't you fire me?"

Babe did hit the ball well that year, compared to other ballplayers. But he did not hit as many home runs as Ken Williams of St. Louis did, and his batting average fell from .378 to .315. He was out of temper often. As a boy he had learned to show respect in the presence of authority, and Babe had not often had any quarrel with umpires—other than making an occasional loud protest over a called third strike. But this season he had an angry dispute with umpire George Hildebrand (George was the very umpire who had called one of Ruth's 1919 home runs on the Pacific Coast a foul because it had curved foul outside the park) and threw a handful of dirt in Hildebrand's face. For that, Babe was put out of the game and fined two hundred dollars. Babe refused interviews this season, snapped profanity at reporters who tried to question him, and fought with his teammates. In his position as field captain of the team, he did not hesitate to find open fault with players who made mistakes on the field. Wally Pipp, the first baseman, had some bad days in 1922 and Babe hardly ever failed to remind him of errors or failures. One day Pipp had had all he could bear, and when Babe came in from left field to deliver his usual "For God's *sake,* Pipp!," Wally, white and trembling, hit the big man right square on the nose. Ruth, yelling with pain and surprise, charged into Pipp and pushed him into a corner. Frank ("Home Run") Baker hurried to separate them and he stopped blows from both directions. Babe was due at the plate and the umpires had turned impatiently toward the dugout. Huggins and Baker together managed to persuade the two gladiators that the game came first.

"All right, you son of a bitch! I'll settle with you in the clubhouse," Babe vowed.

"I'll be there!" Wally promised.

Whereupon Ruth, his nose swollen, his neck red, and his face almost purple with rage, hastened to the plate and drove a pitch clean over the right-field stand. Pipp, who batted fourth in the order, came next and drove another pitch out of the playing field. In the clubhouse, Wally and Ruth shook hands. Never again did Ruth try to act the part of critic of the other men's play.

Babe had lost his temper at a fan who heckled him that season, after Hildebrand had put him out of the game. Outraged that any of those who once admired him should attempt to belittle him, Babe climbed into the stands after the fan and got himself arrested for assault. Up to that point, Babe had been captain of the team. Now he was demoted to private again.

Later in the season he fought again with umpires Bill Dineen— himself a retired umpire baiter who had pitched for the Boston Puritans in the first World Series—and Tommy Connolly, the first man ever to umpire in the American League. For each argument Babe Ruth drew a brief suspension. Each spell away from the game served to sour Ruth's disposition even more. What the hell was the use of living if you couldn't play *ball?* Babe worked off some of his temper on the sportswriters and became more difficult to deal with off the field.

But one writer had decided that Babe needed him—needed someone to help him hold onto his money, negotiate for promotional deals, and cope with all the sharpies who had investments to offer.

This was Christy Walsh, an advertising man, who knew the syndicate and promotion business from the inside and had conservative ideas about investments. Babe would have none of him, would not talk to him on the telephone or sit down with him in the hotel or clubhouse. He had grown far more selective about who was allowed into his apartment and used the Yankee trainer, Doc Woods, as a sort of personal secretary to sort out his mail.

So Christy Walsh pretended to be a delivery boy, got inside Babe's door that way, and soon talked the big man into turning over all his financial affairs to him. That move gave Ruth security for all his life, for Walsh put part of Babe's fat salary into annuities, signed him to advertising and promotional contracts at large fees, and saw to it that the money was collected. (When he first came to New York, Babe, in tearing up the baskets of mail that would pile up in the clubhouse, destroyed at least six thousand dollars' worth of checks for outside deals.)

But this was almost the only good thing that happened to Babe that dismal season, his last year in the Polo Grounds. Even at the plate he found a nemesis, a kid left-hander with St. Louis who seemed to hold some hypnotic spell over Babe. Ten times out of the first fifteen that Ruth faced Hub Pruett, that rookie struck him out with a miserable little curve that Babe just *knew* he could murder. It set Babe to cooking up new combinations of obscenities. But nothing availed him.

The Yankees, despite a lot of snarling and sniping in the clubhouse, with Carl Mays on the outs with practically all his mates and Miller Huggins being hazed and ridiculed by the Babe Ruth faction— which included one of the club owners, Colonel Huston—went on to take the American League pennant by one game from the St. Louis Browns. Once again all the World Series games were played in New York's Polo Grounds, but Babe had the worst Series of his career, making only two hits out of seventeen times at bat in five games. (The Yanks did not win a single game but one was a tie.) He spent most of the time in a rage, not just at the foul insults that were flung at him by John McGraw and the others in the Giants dugout but at his inability to hit the bad pitches the Giant pitchers persisted in throwing him. Why, they even threw at his shoe-tops and Babe would swing at the ball. And miss.

The tie game left everybody in a temper, for it was called "on account of darkness" with the sun still high, and light enough to read even the fine print in a baseball contract. Commissioner Landis (who had finally quit his Federal judgeship in response to complaints about his moonlighting as commissioner of baseball) sat in a front box in this game and got the blame for calling it. Actually he had no say in the matter. Indeed, when he got back to his hotel he offered a few comments in private about the "stupid goddam umpire" who had made the decision. The stupid goddam umpire was the same George Hildebrand who had received a fistful of dirt in the face from Babe Ruth. But some insiders put the blame on Bill Klem, whom Hildebrand consulted before deciding that broad daylight was pitch dark. Klem, recalling that a Brooklyn-Boston game had gone fourteen innings six years earlier, ending in dusk so deep that nobody knew if the final fly ball was caught or not, decided it was best not to take a chance on having that happen again.

But this nonsense did not appease the fans, who were convinced the whole business was just a dodge to work in an extra game with another fat gate. They trailed Landis out of the park, hooting at him as the idiot who could not tell when the sun was shining, and demanding their money back. Safe in his hotel, Landis, without bothering to call club owners or league presidents, announced that the entire gate, about $120,000, would be divided up among New York charities.

With the Series over and Babe Ruth's tail dragging, his new manager, Christy Walsh, arranged a dinner at the Elks Club, where Ruth would have a chance to make peace with the New York writers, who were to be the guests at the dinner. State Senator James J. Walker, soon to win wider fame as the fast-talking mayor of New York, made the major speech at the dinner. He addressed it chiefly to Babe himself, chiding him for letting himself grow soft and fat, for getting his name in the papers as a speeder and a baiter of umpires and a puncher of fans. He urged Babe to change his ways and keep always in mind the example he was setting for the "dirty-faced little boy in the street." Babe received his scolding as if he were himself the dirty-faced little boy, as indeed he had been not too long before. With moist eyes, Babe stood up and vowed that he would keep faith with all dirty-faced little boys and would never again lose his temper, or allow himself to get out of condition, or say bad words out loud.

He actually remembered these vows for a few weeks. And he did devote that winter to his farm, where his little family was now ensconced and where there was wood to saw and split and hills to hunt over.

The country at large and New York in particular was just winding up to enter upon the low-wage "prosperity" that was to create a false glow in many a hungry heart and convince the wealthy that the millennium was at hand, thanks largely to their ability to do as they damn pleased with their money. But the wholesale cutting of wages that was to make profits to grow fat was not accomplished without turmoil. Spring had barely begun, and the old labor contract at the mines had just run out when the coal miners struck throughout Pennsylvania, Kentucky, and West Virginia. Even nonunion workers walked out by the tens of thousands rather than stand still for the 25 percent wage cut the operators proposed.

There was panic in the newspapers and in the halls of Congress over the arrogance of workers who dared desert their jobs. But there was no real panic among the public. Warm weather was just down the street, industry was not more than half stoked up, and everybody had coal enough on hand to last. Even so, authorities in West Virginia—who were largely in the pay of the coal companies—set out to club back to work the nonunion miners who had dared to stay aboveground. One union man was shot dead on the steps of a courthouse, and when miners armed themselves and marched across county lines to protest the killing, they were all arrested and tried for treason. But no one who attended the trials and took a good look at the jury, or watched the accused happily playing baseball with the men who were supposed to be suppressing their rebellion, had any fear that the miners would be convicted.

Politicians, however, begged President Harding to show the toughness Woodrow Wilson had exhibited when he sent federal troops to break a strike. General Billy Mitchell, who would get in wrong in a few years by daring to suggest that battleships were obsolete because planes could sink them, became a hero to many an overstuffed banker when he offered to take a plane up and drop bombs on the strikers.

The New York *Herald* saw to it that the public heard the right side of the story. It offered a long anonymous survey of the situation by a special correspondent who had gone to Pennsylvania. He reported miners in fine clothes disporting themselves on holiday in the cities, spending five dollars on a dinner for the family, attending a movie, loading up on goodies at the shops, and riding merrily home in the middle of the night. He admitted that the men no longer smoked the fifty-cent cigars they had been accustomed to during the war. But they smoked good cigars, bought twelve-dollar silk shirts, and gave their wives money to purchase gaily colored garments. And savings banks were bulging with the wages they had laid by.

Local merchants and all nonminers in the area, he reported, were much against the strike. And if any reader should wonder how shop-keepers could protest the fact that their customers had money enough to buy everything they desired, he explained that a butcher, for instance, could sell only the very fanciest cuts, on which profit margins were small. Cheap cuts, such as miners would be expected to live on, and on which we were asked to believe that profit margins were generous, simply lay unlooked-at on meat counters.

It would take some time, the anonymous writer averred, for it to be borne in upon the strikers that only low wages would restore the proper balance and allow *everyone* to prosper. Meanwhile, he said, the people who did not work in the mines were eating their hearts out with envy.

The miners and their spokesmen were finding it difficult to dis-cover anyone to read *their* side of the story, which could be under-stood by even a third-grader from the simple facts of the case. Anthracite miners had been earning, on an average, $700 a year, about 40 percent of what a government study had decided was required to provide even a modicum of comfort to a modern family. Bituminous miners had been making $1,000, and that was still not enough to live on properly. Men who worked by the ton were being cruelly short-weighted. And nonunion miners were required to sign a yellow-dog contract, pledging never to join a union, on pain of civil penalties. The courts in the mine areas were quick to find union men guilty of violating their contracts. They also ordered the union to clean out an entire tent city where 2,500 folk dwelt in penury, sup-ported by the union, after having been evicted from company-owned houses for "contract violation." Where these people were to go nei-ther the court nor the mine operators cared, as long as it was away.

Rich men also had their hackles raised by the efforts of certain poli-ticians to curry favor with the World War veterans by voting for a bonus—adjusted compensation it was called—to make up for the fact that the boys who went to war made from $18 to $30 a month, while the men who stayed home got rich. This, said the spokesmen for business, was just using the "people's money" to buy political advancement.

These "bonus raiders," as the reactionary press never failed to name them, were bent on wrecking the nation, just as a thorough downward readjustment in the wage scale was getting business on its feet. The boom that was beginning, however, and that was to reach its height in the first year of the reign of Herbert Hoover, was a speculative boom, when men got rich, not by making things and selling them, but by betting on the upward movement of stocks. Farmers were putting themselves into hock and workingmen were borrowing in order to pay their own fare on the Golden Train.

The big cities, especially New York City, were all afester with new freedom, with wild outbursts of crime, with dreams of higher and bigger buildings, more automobiles, and the marvels of the radio— which was no longer called wireless. Families in New York up-to-date enough to own a radio set, with a crystal and perhaps two sets of earphones, had a choice of four stations to listen to: KDKA in Pittsburgh; WBZ in Springfield, Massachusetts; WGI, which broadcast from Medford Hillside, also in Massachusetts; and the station of the Army Signal Corps. A typical day's program on KDKA offered a talk on "Pittsburgh and Its Scientific Importance" and another talk on "Engineering and Happiness," plus some vocal and instrumental selections.

There were sourpusses aplenty who could see no great future in the broadcasting of such thin gruel and who foresaw only bankruptcy for men and women so lacking in sense as to pay out money to promote this folly. Other folk dwelt on the dire consequences to a person's health from all the mystic waves that must pierce his brain when he put on earphones and invited these impulses into both sides of his head. All the same, young folk bought radio sets, or pieced them together from components that were for sale everywhere, while crafty and farsighted adults hastened to buy stock in the company that was specializing in their manufacture, the Radio Corporation of America.

Young people who wanted to get ahead in these years hastened to leave the farms and villages and find furnished quarters in the big cities. Landlords in New York hustled to divide up the ancient flats that families once dwelt in to provide single rooms to house these pilgrims. Rich folk left their midtown homes to the merchants and the furnished-roomers, while they sought more splendor in the new high buildings going up along the Hudson River or on either side of Central Park.

The wealth of New York took any visitor's breath away, for it was flaunted immediately in the vaulted and star-spangled ceiling of Grand Central Terminal, where no coal smoke sullied the air and no champing locomotives drowned all thought. Instead, men and women wrapped in the newest fashions walked on marble staircases and across a gleaming floor past shops whose windows glowed full alight for twenty-four hours every day. It was possible, in this grandest of all railroad depots, to live out an entire lifetime without ever going into the weather. There were three fine hotels attached, where the restaurants were among the best in the city, with chefs of international fame. There was a barbershop big as an assembly hall where only a man of great strength of will could climb out of the chair without purchasing something extra—if not a singe to keep his hair from leaking its vital juices into the air, or a massage to tone up his skin and erase wrinkles forever, then at least a thorough dousing with some restorative guaranteed to grow hair on an egg. There were haberdashery shops and clothing stores; an oyster bar purported to serve the finest oyster stew in the land; men's rooms and ladies' rooms where it was possible to rent a shower bath; telephone operators who would place a long-distance call for you; bookstores; newsstands; drugstores; grocery stores; and a milk bar where for fifteen cents a footsore drummer might purchase a glass of milk and two of the best-tasting ginger cakes in the world.

Of course, through Grand Central, at one time or another, came all the celebrities of the sports and entertainment world, and even the notorious criminals being fetched down in chains from Sing Sing. In a day and an evening there, one might descry close up at different times, Douglas Fairbanks, Harold Lloyd, Babe Ruth, Paul Whiteman, Georges Carpentier, and the bobbed-haired bandit.

It was in Wall Street and its environs—Broad Street, lower Broadway, Pine Street, Cedar Street, Rector Street, Stone Street, and Whitehall—that prosperity was most openly aboil. Here, during working hours, the racket seemed continuous and ever-changing, with hawkers peddling stain removers and other magic potions from baskets, shabby young men offering oversized pretzels for sale while warily watching to either side for approaching policemen, bearded preachers on little wooden stands railing against the open immorality of modern youth, stalled streetcars mournfully beating their gongs to beseech passage, auto horns threatening to force a way, the traders in the crowded Curb Exchange ringing bells, sounding rattles, or waving and shouting to draw the attention of their colleagues in upstairs windows; and an itinerant revivalist with long white hair and a Santa Claus beard singing in a rolling bass: "There is power, power, wonder-working power! There is power in the blood!"

So cheap was time thereabouts, and so hungry were the denizens for new ways to fill it up, that any sight even mildly out of the ordinary would draw a crowd of idle watchers. If a man stopped to tie his shoe at the curb, five or six might stop to eye him. A young man carrying an elk's head would move along with two dozen people at his heels. If one man stopped to make out a face at a high window or to observe a pigeon in flight, twenty more would interrupt their errands and look where he was looking, wondering what they were supposed to see. If he persisted in his search, a whole crowd might finally block the way, with newcomers asking those on the fringe: "What is it? What happened?" Even when the original watcher had long gone his ways, the crowd might linger, hopefully watching heavenward for a portent that would enliven the day.

At noontime, in the Wall Street area, the outturning for lunch would grow so great that the sidewalks would not hold all the men in stiff collars and derby hats, the young women in long skirts with waistlines at the pelvis, and the hurrying lads in caps and knickerbockers who were set loose at the same moment. So the roadways would fill up with people going afoot and the automobiles and trucks would have to bleat their way through the throngs at five miles an hour. In fine weather the steps of buildings, the wide windowsills on the street floor, or the railings that marked off new excavations, even the hose connections that jutted out about knee-high from the ground level of skyscrapers, as well as the many green benches on the Bowling Green and Battery Park—all would fill up with idlers. Along the Battery Wall, men with trays full of binoculars would cry out: "Glasses for use! See the great big ocean liner coming up the harbor!"

The chief concern in Wall Street, however, was the making of money in great gobs by men who might already own more than they could spend. The myriad petty frauds wreaked upon the public in the uptown areas, even the wholesale swindles of the installment houses, were all of little account when matched with the intricate schemes men like Howard C. Hopson and Samuel Insull and Henry L. Doherty had devised to create empires out of paper that might be then cut into tiny sections and sold to the public as if they were pieces of hard goods with unassailable intrinsic value. By creating companies to hold the stock of utility companies and new companies to hold the stock of the holding companies and still newer companies to hold the stock of *those* companies, these shrewd and plausible men made millions of hogsheads of oyster stew with but a single oyster—and that oyster usually recovered by themselves and used to flavor new decoctions.

There may have been laws and regulations to govern and restrict the operations of the men and women who dealt in the changing of money, and the dividing up of businesses into shares, but no real insider ever gave them extra thought. The people who ran the government had made it plain enough that "business" in America meant the making of money, not merely the production of goods. Indeed, factories and mills and mines were busy even then turning out goods while taking care that working people would not have the money to buy them. But as long as the stock rode high and the books could be arranged to indicate even busier days to come, there was no one in high places in business to fret over the far-off future.

Ignorant bankers talked with seeming knowledge of the "new era of equity financing" that would make the whole nation into a gigantic speculative pit. Brokers who were charged with advising their customers and taking care that their advice be untarnished by self-interest were recklessly tossing their own funds and the funds of their customers into upward-swooping stocks without regard for the actual state of the businesses the stocks were supposed to be a piece of. Any and all airplane stocks were frantically sought after, as publicists painted pictures of the land of tomorrow when every businessman willing to look his neighbors in the eye would *have* to own a small airplane to spin back and forth between home and office in. Radio stock shot skyward when the people who made the machines discovered the secret of luring hordes of people to listen to singers and comedians and descriptions of athletic contests through which could be interlarded paid-for advertisements for food, drink, soap flakes, and socks.

If the stock market seemed too complex and esoteric a means of striking it rich in a hurry, there was an incipient boom in the vacant lands of Florida—that sun-baked and sandy peninsula where only the extremely rich had heretofore been able to afford to take their ease and where hotel rates—if was said and not always believed— were often as high as thirty-five dollars a day!

There were of course still forces—besides the Wall Street evangelists—who tried to stay the headlong plunge of the Lost Generation into the roses and raptures of easy money and vice. A bank in Newark laid down the law to the females in its employ: they must either wear shirtwaists up to the neck, sleeves below the elbow, and strictly "non-vamp" gowns, or else stay home from work. And in Arkansas, high-school girls who wore painted eyebrows, rouged or powdered cheeks, short hair, or peek-a-boo shirtwaists were sent right back to mama. When statues of scantily clad females, made by sculptors in the wicked days before the Civil War, were discovered hidden in a museum attic chastely covered with sheets, the museum trustees did not quite yet dare bring them into the open, despite their historical interest.

There were other flies in the generally savory ointment of daily life in the 1920s. A crime wave broke out in Washington Square—where robbers locked A. G. Shattuck and his family in the wine cellar and looted their mansion—and It spread right up past Thirty-fourth Street. Somebody punched a hole in a window at the Saks and Company shop on Broadway at 34th Street and emptied the window of beaded bags and jewelry. Folk on the street saw the thief in the act and chased him down the sidewalk but never caught him. Not far away a man named Cohen, who said he was a clothing cutter, stopped another man named Cohen who was a jewelry salesman. The first Cohen showed the second Cohen a gun and took away $1,135 worth of jewelry the second Cohen was carrying. Promptly caught up by the law, the first Cohen, who was Abe, was arraigned before Magistrate Simpson, who told him men of his type were cowards.

"Life imprisonment," said Simpson, "is too good for men of your sort. Like mad dogs and wild beasts, you should be shot down for the protection of society." Whether Abe Cohen read the lesson that if you wish to rob other people you must do so quietly and openly, like a banker or a politician, it is now too late to determine.

The New York police, now largely manned by war veterans who had learned that guns were not for self-defense but to kill the enemy whenever he showed himself, set out to put down this criminal uprising as swiftly and emphatically as they could manage. When they followed a suspiciously acting man on Madison Avenue one night and saw him remove a spare tire from a parked automobile to toss it into a touring car driven by a confederate, the cops opened fire and scared the thief, Pat McCallum, and his brother into surrendering. They also shot a lawyer dead, but that was a mistake: the poor man just walked into the path of one of the bullets.

Magistrate Peter Hatting extended the boundaries of the battle by declaring that "vampires" of both sexes were also part of the crime wave. Men who flirted with girls just to lure them into autos where the man could make improper advances were criminals, said Hatting. And so were the girls who flirted with men in order to bleed them of their wages.

But young men went on flirting. Girls continued to invite improper advances. The bobbed-hair fever spread apace, despite scornful cries from high places about "short-haired women and long-haired men". Young ladies appeared on golf courses garbed in knickerbockers, cut almost like a man's. Skirts dropped almost to ankle length for a season or two, but they soon began to shrink to the knee and above, until the sights available in a subway train, from the long array of silken legs across the aisle, caused many a young man to ride three or four stops past his destination.

One of the extra dividends of Prohibition was the discovery that as long as one was breaking that silly law, one might as well violate a few more, with the doors being barred, as they were, against interference. So it was possible in the midnight speakeasies, and particularly in some of the Harlem clubs (where black folk were usually admitted only as entertainers and employees), to learn the lyrics of a number of songs that might have brought a blush in a baseball locker room, and to appraise at a respectful distance occasional exhibitions of total female nudity.

But hardly anyone thought of the New York nightclubs and restaurant-type speakeasies as outposts of crime, nor their proprietors as criminals. Speakeasy owners, listed as "restaurateurs," would lend their names to endorsements of candidates or causes. They paid their normal dues to the gangsters who guaranteed them peace. They bought their liquor from the recommended sources. They remained on their guard against intrusion by Federal agents (who were usually not easy to "straighten out" with a simple bribe).

And they might even undertake to arrange for the safe home delivery of helpless customers who had looked too long upon the doctored whiskey when it was red.

Authentic liquor was still imported from Canada or from "rum row"—a line of small vessels hove to beyond the twelve-mile limit, their holds and decks loaded with liquors from Canada or other nations. The wholesale distributors, however, soon discovered that it was madness to offer uncut whiskey to drinkers who could not tell good from bad. So the ordinary speakeasy almost invariably poured its drinks from unlabeled bottles containing an elixir made up of grain alcohol, glycerin, distilled water, and caramel coloring.

Plain people made liquor at home, using fruit of every sort to supply the fermented mash, and distilling it in a tiny "thumper" still that could be set up on the kitchen table. The makings of home brew—hops and malt syrup—could be bought at nearly every street corner, from "Malt and Hops" shops, where you might also purchase some of the paraphernalia. (Occasionally a malt-and-hops shop might undertake to peddle the finished product, too, if the purchaser came properly recommended.)

There was a thriving market in counterfeit labels and bottles of authentic design. (A generation raised on Gordon's Gin looked for its gin in a square-faced bottle and was wary of any other.) At first distributors of imitation liquors, prompted by some lingering sense of the proprieties, did not exactly reproduce the labels, but merely imitated them, so that a gin label that seemed to read "Gordon's" would say "Gorton's," while Peter Dawson whiskey might wear the name Peter Rawson. But the sheer idiocy of trying to avoid difficulties with the Federal Trade Commission while openly defying the Treasury Department became soon apparent.

The real regulation of the illicit liquor traffic, on both a wholesale and retail level, was supplied by the gangsters who found it a richer source of revenue than the standard professions of strikebreaking, gambling, moneylending, and hired sex. The city courts seldom laid the rod too heavily on violators of the Volstead Act or of the various state laws that were meant to support it. Public officials of course were high in their indignation at the thought of flouting any paragraph in the Constitution. Congress actually broke into applause one day when some "dry" legislator reported the shooting to death of three rumrunners off Rhode Island. But judges who had just finished off a prime steak and a cold bottle of ale seldom found it in their hearts to visit a long sentence on some lone purveyor of hard drink, nor were they prone to discern guilt in men and women who had been doing exactly what the jurymen themselves had been guilty of at home. The gangsters saw to it that at least the local police did not interfere with the quiet enjoyment of premises where liquor was sold and that crude competitive methods did not dig too deeply into profits.

Hardly anyone really took the strict enforcement of Prohibition seriously, other than the hordes of innocents who could walk up and down the midtown streets and avenues in New York and not know that on every corner and at ten places in between it was possible to buy hard liquor. Even Calvin Coolidge, the almost invisible Vice-President, who looked like Prohibition incarnate, kept a bottle of good whiskey hidden in a desk that he might warm up the newsmen when they came in of a bitter cold day to interview him. And President Harding, henpecked as he was, still served whiskey to his cronies at the White House during poker parties.

It almost seemed as if everybody in the nation was determined to blame Prohibition on everyone else. Legislators who drank themselves far past the jolly stage every evening still stood up and declaimed their devotion to the cause and their undying enmity for John Barleycorn. William Jennings Bryan was no hypocrite. He fought against hard drink both publicly and privately. But thousands of those who dared not disagree with him out loud remained devoted to the fermented grape in private. Perhaps if it had been possible to take a secret poll of every sentient being in the land, with solemn assurances that no one would hear of any other's choice, a sturdy majority would have admitted that they practiced, privately, the sin of imbibing intoxicating drink. But to ask them, at that stage of the country's sophistication, to endorse repeal of the Prohibition Amendment was like asking everybody in church who favored lusting after the opposite sex with the eye to raise his hand. One desired to make clear he was ashamed, at least, of his own sinful ways and would like them eradicated in others.

There probably were a few baseball players who did not drink strong liquors or illicit brews, but very few fingers would have been needed to count them. A player could be disciplined severely for sneaking a drink in the locker room or for bringing in a cold bottle of beer. Yet the ballplayer who did not drink at all was not deemed a fit companion for man, beast, umpire, or second baseman. Sometimes the whole Yankee club would accept an invitation to a brewery party. And no one imagined for a moment that Colonels Ruppert and Huston—one of whom had built his fortune on beer—had suddenly taken the pledge of total abstinence. Parties for the press were invariably garnished with high-proof liquors, even in the minor leagues. George Weiss, when he operated minor-league clubs in New Haven and Baltimore—long before he became the Yankees' general manager—gave notable parties for sportswriters in which liquor was poured out freely enough to put more than one celebrity literally under the table. (Chief Bender, guest of honor at a Weiss party one night, rose up to speak and suddenly dropped out of sight as if the floor had opened beneath him.) Even Kenesaw Mountain Landis, still wearing the aura of his term on the federal court, stood up at a Weiss party one night, where as commissioner of baseball he was an honored guest, accepted a generous libation of what was labeled "table sauce," lifted the glass high and proposed a toast: "To the Eighteenth Amendment." The whole convocation broke into convulsive fits of laughter, as if a minister of the gospel had told a dirty joke.

Ballplayers did not ordinarily patronize the high-priced nightclubs in New York. They gathered usually at some place like The Dutchman's, a neighborhood speakeasy six blocks from the new Concourse Plaza in the Bronx, where the steaks were better than the beer and where there were no outrageous cover charges, false-bottomed glasses, or lady sitting on a piano to sob out a song of unrequited love. The players would often buy steaks raw from the jolly Dutchman and carry them home to their wives. Babe Ruth, however, was not often to be found in spots like this. He would select one or two friends for company, or he would set off alone for a New Jersey nightclub where he might celebrate in lonely iniquity, sometimes choosing a female companion to warm him through the rest of the night, sometimes eating and drinking and singing songs until almost time to go to the park.

When the team was traveling, Ruth was still assigned a hotel room and a roommate. But the roommate seldom saw Babe except at the ball park, for Ruth had no patience with single beds or male companionship. He used the hotel room to keep his clothes in, to return to for a change of foliage and sometimes to take a meal. He never ate in hotel dining rooms any more.

PART IV

Life with Miller Huggins

BABE now had a sort of comeback to make, to prove his devotion to dirty-faced little boys everywhere. The Yankees had finally built the new park they had promised—not in Astor Place but far up in the Bronx, within sight of the Polo Grounds just across the Harlem River. This was the most splendid baseball emporium of its day, with room enough to seat seventy thousand fans and promise of eventually making room for ten or twenty thousand more. After his winter of abstemious living on the farm, Babe made first for Hot Springs, where he habitually performed his preseason training rites. This season of 1923 he weighed only 210 pounds when he checked in there—his lowest weight since coming to New York. And when he arrived at the Yankee training camp at New Orleans, Babe was ten pounds lighter still after contracting the flu in Arkansas. He was actually weakened by the sudden drop in his weight. His legs, particularly his knees, seemed to give out quickly and he hardly made a safe hit in his first weeks at camp.

There were other omens: Colonel Huston, disgusted with the loss of the World Series, had sold out his share of the Yankees and Ruppert now owned them all by himself. Ruppert promptly told Huggins that Hug was now in full charge, with no danger of interference from above. (Ruppert, although he had actually played some baseball in school, was no expert on the game and he knew it.) Ruth, in his constant bickering with Huggins, was now left without a "rabbi" to run to for support. This did not immediately fret Babe, who was no man to borrow trouble from the days ahead. But it did augur some serious run-ins in the seasons to come. Before the 1923 season even started, Huggins, having watched Babe wobbling about at training camp, sat down with Babe in his Pullman drawing room and suggested that the great man had slipped so badly he might actually be through as a player. Whether this was a bit of devious "psyching" or not there is no telling. Huggins had long been troubled by Babe's utter disregard for club curfews and he may merely have been articulating a fear he had long held in his heart.

Babe, gloomily contemplating his sorry record, could only mutter, "You're crazy!" And he may actually have determined right then to prove to Huggins and the whole world that he was a long long way from through.

The opening game at the new Yankee Stadium attracted the greatest baseball crowd New York had ever seen, most of them turning out to see Ruth try to knock baseballs over these new and more difficult fences. (Babe never did knock a fair ball out of the stadium, nor did any other white player. The incomparable Josh Gibson, the greatest black slugger of any age, did so just once.)

Automobiles were parked helter-skelter along all the nearby streets and in every adjoining empty lot. The mob that swarmed down the long steps from the rapid-transit trains seemed to have no end. When finally signs were posted warning that only standing room was left, the crowd seemed hardly to have diminished. The final attendance was announced as over seventy-four thousand— some ten thousand more than later fire laws would permit.

Along with this horde of plain people, there were celebrities of considerable glitter. Al Smith, New York's new governor, was present. So was Christy Mathewson, the most famous name in New York baseball in the era just preceding the days of Ruth. Commissioner Landis sat in a front box, holding his hat in his hand to show off his luxuriant silver mane. John Philip Sousa himself led the 7th Regiment band as it paraded to the center-field flagpole ahead of the two ball clubs—the Yankees and the Red Sox.

Babe did not hit the ball until his second time at bat. He came up to face Howard Ehmke then, with two men on base ahead of him. Ehmke threw Babe an outside pitch, very carefully placed to avoid Babe's greatest strength. But as so often happens when a pitcher is *too* careful, the ball came in just close enough for Babe to get his enormous bat on it. He pulled it all the way around and sent it on a screaming line to the right-field stands. The Yankee management had been careful, too—about placing those stands where Babe could reach them without strain.

The howl that went up when Babe baptized the new stadium in this altogether fitting manner must have echoed clear into the Polo Grounds. Hats were tossed high, without regard for their landing place. Men, women, and children jumped up and pranced on the seats and in the aisles, yelling and yelling and yelling as Babe trotted from base to base. As for Babe, his broad face almost cracked from the width of his grin as he finished the circuit. He acknowledged the sounds of the crowd by lifting his cap. Then he turned his grin on Huggins. All through, hey?

Babe's home run was his only hit that day. In the second game he got two hits. In the third game he got three. He hit his second home run in a game against Washington, with President Harding in the stands. After the game Babe had his picture taken with the President, who was perhaps more thrilled at the meeting than Babe was.

The immediate effect of Babe's return to top form was increased wariness on the part of the opposing pitchers. After Babe had demonstrated that he was going to hit every good pitch he saw and gather singles, doubles, and triples as well as home runs, the pitchers began to offer him free walks to first base by the dozen. Babe seldom griped about this treatment. He had mighty hitters in the lineup behind him who could send him around to score, and he was as concerned with winning games as he was with hitting home runs. But fans, even in other cities, expressed gathering outrage. They did not pay their way into ball parks to see Babe Ruth get on base on four wide pitches. They wanted to see him clout the ball a couple of furlongs at a time. A few sportswriters urged that the intentional walk be outlawed, so fans would get their money's worth. Had this aim ever been accomplished Babe might have hit seventy home runs. As it was, he was walked 170 times—the record.

But there were also those who suspected there was something strange about the manner in which Babe's batting average began to climb, for he was making many more singles and two-base hits than he ever had before. It took only a cursory inquiry to discover that Babe was using a new-style bat, a present from old Sam Crawford, the famous Detroit slugger whom Babe, as a pitcher, had once fanned right along with both Ty Cobb and Bobby Veach, the rest of the mighty Detroit outfield. The bat was a "built-up" bat, made of four slices of hardwood glued together. Whether it really added any points to Babe's average is doubtful, for even after Ban Johnson, the American League president, called it illegal and Babe had to give it up, he kept right on hitting line drives into safe territory or into the stands.

It was Babe's hitting that led the Yankees to a new pennant, rendering Colonel Ruppert almost incoherently happy, for he owned his ball club to win pennants with, first and above all. The fact that the Yankees led their nearest competitor, Detroit, into the barn by some sixteen lengths was balm to the colonel's soul. He could not stand close races or close games. When the Yankees had a one-run lead, he would often retreat under the stands when the enemy came to bat, afraid of what might happen. "What's the score?" he would inquire breathlessly. And then, fearful of the news: "Don't tell me! Don't tell me!"

The colonel, whose dearest wish, now that the flag was secure, was to beat out the New York Giants, must have spent many moments under the stands in the 1923 Series. The Giants, vituperative as ever and scornful of the Yanks, looked as if they might once more take the world's championship away. McGraw, to illustrate his extreme distaste for the enemy, would not allow his players even to change clothes in the luxurious locker room at the stadium. Instead, they all put on their uniforms at the Polo Grounds and, carrying their spiked shoes, walked across the bridge to the other park.

The Series opened at the stadium, in front of a crowd several thousand larger than could ever have been squeezed into the Polo Grounds. Alas, the Yankees could not take advantage of their tailor-made playground. The game seemed endless. It was actually dusk when the ninth inning opened with the score tied 4 to 4. Then with two out in the top of the inning, a merry young outfielder named Casey Stengel came to bat for the Giants and drove one of Bullet Joe Bush's bullets far, far into left center field, out of reach of Bob Meusel (Babe Ruth played right field in the Yankee Stadium, because left field there was the sun field and Babe did not like to take chances with his eyesight). The ball hit the grass and rolled to the fence, with Meusel, who had been playing left-handed Casey rather shallow, desperately pursuing it. But Casey had taken off the moment his bat made contact and he was well beyond second base before Meusel found the ball. Before Meusel could get it back to the diamond, Stengel had crossed the plate.

The fans begged Ruth, in the final half of the inning, to avenge this indignity. But Babe never got to the plate, for Joe Dugan flied out in the semidarkness, leaving Babe in the on-deck circle.

The second game, played at the Polo Grounds (where the Yankees were perfectly happy to dress in the visitors' clubhouse), returned Babe to the park where he had first reached the mark of fifty home runs. In his second time at bat here, with the score tied 1 to 1, Babe hit a ball high over the right-field stands, the sort of blow only he, of all active players then, had ever been capable of. In the very next inning, Babe hit another. Those two blows were all the Yankees needed to win the game.

The third game, back at the Yankee Stadium, almost broke Ruppert's heart and did drive him into a purple rage. For it was lost by a single run, another home run off the bat of Casey Stengel, who had taken a severe going-over from the commentators on the Yankee bench. When Casey saw his blow drop into the stands, he thumbed his nose at the Yankee bench and kept on thumbing it at each and every Yankee along his way as he traveled all around the base lines. Colonel Ruppert, in his front-row seat, looked wildly about for someone who could rush out and put a halt to this travesty, perhaps arrest the young man and run him out of the park. He finally managed to reach Ban Johnson and demanded that Stengel be severely disciplined for his vulgar display, but Johnson merely agreed to think about it. (In a game at Fenway Park, Boston, between the Red Sox and Giants some ten years earlier, outfielder Fred Snodgrass had thumbed his nose at bleacher fans who had been calling him names. Honey Fitz, in his World Series robes—top hat, cutaway coat, and striped pants—with a squad of police to attend him, thereupon marched out across the field directly to Snodgrass and set out to arrange for immediate discipline. But Fred "explained" that he had just brushed a fly off his nose. The mayor and his retinue then marched back, with the fans who had been booing Snodgrass now pouring howls of derision upon His Honor's head.)

Babe hit only one more home run in the 1923 Series, in the first inning of the final game, and he was struck out later in the game with a pitch, thrown right at his shoe tops, that bounced off the plate. The Yankees won that one anyway and took the championship. Babe hit .368 for the Series. For the 1923 season he had batted .393, the highest average of his career and second only to Harry Heilmann of Detroit, who hit .403.

The joy in the Yankee dressing room at this very first championship in Yankee history all seemed to swirl about the head of Babe Ruth, who was a World Series hero for the first time since he had pitched for the Red Sox. Bubbling over with happiness and goodwill toward everyone alive, Babe climbed up on the rubdown table and made a joyful speech in presenting to Miller Huggins a diamond ring bought by the players.

The more than six thousand dollars apiece that the players took home was the fattest purse since the beginning of time. And for once Babe had earned as much from the Series as he might have made in playing postseason exhibition games. He was voted Most Valuable Player that year and took home the admiration of his manager, the club owner, and all his mates. But the fans felt let down. Babe had hit only forty-one home runs that season and they had been looking for fifty. Was he really beginning to slip? Well, Babe certainly did not think so.

Unfortunately this was Babe's nature—to assume that, now he had hauled himself back to the top, he need not exert any extra effort to stay there. It seemed to be the nation's nature too. The sleekly tailored fellows who manned the financial houses and operated the great utility holding companies, as well as the demigods who directed the doings in the steel and auto and oil industries, were all convinced now that the activities they were engaged in—the solemn telephoning back and forth to arrange more and more new financing, the scurrying about on the stock exchanges to keep the money flowing, the compiling of reports and forecasts, the arm's-length coping with disgruntled labor, the shaving of costs, the fattening of prices—all these were actually supplying the motive power that kept the whole train rolling. Had they been able to look beyond their polished shoes and see past their weedless front lawns into the rest of the teeming nation, it might have begun to dawn on them that, besides the folk who were dashing back and forth in the cars, consuming all the best in drink and provender, "doing business" in numbers too large for a common mind to grasp, there was also a great horde of struggling people who were hauling the train along at great pain to themselves, living on dreams of the day when they might ride.

But this sort of talk was unpleasant, un-American, un-Christian, and unproductive, and those who dared utter it were shunned as poor "wet" slobs who were simply eaten by jealousy. Boys went to college in those days seeking "contacts" rather than education. Selling was deemed the really productive end of any business. Even on the newspapers, lordly business managers spoke indulgently of the editorial side as the red-ink aspect of the operation. And young men who lacked the brass or the presence to sell goods, services, or mere hope of profit to their fellows could look forward to a life without club membership, lavish expense accounts, or the love of fair women.

The death of Warren Harding and the gradual revelation, through the investigations directed by Senator Thomas J. Walsh of Montana, that Harding's Cabinet and Administration had been alive with greedy men who were bent on stealing whatever portions of the public wealth lay under their hands—these things, although they earned black headlines in the newspapers and purple speeches in Congress, seemed to stir the public only mildly. Many of the details of the Teapot Dome scandal, which involved the handing over of part of the naval oil reserves to oil millionaires Edward L. Doheny and Harry F. Sinclair to exploit, hardly reached the public ears and eyes at all. The press of the nation generally supported the Republicans and took care not to overburden its readers with matter that might rile up the blood.

Harry M. Daugherty, Attorney General under Harding and Coolidge, and one of the more arrogant of the thieves, went to special lengths to silence those in Congress who were most strongly bent on airing the scandal. He arranged for his operatives to shadow them, to eavesdrop on their telephone calls and to break into their offices, in search of any personal secrets that might be traded off for silence. Ned McLean, playboy publisher of the Washington *Post,* connoisseur of racehorses, fine whiskeys, and lissome ladies, consented to help cover up the crime by supplying a worthless check for $100,000 to be used by Albert B. Fall, Secretary of the Interior, as proof of a "loan" that had made him suddenly rich. But the Senate investigators were too spry to be taken in by a move as hoary as that. They soon made clear that Fall, that gruff, swaggering, and grasping old man, who had signed Teapot Dome over to the Sinclair interests, never cashed any such check but instead had taken lavish gifts from Doheny and Sinclair that were "paid for" by money advanced by Sinclair himself.

Archie Roosevelt, trifling son of the great T.R. and brother of Assistant Secretary of the Navy Theodore, Jr., had been given a job without work by Sinclair as a means of buying a little influence with the older brother. But Archie, in a panic, hurried to clean his own skirts by blowing the whistle on Harry Sinclair. There were, he revealed, checks made out to Fall by Sinclair that covered all but a few dollars of the "price" Fall had paid to buy a ranch, a hydroelectric plant, and a pasture full of cattle from the oil millionaire. With this, the guilty went scattering. Dougherty quit, Sinclair fled across the seas in hopes the heat would diminish, Secretary of the Navy Edwin Denby found he would prefer to return to civilian life, and Theodore Roosevelt, Jr., who, some cynics said, was light enough to float off into space, also hastened to shed the burden of public office.

Harding, some whispered, had died of shock when he heard that this scandal was about to come out. And one or two even hinted that someone had silenced the genial gentleman by dropping a teaspoon of arsenic into his highball. Yet little Cal Coolidge, who had, with needless melodrama, taken the oath of office by the light of a kerosene lamp in the parlor of his father's Vermont farmhouse, climbed out of this mudhole as clean as he had gone in.

One knew that Cal sat in the Cabinet with the crooks, that he could not have been ignorant of the leasing of the lands, and that he would have had to be deaf and blind not to observe that the Secretary of the Navy had even sent a detachment of Marines to keep a rival oil company from moving in on Harry Sinclair's private preserve at Teapot Dome. But Cal never uttered a word of indignation or reproval when the horrid facts came out. He accepted the resignations, vowed that he would keep his Administration clean and run all the guilty to the ground, then went back to saving nickels and dimes by turning off the lights in the White House and reusing all the postal pouches until they were ready to come apart.

"I'm for economy," he told the country. "Then for more economy."

Meanwhile Cal took care to accept his own profits from the

Morgan preferred list and to keep his own counsel about the men with whom he had shared office under the late leader.

As a matter of fact, an even greater scandal was uncovered in the Veterans' Bureau, where almost half a *billion* dollars had been stolen or thrown out the window by Charles R. Forbes, an old drinking buddy of Harding's who had no more right to the job as head of the bureau than Harding's illegitimate daughter. But he had known good old Warren since Warren was a hell-raising Senator from Ohio on the loose in Hawaii, where Forbes had drifted after deserting from the Army. A rough-and-ready, well-met, hard-drinking young man who could tell a good story, find willing girls, and mix a dynamite cocktail, Forbes hit it off so well with Harding that the two were seldom apart. When Harding became President, all Forbes asked him for was appointment as head of the Shipping Board, where the pickings were probably rich. But Forbes's lack of qualifications even to paint a rowboat was too plain for even Harding's advisers to ignore. So good-time Charlie became the boss of the Veterans' Bureau at a salary of $10,000 on which he entertained as recklessly and regally as Ned McLean ever did, staging parties so spectacular that they must have made good old Warren gasp. Charlie let contracts right and left for the building of hospitals, always with the understanding that he receive no less than 10 percent of the total cost. Charlie sold his friends surplus stocks from the hospital at prices about one-tenth of market. Oiled paper that cost the government sixty cents a pound went to friends of Charlie for a nickel. Charlie sold ninety-eight thousand pairs of pajamas, unused, which had been donated to the "poor boys" by American women, for thirty cents a pair. Charlie let his friends buy "surplus" bed sheets, never even unfolded, at twenty-six and twenty-seven cents each, although they had cost the taxpayer $1.37. Then Charlie bought twenty-five thousand more sheets from another friend for $1.03.

When the investigators caught up with Forbes, his "legal adviser," Charles Cramer, committed suicide. But not Forbes. He had lived through worse troubles than this. Why, he could do *his* stretch in jail on one leg!

Charlie's cool may have transmitted itself in some degree to the electorate, for there was mighty little public indignation over any of these larcenies. The inside story of Albert Fall's acquisition of a shipment of heifers and a prize bull attracted far more notice. *That* was the sort of small-time graft a fellow could wrap his mind around.

With Harding dead, it was easy enough to pretend that all the evil that had been done in Washington had been buried with him. Little Cal, God knows, was no sybarite. He traveled in an ordinary Pullman when he went anywhere by train. He staged no grand parties, cultivated no drinking buddies, set no light ladies to swooning at the sight of him. If he ever put on golf clothes, it must have been in his bedroom closet, for he seemed to have been born in a stiff collar. Even when he had his picture taken in a farmer pose, as he did on several occasions, he often wore his polished city shoes in the hayfield. His athletics were limited to bouncing up and down on a mechanical horse that was supposed to provide all the benefits of exercise with none of the effort. He drew the scorn of sportsmen when he allowed that he took trout on worms. And when someone brought home a fish alive from a fishing trip and presented it to the President, Cal set the creature to swimming in his bathtub. It seemed altogether fitting that the President should live an abstemious, quiet life, setting the nation an example it had no intention of following. Cal early let it be known that he intended to run for President on his own in 1924, and no one in his party seemed inclined to challenge him. He was set as solidly in his chair as if he had been sculpted there: the diffident, mind-my-own-business, nickel-nursing, early-to-bed keeper of the keys in a castle given over to the twenty-four-hours-a-day celebration of the constant influx of easy money.

Babe Ruth had not found his thousand dollars a week as easy to come by as he hoped, for it required now some far more careful attention to the state of his physical strength. But he had learned from Christy Walsh to get by on only five hundred a week (borrowing as needed from willing teammates), letting the other half of his salary accrue until it could be paid him in a lump at the season's end. That way, he was certain to salt a fair portion away before it could trickle out of his lavish paws.

Babe's health, despite his devotion to the regimen at Hot Springs, cracked once more at the very start of the 1924 training season. "Taking the baths" did not seem to boil the badness out of his system at all. Or perhaps he did not thrive on sharing the infections of the many infirm who took the cure along with him. He contracted a heavy dose of flu in March that laid him low enough to start another rumor that he was dead for sure. (The radio still had not grown strong enough to outrun the word of mouth that so often corrupted the news before it could reach home base.) But he pulled out of this attack handily enough and arrived in New York all glowing and strong, ready to scare pitchers right out of the league.

Babe was set upon at once to help promote one cause or another; and with his almost unfailing good nature, his wink, his grin, and his ready handshake, he said yes to almost all, even those he could not quite understand. He set the youth of the land an example by joining the National Guard in public (a duty he had missed out on when the war was in progress) and, without even a wince or an acknowledgment of the irony of the move, he let himself be put on exhibition as the prize pumpkin in a "Safe Driving" campaign (He did annoy a few clothing merchants by riding hatless in the parade.)

Babe also hit the ball steadily again, for distance and for average, and wound up with the most home runs in the league and the best batting average. But the Yankees missed the pennant. Their priceless new lead-off man and center fielder, Earle Combs of Kentucky, who had hit .380 in the minors, broke a leg sliding into home plate, after playing in only ten games. One or two of their veterans, but not Babe Ruth, seemed to take victory for granted, as if it were among the world's verities, like the supremacy of the white man, the stability of the Republic, the increase in the value of everything, and the permanence of prosperity. Even Manager Miller Huggins had a hard time convincing himself that his perfectly balanced ball club could be beaten.

Huggins learned a lesson from the Yankee failures in 1924—that you had to keep struggling to stay on top. But hardly anyone else in the country believed that any special care needed to be taken to keep the economy booming. There was time for all sorts of foolishness, now that profits were flowing in an endless river and the little man in the White House allowed no leaks to develop. Men who could not hit baseballs long distances or outrun their neighbors, or lick any considerable number of fellows their own size, discovered that fame could still be won by climbing up on flagpoles and staying there, without even toilet facilities, until they had outlasted every other fool who had tried it. Young people engaged in dance marathons, staggering about a dance floor, holding each other up from complete collapse, to the tired tunes of a relay of musicians, just to earn a thread or two of notoriety that they could hug to their bosoms for the rest of their lives. To maintain the universality of this type of madness, a man in Holland made his way to Marseilles, turning somersaults every few feet of the journey.

Those who could not lay a hand on any of this counterfeit fame by themselves sometimes struggled to touch the body, or collect a signature, or snatch a bit of clothing away from someone whose name they could pair with their own for a while, so they might be airborne together.

Yet throughout the land there were hundreds of thousands of men and women who had never known any but hard times. Farm prices sank, even while profits and dividends climbed. Wages dwindled as new factories were built and even when long-cold smokestacks suddenly filled with smoke again. And to be born black in that day was to know from early in life that you had no right even to breathe the air without the consent of your betters. After a black man in 1924 broke into a house in Homestead, Pennsylvania, and ran away when the owner found him, the police in the morning picked up thirty suspects. All were brought to court and all thirty were sentenced to a month in the workhouse. That was better, the judge obviously felt, than taking a chance of letting a "nigger" believe he could get away with something like that.

There was no such wholesale punishment of the upstanding fellows who stole the public moneys. Two, it is true, did commit suicide rather than face the shame. (Besides Charles Cramer, Charlie Forbes's legal adviser, Jesse Smith, assistant to Attorney General Daugherty, did away with himself when his brisk trade in presidential pardons and permits to withdraw bonded liquor was exposed.) But Daugherty, who almost single-handedly had made Harding President and then set up shop in the Justice Department, where pardons and permits could be had for fat fees, never went to jail at all, thanks to hung juries. Harry Sinclair, who had bribed the Secretary of the Interior and God knows how many others, was caught in the act of trying to fix his own jury, and he went to jail for *that*—but not for bribery. Edward L. Doheny, the California oil magnate who had passed a $100,000 bribe to Fall, was acquitted of the deed, although another jury found Fall guilty of accepting the bribe. Fall had quit the Cabinet soon after he put the money in his pocket, and spent his remaining years, up until he was taken to jail, living the life of a big spender.

But big spenders, particularly in New York, were common as pigeons in that day. Even baseball players were making more than enough to live on, or at least the best of them were, thanks largely to the manner in which Babe Ruth had pushed up the ceiling on wages. Travel for most big-league clubs now was always by Pullman and the trips were filled with fun. When the Yankees went west by sleeper, their car was always the last on the train. There being no air conditioning in that era, the men sat around in their skivvies, playing hearts or singing, merely arguing with make-believe ferocity, or yelling jokes at each other. Occasionally young ladies, bent on catching a close-up view of some headline hero, would run back out of the vestibule shrieking at the sight of this squadron of nearly nude males. Babe Ruth always took his little portable phonograph along, to play some favorite song over and over. Or he might lie back with his ukulele and beat out the chords of some well-worn number, which he would render in his resonant voice.

The world then, despite divers alarums that seldom penetrated inside the batting cage, seemed well ordered and benign. Barbers, bellhops, redcaps, Pullman porters, bartenders, waiters, taxi drivers, cops, conductors, room clerks, bus drivers, salesgirls, and even street beggars seemed docile, and if not content at least resigned to their lot. To be young, and rich, and a famous ballplayer was to move through life—at least when away from the ball park—without a cross word flung your way, with every door swinging open before your face, and with a dozen hands always offered to make you welcome or ease your steps. It seemed to Babe Ruth, as 1924 turned into 1925, and he, in adding another year, reached thirty, that only good things could await him. The club had done badly but he had done well. The fans, who for a few weeks had seemed to drift away from him, had thronged close again. It was still impossible for him to move anywhere on foot without a mob gathering.

Whatever resolves he may have made about his physical condition had long since trickled out of his conscience. He filled himself full to bursting night after night with yeasty beer and broiled meat. While he did not habitually eat the gargantuan meals some gossips later described, he did now and then yield to some offhand challenge and consume as much as a small horse could hold. And he further assailed his gastrointestinal tract with the constant tiny overflow from the chewed end of his fat cigars or the bulky quid of plug tobacco often snuggled in his cheek. (Hundreds of thousands of men, including President Harding, chewed tobacco then; spittoons were more common than ash trays.)

At Hot Springs in 1925, Babe Ruth weighed nearly 250 pounds, the top weight of his career. And no steaming himself or soaking his bulging carcass in the baths was going to melt that too-solid flesh. He did sweat himself enough on road work and gymnastics to take his weight down below 240 pounds. In the process, however, he pulled a muscle in his back and could not hike over the hills any more. When spring training opened, Babe seemed hardly fit to run from first base to home. Very early in the workouts he broke a finger, so that he put in very little playing time. Still Babe moved serenely through the warm days, eating all he could take aboard, ignoring curfew, reaching out for whatever full-grown females chanced to cross his course, sampling anybody's beer.

Still, when the regular spring series of exhibition games with the Brooklyn Dodgers began, Babe seemed to slip right back into gear. Against the Dodgers in Birmingham, he hit two home runs, a double, and a single in four times at bat. In Nashville the next day, Babe staged one of his favorite festivals. He invited all the kids from the orphan asylums to come watch him play ball, and seven hundred appeared, bringing their own brass band. Babe bought every kid a bag of peanuts and bought everyone, including himself, a paper hat, then moved among the kids with his wide grin never failing. He sat down with the kids' band and borrowed the cornet player's horn, then tootled it right through the next tune. Never had the sun shone any brighter or the spring seemed any more sweet. Babe hit a triple and a double in the game and left town with no more to fret him than his failure to deliver the kids a home run.

The clubs played in Atlanta then, where Babe could produce only a triple as high as the Tower of Pisa. He came down with the shaking chills right after the game and soon took to his bed. At three o'clock in the morning he had to call the hotel doctor to come tend to him. Yet when the call came to make the train to Chattanooga, and someone asked Babe if he thought he could manage it, Babe bellowed: "Goddam right! We play a game today, don't we?" So there he was, swathed in sweaters, on the station platform, just as the trainmen were calling out, "All aboard!"

In Chattanooga, Doc Woods, the Yankee trainer, would not let Babe take batting practice. But it would have taken ten trainers to keep him off the field. There were too many fans in the park who had paid good money to watch Babe Ruth hit home runs. Babe provided two homers for them to yell about, then he went back to bed.

Next stop was Knoxville, with Babe feeling almost well, the aches gone out of his bones, his fever down. Here he beat red-faced Dazzy Vance, the Brooklyn pitcher (after Dazzy had struck him out once), with a home run that cleared the left-field fence by ten feet and broke a limb off a tree beyond the fence—a tree abloom with little boys who clung to its branches to see the game free. Fortunately, the limb that Babe broke off was not wearing any children.

The two clubs moved on then to Asheville, North Carolina, where, on the railroad-station platform Babe fell in a faint. He was promptly hoisted on a stretcher and taken unconscious to the Park Hotel, where two nurses and a doctor ministered to him. By early evening the nurse on duty reported that Babe was a great deal better, but Huggins decreed that Babe would play no more baseball on the tour. He arranged for Paul Krichell, the Yankee coach and chief scout, to accompany Babe back to New York. This time there were no protests from Babe. "Every goddam bone in my body aches," he told the sportswriters. The hotel doctor had described his ailments as "severe grippe and nervous attack." What Babe had to be nervous about, no one could imagine. His teammates suspected he had simply been riding the night circuit too long.

Against the advice of the doctor, Babe took the train home next day, leaning hard on Krichell's arm and helped on to the Pullman by two or three newsmen. "I'll be in the opener, anyway," Babe promised the writers. "Don't worry." Earlier he had insisted that the local photographers be admitted to his room to take pictures of the Babe in bed.

From that time forth disaster seemed to dog him. When the train approached New York, Babe felt well enough to dress up in his best so as to reassure his wife and his daughter, Dorothy, who would meet the train along with Dr. Edward King. As the train pulled out of Manhattan Transfer, the last stop before it dodged into the Hudson River tunnel, Babe, grooming himself in the washroom, sent Krichell back to the berths to fetch a comb. While Krichell was gone, Babe fainted again and struck his head on a washbowl as he fell. Krichell came back to find Babe bleeding and unconscious, breathing like a down horse. The train sped to the station and there was held for an hour and a half on the main track while arrangements were made to patch up the Babe and transfer him to an ambulance. His wife and daughter came aboard to find Babe still dead to the world, bandaged, bleeding, and breathing heavily. Was his skull fractured? Was he dying? No one could be sure.

Finally, with much hoisting and twisting and six men to hold Babe's carcass secure, he was lifted out of the Pullman window to be taken to the ambulance. But as he was moved out of the train, Babe went into a sudden convulsion, flinging his arms and legs wildly like a man in torment, and muttering words that made no sense. It took all the men in the party, using all their strength, to keep Babe from leaping right off the stretcher. Tough Ed Barrow, when Babe had been quieted, tenderly stroked Ruth's cheek. The ambulance from St. Vincent's Hospital, it then developed, had broken down on the way and one had been sent for from the New York Hospital. Babe was taken by freight elevator to the baggage room in Pennsylvania Station where he opened his eyes and recognized his wife.

"I feel rotten, Helen," he told her, then lapsed once more into unconsciousness. Babe lay there for half an hour waiting for the new ambulance. As he was being lifted into it, he was seized again by some feverish impulse and began to thrash about and struggle to escape. All the men together held him firmly to the stretcher while the ambulance doctor gave him a jolt of morphine. The ambulance driver then discovered that his siren was out of whack, and they had to poke along through the traffic-choked streets, with the horn feebly petitioning that a way be made clear. On the way, Babe once more suffered a wild seizure and had to be forcibly restrained. But once he was snug and safe in his bed at St. Vincent's and had begun to regain his senses, Dr. King gave out word that the Babe was not seriously ill at all. (Newspaper and radio reports had already proclaimed of course that Ruth was dead. London newspapers reported Babe's demise on their front pages.) No, he just had two degrees of fever with a light case of flu; he had been eating too much, and needed a rest. Steaks for breakfast and lunch, cheese sandwiches at midnight—these would have to stop. The doctor said nothing about beer or sex.

Babe quickly turned cheerful and the next day was talking about going to the stadium soon. Outside the hospital a crowd of newsmen and photographers, along with half a hundred fans, stood watch. Motorists going by would slow down and call out for some word of the Babe's condition. Within two days Babe announced his decision to get up and go out to see the game, even if he couldn't play. He was also getting goddam tired of eggs, milk, and weak tea three times a day. But the doctor, with the help of Babe's wife and daughter, persuaded him to lie still and listen to the game on the radio.

Then, of a sudden, the doctors announced that Babe was not nearly so well as he seemed: He had an intestinal abscess and would be operated on right away. This was the first time Babe, who had suffered previous attacks of boils and carbuncles, had ever had to be sliced open for an infection, and his big grin faded somewhat at the prospect. All the same he was scrubbed and shaved and hustled off to the table at 8:30 the next morning, dosed with ether, and worked over for thirty minutes. He lay unconscious until noon. When he came to, the doctor told him he was well again but that it would be six weeks before he could play ball. Babe lay enraptured by the magnificence of his own illness and had to be told every detail of the cutting and sewing to keep him still.

Long before the six-week sentence had run out, Babe was straining to swing a bat again. He was bound to get away from the bedpan as soon as his legs would hold him. Within a few days after the operation he was wobbling about the hospital corridors with a cane, some twenty pounds lighter than he had come in but with his good nature undiminished. He pestered the doctors until they agreed he could light up a cigar. After that he kept chugging away at rich Havanas as if he had never been ill.

Five days before his allotted term was up, he had put on his uniform and was sitting on the bench at Yankee Stadium. Then, on the first of June, Babe took up his place in right field. He failed to hit in two visits to the plate and sat down for the final half of the game. The mighty Yankees, he noted, had started to come apart. Aaron Ward, his buddy, had to be taken out of the lineup for failure to hit. Wally Pipp, who followed him at bat and who had once punched him in the nose, was taken out of the order too and his job was given to a big strong Bronx boy named Lou Gehrig who had a habit of bringing into the clubhouse goodies (like pickled eels, for cripes sake!) that his mama had prepared at home.

With no strong boy to blast home a handful of runs at a time, the club had sunk to seventh place and Huggins was struggling to put some beef back into the lineup. The old-timers who were shunted aside refused to adjust to the change, and they began to share their gripes and vent them together on the little manager. They ridiculed his decisions, refused to follow his instructions, took care to remind him of his own big-league batting average (.265, with nine home runs in thirteen years), and shoved him around the locker room as if he were a pestiferous kid brother. Babe, as a member of the old original Polo Grounds gang, took an active hand in the hazing of the manager, and loudly assured poor Miller that he would be looking for a new job next year.

With his health, he imagined, completely restored and his insides all made brand new by a fancy surgeon, Babe resumed his accustomed rounds. He frequently took dinner at his pet speakeasy and drank beer as long as he felt any thirst for it. He gloried in the bright pink incision scar along his great belly and offered it for inspection to his mates as if no man alive had ever before been cut so wide open and survived the experience. The horrors of the operation all grew darker and deeper in his memory, until he seemed to have been hauled barely breathing out of a shellhole and carried in fearsome pain to a field hospital.

(Actually, some of his mates reacted to Babe's crisis with an almost total lack of dismay. When word came back to the Yankees that Babe, on his way home, had collapsed and died in a Pullman washroom, Bob Meusel, never a man to utter an extra sound when there was no need for it, shook his head. "I hope he didn't," he muttered. "That'd be another buck for flowers.")

Although Babe took a long time to start swinging his bat with the old authority, he fell quickly back into the routine of going out to "see a party" every night. The "party" was invariably female and often there were more than one. Proud of the mighty constitution that had withstood the surgeon's knife so valiantly, Babe never imagined that *this* sort of thing could slow down his recovery. Yet he did continue to find his legs giving way in the later innings of ball games and frequently he had to sit on the bench and let Bobby Veach finish for him in the outfield. If Babe hit anything less than a home run (and he hit only twenty-five that season), he sometimes had to sit down and allow some other player to run for him. One day he even had to let Bobby Veach *bat* for him—the first time he had ever made way for a pinch hitter since he had given up pitching.

Huggins kept warning Ruth of what his post-curfew prowling was likely to do to his playing skill, but Babe never heard a word. The manager gradually made up his mind that he was going to have to give a sharp yank on the reins. It took Huggins several days to develop the courage to face down Ruth. First he consulted with his boss, General Manager Ed ("Simon Legree") Barrow, who agreed with him that the bad boys in the family would have to be reminded that papa was still calling the tune.

The old-line Yankees had never been a docile crew. They had not only roughed up their manager but had more than once taken to clouting each other about the head and neck. The real roughnecks, however, notably Al DeVormer, Braggo Roth, and Carl Mays, had long since gone their ways. And tough Wally Pipp had been laid low by a hard pitch to the head. But the lads who were left, irritated by their own failures and pulled apart by jealousies, had all begun to play with half their hearts. So long as they were winning, it was useless to argue that they were injuring either the team or themselves. But they were losing. And Babe was batting less than .250. How the hell, Huggins must have asked himself, can it be any worse than it is now?

The club was playing in St. Louis, quartered at the Buckingham Hotel, when Huggins found the opening he had waited for. Big Jidge had hardly ever totaled many hours in his hotel room when the club was on the road, often checking in just about in time to change his shirt. (In St. Louis, where it always seemed 100 degrees at night and just below the melting point of lead in the afternoon, Ruth had once used up twenty-two silk shirts in three days and left them all behind for the chambermaid to treasure.) This trip, Ruth was not even seen about the Buckingham Hotel for two whole days. He had a favorite whorehouse in St. Louis and a lady in town who could do spare ribs exactly to his liking, besides two or three "parties" with whom he often made evening appointments, so his spare time was completely booked. On the third day, Babe breezed into the locker room minutes after the rest of the club had taken the field. Only Huggins, solemn-faced and white-lipped, awaited him.

"Sorry I'm late, Hug," Babe boomed out, with no more show of worry or regret than a king might show who kept his equerry waiting. "I had some personal business."

Babe's personal business had been a visit to a local lady who kept him involved until long past midnight, and then a long, long ride out into the country in the lady's car, to court some cool air. Huggins knew well enough what the flavor of Ruth's "business" was. His voice trembled as he replied:

"I know. Don't bother to suit up. You're suspended."

Babe, who had conducted so many profane shouting matches with Huggins that he hardly heard any more what the little man shouted back, now stood with his mouth open. Was this guy out of his MIND?

"I'm what?!!" Jidge roared. "Why, you miserable little son of a bitch . . ."

Huggins had stood up and had turned altogether as white as his undershirt. He gripped his belt with both hands.

"What's more," he said, "you're fined five thousand dollars."

Once more Babe's mouth worked wordlessly before he could speak.

"I'm fined? I'm *fined!?* Like *hell* I am! I'll see Jake about this! You think Jake will let you get away with this? You're crazy! Five thousand DOLLARS? Why, you little bastard, I'll never play for you again! I'll see Jake! He'll throw you out on your ass!"

"See Jake, if you want to. Now go on home."

Huggins walked out of the locker room before Babe could find another dirty word to hurl after him. But Babe soon found some sportswriters to listen to him and he treated them to a long diatribe about Huggins, his stupid strategy, and his inability to win ball games. Why, this would be his finish. When Jake Ruppert found out what this little prick had tried to do, Jake would give him the old heave-ho. I'll go right straight to Ruppert when I get back! If Jake wants to keep this stupid little son of a bitch, then he'll have to get himself somebody else to play the outfield! And he's not *that* crazy. I won't play for this little prick ever again, no matter what he says!

Then Ruth had an even better idea. The whole damned thing was so outrageous. And the fine just so goddam *crazy.* Just for taking a little spin when it was too hot to sleep! He'd see *Landis* in Chicago. The old guy always stood up for a ballplayer who was getting the shitty end of the stick. By Jesus, *Landis* would straighten this out! Wait until *Landis* got through with Huggins! We'd see who was suspended!

When Ruth reached Chicago, however, Landis was on vacation in Michigan. When he heard Ruth was looking for him, he suggested

Babe come out to the Landis lake cottage. He even suggested some trains. But Babe wasn't all that eager to make this a federal case. Instead Ruth held court for the Chicago sportswriters. Puffing thoughtfully on his big cigar, Ruth explained what was *really* going on. Here was this incompetent little manager who had been handed a championship team and then ran them into the ground with his nagging and his silly advice. Now, to cover up his own failures, he was trying to make it look as if Babe Ruth's missing bed check a few times was what was holding the team back. Well, it wouldn't work. All you had to do was look at this guy's record . . . Anyway, if Huggins stayed on, Ruth was through. Never would he play a game of baseball with Huggins as his manager. Never!

In New York, what with all the lead time the story had had to build into a national scandal, there was a throng worthy a returning war hero to greet Ruth's train. Jake Ruppert had already announced that Huggins had his complete support and had done just right in showing Ruth that the management played no favorites (especially if the favorites were batting only .240). So the imminent confrontation would surely make the walls to tremble.

Babe ducked away from the thousand or more fans who awaited him when the Twentieth Century Limited brought him into Grand Central. Grinning, fit, and dapper in his sparkling new camel's-hair cap and belted overcoat, Babe stopped for one picture to be taken, then waved his smoking cigar at the crowd and trotted off to a taxi. Newsmen and photographers clattered at his side and heels.

"See you at the apartment!" he told them. They piled into separate taxis, like bit players in a Mack Sennett comedy, and made a parade of it as they spun uptown to Babe's West Side hideaway. Here Babe outlined his stand as he had to the Chicago writers. The telephone bell interrupted him and he plunged for the phone. "Tell him I'll be right down," he ordered the little open mouth. He did not need to explain to the newsmen that it had been a summons from Jake Ruppert. Repeating his vows to quit the club before he ever took orders from Huggins again, Babe, hulking, confident, leading his retinue, made off for the Ruppert Brewery.

The office of Jake Ruppert seemed designed to strike simple men solemn. It was paneled in funeral-parlor wood, hung all about with dreary photographs of brewery buildings without a human face showing. The colonel—stiff collar, dark tie, bright stickpin, and somber, iron-creased clothing—sat like a judge, behind a desk that would have suited Mussolini. At his side sat Simon Legree, jut-jawed, unsmiling, and almost as big as Ruth himself. The door closed behind the Babe and the reporters disposed themselves about the outer office to listen to the ticking of the clock. Not a sound came from the sanctum. When the door opened less than half an hour later, the reporters were admitted to a scene that looked for all the world like a bad boy sitting before the principal's desk. Ruth, shame-faced, silent, seeming on the verge of tears, said nothing. Ruppert, in his slightly German-accented English (although he was American born and educated), spoke the first word.

"Ruth, ' he said (it sounded more like "Root"), "has changed his mind. Haven't you, Ruth?"

Babe, in a subdued voice, allowed that he had. Ruppert said Babe would report to the team next day; whether he would play again would be up to Huggins. As for the fine, that still stood. Ruth then spoke his own piece to the sportswriters. His repentance was obvious and absolute. In a manner wholly typical of the Babe when he knew he was wrong, he swallowed all his bad words, recalled all his threats, and expressed the hope that Huggins would let him go back into uniform.

"I'll apologize to him right away," Babe promised. And Babe did apologize, or try to, sticking his big hand out to Huggins at the stadium and loudly declaring that he hadn't meant any of those things he had said when he was mad. But Huggins, who had been far more deeply shaken by the affair than Ruth had, and who had a long train of abuses and usurpations on the Babe's part to count over, was not quite ready to open his heart.

"Get away from me," he told Babe. "You're under suspension and I don't want you in the clubhouse. You can't play again until I say so."

Really jolted now, Babe stood with his mouth open and his eyes moist.

"Can't I even do some hitting?" Babe asked.

"No. You can't even put on a uniform."

It took several days for Babe to wear Huggins down with pleas by telephone. Huggins had at first insisted on a public apology, before teammates and newsmen. But he soon decided not to subject Babe to this humiliation. When the club left for Boston on September 7, he gave Ruth permission to come along. There had been some strong hints that the whole business had been exaggerated anyway, to ensure a fat gate when the Athletics came to town and Babe staged a triumphal return. So Huggins had made up his mind not to use Babe until the club was in Boston. In Fenway Park, Babe trotted out to his old position at the foot of Duffy Lewis's left-field cliff to a loud roar of welcome. (His previous appearance here had brought only howls of derision.) Babe made just one hit in that game and let a ball elude him in the outfield, but no one even offered a boo. And from that time on, for the remaining three weeks of the season, Babe wielded his big bat like a man possessed, determined to demonstrate his complete devotion to the ways of righteousness. And also hoping the fine might be remitted. *That* part of the deal he could not get out of his mind.

"Five thousand bucks!" he would complain ruefully. "Why, I know guys that killed guys that didn't get fined that much. Even *bootleggers!* They don't get fines like that!"

Well, hardly anyone in the big cities was angry with bootleggers. But Huggins saw the fine as a symbol of his authority and he would not even talk about remitting it. A few years later, when Huggins was dead, Simon Legree Barrow gave Ruth back the money.

But for the remainder of the 1925 season Babe tried to win his way into Huggins's heart with his bat. There really wasn't time enough for him to climb to the peak again. At least he lifted his average from .240 to .290, but his total of twenty-five home runs that season did not equal silent Bob Meusel's and was just a few more than the big awkward kid named Gehrig put out of the park himself.

The experts of the day considered that .290 batting average the sign of the decline of Babe Ruth. Too much money. A swelled head. A body wasted by dissipation. And he was not a kid anymore. No, the great days of Babe Ruth were all behind him. Another athlete spoiled by too fat a payday.

The rest of the Yankee club had not responded to Babe's reformation. They continued to growl at each other in the locker room and work at cross-purposes on the field. Each man knew *he* was all right. It was just those other goddam dubs who kept making it impossible to get the club rolling.

The fact was that a number of the players were truly over the hill, even though Babe Ruth wasn't. If George Weiss had been operating the Yankees, as he would be about ten years later, the club would have had replacements all ready to move in to take over from the outworn troops before disaster overcame them. Weiss, who was

operating the New Haven club at this time, would make it his practice, when he became general manager of the Yankees, always to
have *three* New York lineups: the team on the field, the team on the
bench, and the team in the minor leagues. Often members of the
team in the making would not even all belong to the Yankees. But
George would have them spotted just the same and, planning three
and four seasons ahead, would start the maneuvers that would
bring them to the stadium when they were needed—a Joe DiMaggio to take over when Ruth had faded; a Mickey Mantle to replace
DiMaggio; a Roger Maris to provide that left-handed power that
made the handy right-field seats pay off.

But Ed Barrow, shrewd as he was and as tough a man as he was
in a trade or a salary negotiation, had not been looking far enough
into the future. When the Yankees began to crack, the replacement
parts did not match the originals. Pee Wee Wanninger was no
Everett Scott, nor was Benny Bengough a match for Wally Schang.
And Hank Shanks, Lord knows, was not built in the image of Aaron
Ward. But once the season had tumbled in about their ears, Barrow
allowed no sentimentality or self-doubt to restrain him from empty-
ing out the stable. When it became clear that his steeds were not
even straining to get first to the wire, he told Huggins to turn them
loose. And he ordered his scouts—led by the wily and indefatigable
Paul Krichell—to recruit him a new set of heroes immediately.

Witt, Pipp, Scott, and Schang, and later Aaron Ward, were all
dumped on the market. The clumsy Bronx kid, the one who had just
never fit into the gang, that Lou Gehrig from Columbia, became the
first-string first baseman, no longer just filling in until Pipp got over
his headaches. Tony Lazzeri, who had hit sixty home runs in 1925 as
a shortstop for St. Paul, and whom the Chicago Cubs passed up
when they learned he had epilepsy, was bought for $50,000 and a
carload of ballplayers to become the full-time second baseman. At
third base, Home Run Baker had already been permanently replaced
by Run-Home Joe Dugan, who suffered from a wobbly knee and
spells of homesickness that prompted him to hightail it without
warning sometimes for Papa Dugan's fireside. But he had his knee
operated on and his hand held by admiring teammates until he overcame both ailments and surpassed Baker at the job. Mark Koenig
was brought in from St. Paul to become the regular shortstop and to
add about forty points to the batting average at that spot. A re-

formed and revitalized Ruth in left field promised to provide both the power and the confidence the club had lacked in 1925.

Babe was leery of Hot Springs now as a conditioning spot, so he did his hiking that fall in the New Brunswick woods, pretending to be a hunter. But what really made Ruth new again was his turning over the care of his burgeoning carcass to Artie McGovern, a tough ex-pugilist who ran a gymnasium in New York City. McGovern made Ruth sweat until the big man moaned. This was no taking-the-baths and poking-around-the-golf-course regimen. This was brutal muscular labor. After two weeks of boxing, wrestling, pulling on the rowing machine, and batting a handball about every single day, Babe weighed only 224 pounds, a good playing weight. His legs were strong, his eyes bright, and his wind sound.

When it was almost time to report to the new training camp in St. Petersburg, Babe went there ahead of everyone else and nursed his new physique along by spending all day on the golf course. He fell off the poached-egg diet that McGovern had bound him to. But he kept his figure lean and his muscles hard. Perhaps the sudden vision that Ruppert had given him of a nonplaying ballplayer with no money in his pocket had frightened him enough to ensure his walking the line from now on. But more likely it was the taste he had had of not being *allowed* to play ball, of having to sit like some slob high in the stands (Babe watched the games during his suspension from the back row of the mezzanine) and never getting into the clubhouse again to raise hell with the guys. That was a fate that really frightened him.

The world meanwhile moved along as if Babe Ruth had never had a stomachache. Fathers told their little ones that Babe had been felled by an overdose of hot dogs and soda pop. Babe, however, had no taste for such fare. His breakfast on the morning he took sick had been steaks with fried potatoes. When he overloaded *his* stomach it was with food a man could relish, not with cheap appetite killers that were meant for kids.

Kids in that era were growing up too fast, some parents felt, what with all the truck that was fed to them now on the radio and the trashy books they could lay hands on. It was true that the radio-broadcast of the 1924 Democratic national convention, where 103 dreary ballots were needed to select a loser, had smartened many a youngster up to the pompous idiocies of the grown-up world. But a number of young people clung tight to the earphones through ballot after ballot, not bored at all, but learning to chant "Al-a-ba-ma! Twenty-four votes for Oscar Underwood!" as if it swung with as fine a lilt as "The March of the Wooden Soldiers."

But what caused parents most to despair were the shockingly sexy songs like "You'd Be Surprised!" or "Louisville Lou" and "Red Hot Mama," or the novels like Warner Fabian's (Samuel Hopkins Adams's) *Flaming Youth* or Elliot Paul's *Imperturbe* that suggested sin might not be ugly after all. There was even a horrid little book called *The Plastic Age* by a college professor named Percy Marks (who would soon be denied a new contract) in which words like "bastard" were spelled right out and characters were made to talk about having sex outside of marriage.

Typical, some folk held, of what all this sparing of the rod was doing to the younger generation was the dreadful murder of Bobby Franks by two young "geniuses" in Chicago. This fearful crime—fearful in its cold-bloodedness and in the utter lack of remorse displayed by its perpetrators—occupied the public mind more intensely than anything that happened on the baseball field. Men and women spelled over to each other each new horror as it was offered up in the newspapers and children read the details with prickles of real terror growing in their insides.

Nathan Leopold and Richard Loeb had obviously been "spoiled," street-corner psychologists decided, by being brought up with all their wants fulfilled, with ten-dollar bills handed them for the asking, and with carloads of goodies provided them and nothing asked in return. Their having been raised at arm's length by their parents, given almost from birth into the care of mildly sadistic and discipline-oriented nursemaids and governesses, was counted one of the "advantages" of being rich. There had been no one around to tell of it when the little babies screamed themselves to sleep, sternly neglected in the name of "training," so they might learn that the world did not come running when they were hungry, wet, or in pain.

That they grew up into two normal wealthy psychotics who could torture little children without qualms should have surprised no one. But it did surprise all who knew them. They had been such *lovely* boys—well-spoken, considerate, freely giving their time to edify kids younger than themselves, Leopold by taking boys on bird walks every week and Loeb by teaching water sports at a summer resort in

Charlevoix, Michigan. Their homosexual relationship was just one more secret they cuddled to their hearts, as they plotted ways of illustrating to the world their own social and intellectual superiority. Their "perfect crime" was meant first to be committed on a Rosenwald grandson, a far more glittering target than poor little Bobby Franks. But the little Deutsch boy did not come to school on the chosen day and Bobby became the target of opportunity.

One of the ironies largely missed on the sidewalks of the day was that the two young monsters actually did come within a whisker of outwitting the grown-up world. They had rehearsed their alibi story so carefully that the police were able to find no contradiction between them. And had Leopold not accidentally dropped his glasses at the scene, the cops might not even have dug deeply enough to discover that the boys had not taken the auto out of the garage and so could not have gone riding together as they said.

But blood was chilled as the tale came out of how utterly cool the boys remained even when discovery was imminent. Leopold, knowing his glasses had been found, still took his little charges on their bird walk, then delivered each one to his parents, explaining that he knew that the parents would be worried over the dreadful Bobby Franks story and so he had chosen to take each child right to the proper door. Loeb assured the newspaper reporters that they would never be convicted, because their parents had money enough to sway any court. The parents of the boys however vowed that they would not use their wealth to get the boys off. Then they hired Clarence Darrow to save them from the electric chair—and refused to pay his fee when he delivered them over to life imprisonment.

This sort of sport, along with the other bloody crimes that livened the front pages of the big-city newspapers, probably involved more hearts and minds than the stock market did. The hunting down of killers and the taking of condign vengeance upon them by the state did quickly attain the status of entertainment. When the middle-aged lovers Ruth Snyder and Judd Gray conspired to murder the uncooperative Mr. Synder with a sash weight, they earned a tankful of sympathetic tears along with rabid howls for their prompt eradication. And fans who followed the trial bought miniature sash weights, as if they had been toy baseballs, as mementoes of the game.

The big city was still in many ways but half grown-up. One day in 1925 a policeman actually had to leap twice from a moving auto to stop a runaway horse—much as policemen and other heroes had done in the storybooks of an earlier generation. And it was not until that year that auto traffic on Manhattan avenues was deemed heavy enough to require the ordering of stop and go lights at every corner. Theretofore, the traffic lights had always shone green in both directions, barring some emergency, with an amber light to indicate whether north-south or east-west had the right of way.

Traffic cops were soon encased in glass cages atop four-legged metal towers right in the middle of Fifth Avenue, to keep watch over the coming and going of autos and trucks and to shift the lights when need be. What police were not needed to keep the wheels moving were sometimes assigned the task of stilling the unseemly protests of those who might find the current divvying up of the national income not altogether to their liking. In early April 1925 the Teamsters Union scheduled a meeting at a hall on East Fifth Street, amid whispers that they might be planning a strike. Police Commissioner Enright nipped that notion in the bud by dispatching policemen to order the incipient rebels to disperse. And disperse they did, for none of them was yet ready to risk a term on Welfare Island.

Preventive action against people who might do wrong was everywhere endorsed as the safest way to promote domestic tranquillity. When rumrunners carrying liquor in from the ships of rum row chose Atlantic City as their port of private entry, federal agents were ordered to "shoot first and ask questions afterward." Private Paul Crouch of the 21st Infantry was sentenced to forty years in the brig for "defending communism" in letters to the Honolulu papers. And New York City policemen were generally granted the privilege of employing fist and rubber hose to discipline suspects who would not confess or loiterers who could not account satisfactorily for their presence on the streets. Even so, when Mr. and Mrs. Philip McFadden returned from a big-game hunt, they assured reporters that Broadway was more dangerous than the jungle. "Animals," said they, "do not attack."

Senator William E. Borah of Idaho deplored the "furtive eye of the government peering into our private lives." But hardly anyone listened. Innocent people, it was generally granted, had nothing to hide—except perhaps a few bottles of illicit gin. (The private railway car of the opera singer, Geraldine Farrar, was raided just after it crossed into the United States from Canada and found to contain a stock of liquor. The liquor was seized and Farrar made no protest, although she vowed later that it had belonged to others in her party.)

Henry Ford startled the nation in the twenties with his announcement of a five-day week with no reduction in pay. Such spoiling of the working class was bound to spread discontent, other business leaders prophesied, and it would surely create a new supply of idle hands for the Devil to find use for. The men who worked in the Ford plant, however, were somewhat less than enraptured at this new deal. While giving them these extra days off (only in the twelve-week summer season), Ford did away with the paid vacation, swapping twelve half days (for the plant operated only half-time on Saturday) for twelve full days, thus coming out ahead, as he generally did. Henry also took upon himself the regulating of his workers' private lives by authorizing gate guards to sniff the breaths of all who reported for duty and offering rewards for inside operatives who would squeal on all those who spoke favorably of unions or admitted to being Jews.

Ford had his own newspaper, the Dearborn *Independent,* in which he did his small part in awakening the nation to the perils of Zionism and the other many machinations of international Jewry. By articulating and lending I-saw-it-in-the-paper respectability to nearly every whispered lie ever used to keep plain people from living at peace with their neighbors, crackpot Henry, now one of the richest men in the world, helped make the world safe for war even while he preached Prohibition and peace.

Generally, however, men and women who had no need to slave in auto plants or on farms or in laundries or mills or mines were too concerned with the spending of money, and the hasty gathering of it, to find room in their minds for much more than the conventional workaday wisdom needed to conform to the expressed beliefs of their fellows. In those days it gradually became the fashion to make everything bigger, on the grounds that spending, consumption, the using up of resources and manufactured goods as rapidly as hands and jaws and feet could operate, was God's own chosen method for spreading the wealth. The more the rich ate, in short, the more would tumble down to the poor. Few people actually put it to themselves this way, outside of executive bull sessions and solemn talk at speakeasy bars. Most people just consumed heartily because it was the style.

Automobiles that had been set up square and high as buggies began to grow long and low until a chauffeur had to walk a rod and a half to get all the way around the rear of his car and open the door for the master and his lady. Tires ballooned to almost twice as wide as they had been. Engines grew from four to six to eight to twelve and, by the end of the 1920s, even to sixteen cylinders. Clothing was cut so full that grown men in their best looked like small boys wearing their papa's or big brother's clothes—the trousers wide enough and long enough almost to cover the shoes completely, the jackets cut wide and padded and draped to conceal the fact that there was not flesh enough to fill them out, the overcoats reaching nearly to the ankles and tied with belts two feet longer than they needed to be, with lapels so large and collars so deep that two men might have found cloth enough in one coat to hide from the cold in.

Buildings were planned to push higher and higher into the sky, to put to shame such pathetic antiques as the Woolworth Building, which had earlier been one of New York's wonders. The Waldorf-Astoria Hotel, then on Fifth Avenue between Thirty-third and Thirty-fourth, where men and women used to show off their expensive clothing to each other, was to be torn down to make way for the tallest building in the world, atop which a mooring mast would grow, where dirigible balloons from all over the world would stop and unload passengers into the very center of the city. (The fact that air currents would rip to pieces any balloon whose commander was crazy enough to leave it hitched above the streets did not enter into any calculations, for there was no room in that day for "destructive criticism.")

In the naughty nineties, when rich men had lighted their cigars with paper money, conspicuous consumption was considered just a vagary of the *nouveaux riches,* who wore outsize diamonds and billowing furs and drove four-horse equipages to flaunt the fact that they had come into more money than was good for them. But now every man who wanted to avoid looking like a freak on college campus or in city club took care that his trousers were cut wide, his jackets padded and his knickers ballooned out until they drooped inches below the knee. Gradually since the Great War, wrist-watches—once a sign of effeminacy—had begun to replace the pocket watch, so there were few chunky gold watch chains or diamond-studded fobs to proclaim a man's affluence. But cigarette lighters made in precious metals could be exhibited quite casually a dozen times an evening.

Motion-picture theaters were built in the shape of palaces, with lavishly gilded railings, overupholstered seats, mirrored lobbies, and ushers decked out like Graustarkian troops. Department stores grew impatient with common customers and sought out ways of concentrating on the "carriage trade." A. T. Stewart, one of the oldest, made a survey of its charge customers, learned that most of them lived now in the upper reaches of Manhattan, and set out at once to move out of the dingy thirties into the affluent fifties. It settled down there with much fanfare, then slowly expired. Dobbs & Company, the hat store, built itself a marble palace far uptown and nearly went broke amid its grandeur. Even Whyte's, the famous luncheon spot for bankers and brokers and a few affluent newspapermen, sought to shake the dust and manure of Fulton Street off its heels to reopen in grander surroundings in the forties—only to discover that its pristine dinginess and antique unhandiness had provided most of its charm.

But these minor misfortunes did not typify the age. Restaurant-speakeasies grew wealthier, and became more exclusive, lifted their prices to keep out the beer drinkers, and tightened their security against the unfashionable, the nonfamous, and the people of no account.

Barney Gallant's speakeasy on University Place became a haven for judges and lawyers and grew rich not merely on its fare and its drink but through the proprietor's discreet methods of recruiting willing ladies to come entertain his favorite customers in the private rooms upstairs. There was a Merchant's Club in the Thirties where admission was through introduction only, where there was a tiny quiet bar, private rooms on several floors and even a sewing room where a patient lady repaired garments that had been torn or come unstuck during some revelry. And one speakeasy even took to advertising in the weekly papers that circulated in the wealthy suburbs—using just a picture of a half-open iron gate with the legend "When in town, Don't forget—Twenty-one West Fifty-second Street."

Although there were still many spots—like the Dutchman's, where the ballplayers went for steaks—that stood open to any who might push the door aside, the Manhattan saloons had all, since Commissioner Enright's crackdowns, pulled in behind locked doors, through which muscular men peered out to identify any who sought entrance. And to be recognized by one of these bouncers was a social accolade of far more worth in New York political, business, and theatrical circles than a listing in the sacred Social Register. Indeed, a few of these bouncers afterward exploited the "friendships" they had built up as janizaries of the high-priced saloons and opened restaurants of their own, where they tried, often unhappily, to play the part of big-spending host. One large flat-footed husky named Shor who had long guarded the doorway at a speakeasy called Billy LaHiff's attained far more fame as a saloonkeeper than his employer had ever owned.

Some speakeasies maintained large files of customers' names, but most depended on the doorman or bouncer to recognize the face, or at least to select the ones least likely to be on the prowl for evidence to be used in a raid. One famous place in the fifties, called the Aquarium because it served drinks across a bar atop a long tank full of tropical fish, used to identify its customers by their birthdays, matching names and dates before opening the door.

Usually these run-of-the-mill places offered good meals for about a dollar and drinks for fifty cents, serving as restaurants for those of the middle class who sought something a bit more sophisticated than the "tea rooms" that bloomed on every block in all five boroughs. The Manhattan tea rooms of course were far more fussily decked out than the dollar-dinner spots in the outlying neighborhoods. Out-of-town ladies who wanted a quick taste of New York without any hint of gangsterism, either in the ambience or the bill, crowded into Alice Foote MacDougall's places and sat with breath bated and eyes aglow at candlelit tables while plump "gypsies" wandered about offering serenades.

But the New York known to the big spenders and the hep crowds had hardly got its eyes wide open when the gypsies were in full voice at Alice Foote MacDougall's. The loudest and liveliest nightclubs of New York were all big-league speakeasies where half-size drinks were served in oversized glasses at double what a full drink brought in an ordinary saloon. Only a rank yokel or an utter innocent would be so naïve as to protest either the stinginess of the drink or the breathtaking arrogance of the price. When you were out for a big time in New York, you expected to be overcharged—even "clipped," as the current jargon worded it. The most famous nightclub hostess of the era, Texas Guinan, set her customers to laughing every night by bullying them into spending more money. Her "Hello, sucker!" was a greeting more sought-after than a smile from President Coolidge.

The conviction persisted throughout all New York that ownership of a business conveyed a license to peel the hide off any customer who dared cross the threshold. The Bronx and upper Manhattan were crowded with installment-purchase houses where people were shamelessly misled, where guarantees offered in a newspaper advertisement were laughingly disowned, where cut-rate specials turned out to be pieces of obvious junk that the salesman would not let go of unless you put a gun on him, they being so vital to the luring in of prospective customers. Installment rates were outrageously usurious, yet nothing short of a court order could earn for a customer the right to have the interest rate (at least 20 percent and usually far more) explained to him. There were dozens of houses that specialized in repossession, that hardly knew how to deal with a customer who met all his payments on time, and that used the city courts as collection agencies, throwing the required summonses in the sewer and bullying debtors with fake legal documents, early morning or late-night collection calls, and forcible repossession of furniture or appliances (to be promptly resold). The classified advertisements of the big morning newspapers (the *World,* the *American,* the *Times,* and the *Herald Tribune*) were filled with distressful notices of the need to "sell out contents of beautiful apartment" at heartbreaking losses. What the seller knew and the newspaper knew—but the buyer didn't—was that this "beautiful apartment" was a display room for a furniture retailer, who would fill the place right up again as soon as enough buyers had come to take advantage of his distress.

The auction rooms on Forty-second Street and throughout the Times Square district were merely retail outlets for junk jewelry, chinaware, and haberdashery, with make-believe bidders on hand to keep the prices high and an angry auctioneer to shout down any "rube" who dared question the methods. Strangers who walked the streets in this area were often amazed at the amplified voices squawking "going once! going twice!" to almost empty rooms. Street hawkers too, shouting "Advertising! Advertising!," strode along with a whole covey of make-believe buyers circling around them, passing out "gold" watches for a quarter each and occasionally luring a live customer into the flow to send him off with a prize that not only would not keep time but could not be wound up.

Signs that seemed to announce "Auction Sale" of rugs or linens or tableware or furniture sometimes turned out to say, when you looked at them again, "Action Sale"; and "Going Out of Business" signs usually said, to those who came close enough to notice, "Going Out for Business." The device of the "loss leader"—the no-profit item used to lure customers through the door—was carried everywhere to its obvious extremes. Either the item did not exist at all or was available only to those who made substantial purchases of other goods. Real-estate agents all had flimsy shacks for rent or sale in some mosquito-ridden area, so that they might be advertised as "six-room bungalows" at incredibly low prices.

Loan companies beseeched working men and women to borrow years ahead on their salaries so they might own and enjoy all the goodies usually reserved to the rich. This was the era of the co-maker, when unwary friends, who thought they were just offering a sort of business reference, found that they were the party of first recourse when the debtor let a payment slip. Nobody really knew what interest rates he was paying, and the operators of various "plans" for sinking painlessly over your head in debt fought valiantly against every legislative effort to force full disclosure. Why, the poor customer simply would not "understand" all that complicated arithmetic! It was for his own protection that he was kept in ignorance. And it was from similar motives that "orange-juice" stands neglected to identify their product as orange-flavored and slightly sweetened water, while root-beer stands filled foot-high and inch-wide glasses with foam and said it was something to drink. The poor man who had vowed never to go to the Bowery anymore would have found all the practices that had dismayed him moved uptown in the twenties and multiplied by ten—from the fast-talking auctioneer who sold the box instead of the sox to the barber who clipped your wallet as closely as your head.

Gyp cabs were easily recognizable by the street-wise New Yorker but not by the tourist, who could not know that the "gyps" had paid off the doorman and the policeman on the beat to permit them to monopolize the cab line outside a busy nightclub or big hotel. But even the legitimate cabbies, who often had to pay tribute of some sort to acquire access even to the second-rate sources of calls, had all devised ways of skimming off a few extra (and often desperately needed) nickels and dimes. Some would take an out-of-towner all through Central Park to bring him back within half a block of where he started. Others would steer customers, for a fee, to speakeasies, whorehouses, or spots where action was to be had at cards or dice. There was so much easy money afloat in the city then that it seemed indecent not to lay hold of at least a little of it, and the town was full of friendly garagemen, bus drivers, special cops, doormen, janitors, and bellhops who could either get something for you "wholesale" or put you in the way of getting through a secret door to sample some illicit joy.

These were the final great days of vaudeville, although the practitioners of that art were all convinced that they had attained a fleshly immortality, or that at least the big money would last them far past the grave. Young ladies in dancing classes still dreamed of playing the Palace—the Olympus of vaudeville—and so did brash young men who were frantically singing "I Wish I Was a Monkey in the Zoo" at a 10-20-30 theater in Fall River, Massachusetts. So great was the thirst for entertainment, and so little had radio infringed upon the custom for the vaudeville stage, that many of the silliest acts ever conceived still managed to find stage room all over the nation—and particularly in New York, where half a hundred movie houses fattened out the bill each week with several acts of vaudeville. A few of the veteran performers, working the same tired routine that had earned them a good living for a decade or more, did not even trouble to relate their lines to the business on the stage, chanting the same lyrics that had "killed them" all over the country, even though they no longer made sense.

There were great performers at the Palace too—men and women who would make fortunes in the talking pictures before another ten years had gone by, and others who had grown famous and wealthy by dint of a long run with the Ziegfeld Follies or at some speakeasy-nightclub.

The corner of New York where the Palace stood—Forty-seventh Street and Broadway—was often characterized as a spot where you could find a man who would do *anything* for money. And it was true that, besides the young ladies in orange stage make-up and the young men with funny haircuts who stood outside the theater to chat with their kind or yearn after the day when *they* might walk in and out that stage door, there could often be found pimps, male prostitutes, pickpockets, small-time thugs, bookies, glum gangsters in snap-brim hats, and hustlers who would accept almost any sort of errand that promised a quick payday.

The hotels up and down the side streets off Broadway in the forties and fifties were aswarm with theater folk and speakeasy employees, many of whom made these places their homes. But the hotels also offered lobbies where prostitutes could display their qualifications and where rooms could be signed for without fear that any officious night clerk might undertake to enforce the True Name law. (Ty Cobb, taking a night off to celebrate his signing as manager of the Detroit baseball club, once checked into the Knickerbocker Hotel as T. R. Call and turned purple with rage when the bellhop addressed him as "Mister Cobb.")

Oddly enough, the great commercial hotels in the Grand Central area conducted endless guerilla warfare against those who dared attempt to employ their beds in the commission of some mortal sin. There were floor clerks to eye with suspicion any guest who walked by with an unregistered lady at his side and a house detective who was sometimes rendered breathless as he endeavored to root out every single-occupancy male who was "entertaining a lady." There were even mirrors to give the floor clerks a view of those who tried to use the staircases to smuggle dear friends in to bear them company. (In the Broadway hotels an elevator operator might wryly suggest that the fire bell was used simply to signal "Everybody into their own rooms!")

All throughout the theater district, and to a lesser degree throughout all Manhattan and Brooklyn, an air of phoniness persisted that sophisticates actually took pride in. A current song, sung by a gravel-voiced young man named Jimmy Durante, declared the whole street "a fake and a phoney" but still "My street! The Heart of the world!" "Blind" men and women working the street would often steer themselves deliberately into a knot of idlers with their canes thumping and their little trays of pencils inviting contributions. Then, when business was done, they would unblushingly fold their trays, remove their dark glasses, tuck their canes under their arms, and head briskly for the subway.

The sight-seeing buses parked along the curbs around the Times Building would always carry a half-dozen professional passengers, who would hold their seats only until a few real passengers had been ensnared. Then the decoys would all file somberly out the door and into the empty bus that was scheduled to move out next. A block away, along Sixth Avenue, penny arcades offered nonexistent delights to those who would drop a penny in the picture machine and turn a crank; shooting galleries featured targets that could not be knocked down; "strength meters" would hit the top figure only for men who knew just where to land the blow. And the subways were infested with men who filed through the trains dropping little cards with nail files attached, into the lap of each passenger, so that those who were moved by the message on the card (I have diabetes or I have an incurable disease) could contribute a small something when the man walked back to pick up all the cards.

Petty crimes in this era, such as public drunkenness, snitching merchandise from a newsstand, dropping a slug in a subway turnstile, or hawking shoeshines near the train terminals, were usually dealt with by the police, who would punish the perpetrators by cuffing them about the head and ears, earnestly belaboring them with nightsticks, or idly torturing them by knocking them down and stepping on their fingers. But a man who fell into the hands of the special police who worked for the transit companies would have welcomed a session with the city cops. For the boys in the light blue uniforms, with no one to answer to except the boss, would occasionally amuse themselves by beating bloody with handcuffs some fellow they caught trying to sneak through the gate without paying his nickel.

Despite rising prices that were supposed to signal blossoming prosperity, a nickel was still a coin worth counting in many a pay envelope. Wages in department stores were usually less than twenty dollars a week, with nothing offered for required overtime except fifty cents "supper money." Managers of chain bakeries might bring home thirty-five or forty dollars and assistant managers in the five-and-dime were supposed to keep their eyes on the riches that awaited them when they made manager, and to forget the tiny salary they were granted to live on.

As a matter of fact, hardly an employer in the city gave any thought to whether or not his employees could live on what he might allow them. Labor was simply a commodity, to be bought up like wrapping paper when there was need for it, from whatever supplier offered the lowest price. Employees in the large retail shops or beehive offices, even though they might be often apostrophized as "fellow workers," were deemed a sorry lot on the whole, who had no right to anything, even frequent trips to the toilet, that might interfere with the brisk accretion of profit. Whether they lived in a tenement, a gutter, or a tent, and if they ate beans for supper or good roast beef, was of less concern to the man who owned the business than the color of their socks. Indeed, more than one prince of industry took pride in setting up codes of dress for employees, which might actually dictate the shade of stocking, the color of necktie, or the length of the skirt.

Hardly anyone looked upon these intrusions as curtailment of liberty or unlawful interference in a person's private life. If anyone objected to the terms of employment, he could simply go look for another job. If there were none to be had, that was merely an illustration of the fact that it behooved a working person to do as he was told. Freedom, in the lexicon of big business of the 1920s, was freedom for employees to go look for a job and for a businessman to spend his money and run his operation as he pleased.

There was also the freedom to take your savings and try to run them up into a competence by buying common stocks. No one in this era, not the shoeshine man or the lady who ran the elevator, was exempt from laying small bets on the upward movement of stocks. It was like playing a lottery that had nothing but winners, or betting on a race where every horse came in first at long odds. Dayton Airplane and Engine, the name of a stock that had hardly anything but stacks of paper behind it, might sell at five dollars today and twenty-five dollars the following Monday, while every other stock on the board went climbing too. The very name of capitalism made a joyful sound, for every man was his own capitalist and no one, looking from Trinity Church clear down to where Wall Street turned a corner, could see any possible end to all this except exultant prosperity, with every man a king and with the ultimate coming of a new heaven and a new earth, all built in the image of the New York skyline, where there would be no more sea.

Most of Babe Ruth's playmates, like everybody with extra cash, were buying common stocks too and eagerly opening the morning paper to the financial pages to see where their favorites had finished. But they were saved from the disaster that befell most of the nation because their manager, Miller Huggins, being so far removed from the conventional wisdom that inundated all who dwelt too close to the financial district, saw the bust coming. Riding in a taxicab from the railroad station to the hotel in Chicago one day, Huggins told the players who had crowded into the cab with him that he had just sold all his own stocks and all his land in Florida. The whole thing had just climbed too high, said little Miller, who had more good sense than any two other baseball managers. The fantastic stock values had no justification in earnings. It was the time for all who owned stocks to unload them and for those who had contemplated buying more to put their money back into their pockets. The ballplayers took his advice.

Babe had no time for complex matters like that, however. If he wanted action for his extra cash, he simply telephoned one of the two New York handicappers whom he and Joe Dugan favored with their custom, then bet on their choices, and let the horses work things out among themselves. What money Babe failed to spend was all tucked conservatively away where it would draw the breath of 6 percent through all eternity.

Most young people of that day were concerned with living in the style of the current aristocracy—the motion-picture actors, the nightclub heroes and heroines, and the playful rich. It being generally recognized that all such folk, in the New York area at least, dwelt in penthouses, the youth of the city, what part of it had come upon an easy way of making a living, competed earnestly for any apartment that, because it was perched on the roof of a high building, even alongside the water tank, could be described as a penthouse. Those who could only pant after such dwellings usually bedded down in a furnished apartment, for it was considered folly to "tie oneself down" with such accoutrements of the horse-and-buggy age as furniture or homeownership. Some new families even undertook to raise their young in two rooms in a theater-district hotel. Brooklyn, upper Manhattan, and nearby Queens were laced with large buildings where apartments could be rented with fashionable front doors, cheap and scanty furniture, and rooms all cut up small enough to permit three or four or five young people all to live together with some remnants of privacy. Neighborhood bootleggers grew rich running bottles of two-dollar gin night after night to such communes.

PART V

Jimmy Walker Days

THE city had a new mayor now, a slim, sharp-featured, snap-brim fedora type who could fashion a wisecrack in a trice, could charm an enemy, con a friend, or silence a heckler with a deft ad lib, who looked like the valedictorian of a Catholic high-school graduating class, sounded like a born New Yorker, and comported himself like a vaudeville hoofer. This was Jimmy Walker, whose very name became a sort of shibboleth in his campaign to separate the city-bred from the carpetbaggers. "Vote for Walker, a real New Yorker," went the slogan. And if you couldn't make that rhyme, why you'd better go back to Utica.

Jimmy was a penthouse man himself. That is, when he sought out a hideaway where he could lodge his lady love, a pretty actress named Betty Compton, he found a rooftop apartment in the East Thirties hardly a stone's throw from the townhouse of J. P. Morgan. With most of the city reporters earnestly averting their eyes, Jimmy used to flutter to this nest whenever the burdens of office began to cut creases in his shoulders. Because Jimmy's crowd ruled the town, directed the police, controlled the courts, knelt down in the proper church, exacted tribute from the whorehouses and speak-easies, and granted unwritten licenses to gangsters, gamblers, and grifters of every caliber, Jimmy had no real fear of exposure or shame as long as he trod his own turf. Once, when he took a cruise with Miss Compton and suddenly found himself exposed to the un-jaded eyes of outside reporters, Jimmy hastened to contrive a breathtaking cover story by explaining that Betty was off on a wedding trip. And then, by all that's unholy, he persuaded his actor friend, Eddie Dowling, to submit to the marriage ceremony, with the ship's captain offering the vows and Jimmy himself standing up for the bewildered bridegroom.

Not all New York shenanigans were as bare-faced as this but many of them were, for a "right" guy could commit small sins of almost every sort and still find ways of keeping his tracks covered. Jimmy campaigned earnestly against all bluenoses and reformers who would take the fun out of life by trying to lay bare the actual sources of the income that made his own life so merry, or by attempting to enforce laws against his friends just as if they were nobodies from some tank town up the Hudson. Reformers, Jimmy averred, were people who liked to ride through sewers in glass-bottomed boats. And most of the town's sophisticates agreed that there was something decidedly unlovely about a person who was always trying to uncover activities that decent people simply did not talk about in company. Of course politicians took bribes. That was the American Way! But you didn't have to keep printing it where kids could read it.

No one at the time was trying to run Babe Ruth's lady loves to earth, else they might have come up with two dozen different hide-aways, not one of them a penthouse. Babe at about this time was counting over the woes that had beset him and wondering if anything would ever go right. His wife, Helen, had finally given up trying to pretend there was any such thing as a family life with Babe and she had started action for a separation, asking $100,000.

It seems ironic that Babe, who was always alert to others' pains when they were presented to him directly, and who would jump privately into a cab or drive his own car recklessly at almost any hour to go see a sick boy in a hospital who had "asked for him," should have been so insensitive to the misery he was inflicting on his wife—not simply by his attention to light ladies throughout the circuit but by the manner in which he sometimes flaunted his adulteries. One time, before Helen and he had even been legally separated, he brought another woman with him on a trip to Binghamton and stood smiling by as she accepted a gift (a silver service or some such thing) as "Mrs. Babe Ruth."

One lady to whom he devoted much of his attention while he was off the home range even wrote letters to his wife reporting the lavish gifts she had most recently accepted from Babe's always open hands. And, in cities other than Boston, Babe made no secret of his preference for the public companionship of ladies other than his wife.

Yet when Helen made the first moves for the separation, there was such a rushing to and fro of Catholic clergy of every rank that one might have imagined a bishop was about to defect to the Protestants. Even Babe's devoted patron from St. Mary's Industrial School, Father Matthias, hurried to New York to see if he could save Babe from damnation, protect his public image, and incidentally keep the most prominent Catholic layman in the land from hanging his tattered laundry in the front yard. Babe bought Father Matthias a brand-new automobile and gave polite ear to what the other priests expounded. But, living as he always did for the very moment and in the world that lay closest to his hand, Babe was not moved at all by pictures of what tortures might await his soul in the world to come. If it was going to cost him his baseball career, that might have been different. But he was just having fun and meant no ill to anyone. Besides, he provided his wife a comfortable home and all the money she could use. Did women need more than *that,* for God's sake?

Helen thought she did. She left the South Sudbury farm, which Babe had had all refurbished, with a redecorated house, concrete floors in all the outbuildings, and a resident caretaker to keep the whole shop running, and moved with Dorothy into the home of a friend in nearby Watertown. Babe began to look for a buyer for the farm, while he bade good-bye to his Boston self altogether. When the Yanks went to Boston, Babe would bring Helen and Dorothy to his hotel suite and make feeble and awkward efforts to play the family man.

But Babe, with his life centered now in New York, was learning to act the part of a suave citizen of the greatest city in the world. His clothing, while still occasionally outspoken (he loved colored silk shirts and two-toned shoes, and when he wore a panama hat it had a colored band on it), was always in good taste.

Also, he was doing his best to cope with long words and to polish his idle conversation. At Hot Springs in an earlier day, while sitting on the porch with other players and their wives, Babe had excused himself suddenly, remarking as he left the porch, "Jesus! This water here sure makes you piss!" A teammate headed Babe off on his way back to the porch and reproved him for using such language in front of ladies. "If you *have* to say something like that, for Christ's sake, the word is 'urinate.' "

Babe was truly mortified at having caused distress to anyone and he hurried out on to the porch as if he was going to mollify a manager. "Jesus!" he told the assemblage. "I'm sorry. I meant to say 'urinate'!"

Now he was practicing words like that so he could fit them into polite talk without a stammer. Still, Babe never did develop a complete sensitivity to the company whose attention he was holding. Near the end of his career, when describing, to a writer and the writer's gentle wife, that great moment when he had driven a home run right to the spot he pointed at, he went through the motions of swinging an imaginary bat, while he explained in excited tones how he "knocked the fucken ball right into the fucken seats!"

Still, Babe was striving to outgrow that sort of thing. And while he would all his life, when he became deeply involved in a story, flavor it with his favorite obscenities, he could exchange casual talk with the grace of a courtier when need be. He was still convinced that his own experiences and emotions were as enthralling to others as they were to himself, but Babe's heart was really as soft as whipped cream and if he learned he had hurt some innocent or inadvertently embarrassed a friend, he could not rest easy until he had set matters right.

The spring of 1926 was a joyous time for Babe, even though he did not hit all the home runs he wanted to. The Yankees, after winning six exhibition games against assorted ball clubs, took twelve games in a row from the Dodgers, beating them all over the South, from Atlanta to Richmond, then taking them home to the Yankee Stadium and pounding them into the sod. Babe, on the way home, and despite the fact that he could produce only a long long triple for his loving fans in Asheville, was all abubble with joy and optimism. If we keep on beating these guys, he vowed to his mates, we'll go right on and take the pennant! *He* wasn't hitting yet, or not hitting his best, but young Tony Lazzeri and Koenig and Dugan and Meusel

Mayor James J. Walker. October 18, 1926. (*Wide World*)

Mayor James J. Walker of New York City in Hot Springs, Virginia, March 25, 1932. (*Wide World*)

George M. Cohan was the first customer to buy a flower when Mrs. Betty Compton Walker opened her flower shop in midtown New York City on February 3, 1938. The wife of former mayor Jimmy Walker was herself once a star of the Broadway stage. (*Wide World*)

Babe with his pet calf "Flossy" on his farm at Sudbury, Massachusetts, December 12, 1924. (*Wide World*)

The slugger and his wife on their farm at Sudbury, Massachusetts, January 1, 1929. (*Wide World*)

Babe Ruth hitting his 60th home run of the 1927 season off of Tom Zachary, Washington pitcher, at Yankee Stadium, September 30, 1927. (*Wide World*)

Parade in honor of Charles Lindbergh. (*Wide World*)

Charles A. Lindbergh.
(*Wide World*)

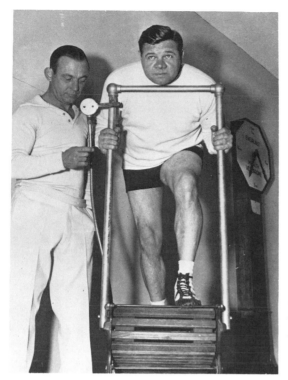

Babe with Arty McGovern, who had the job of keeping the Babe in good physical shape. *(Wide World)*

Cheerily acknowledging the plaudits of the crowd, Mayor James J. Walker is shown in center accompanied by John J. Curtin, his counsel, leaving the State Capitol at Albany, New York, August 18, 1932, at the completion of the day's hearing before Governor Roosevelt. *(Wide World)*

Here are (left to right) John H. McCooey, John F. Curry (Tammany leader), and Mayor James J. Walker of New York City as they were photographed in Chicago, June 26, 1932, at the caucus of the Democratic delegation to the National Convention. (*Wide World*)

Entirely oblivious to the surrounding welcoming crowd, James J. Walker (right), former mayor of New York, is shown as he conferred with John H. McCooey (left), the Brooklyn leader, and Tammany chief John P. Curry (center) on the pier after arriving in New York, October 9, 1932. (*Wide World*)

President Franklin Roosevelt, an old master at press conferences, held 998 of them. This one, on August 25, 1939, was the first to which a cameraman had been allowed since Roosevelt's first conference in 1933. *(Wide World)*

WPA sit-down strike in front of 701 Eighth Avenue in New York City, December 1936. *(Culver)*

Bruno Richard Hauptmann (left), a Bronx carpenter, died in the electric chair for kidnaping Charles A. Lindbergh, Jr. H. Norman Schwarzkopf (center), as head of the New Jersey State Police, directed the search which led to Hauptmann's arrest. Harold G. Hoffman (right), who died in 1954, was governor at the time of the trial and granted Hauptmann one thirty-day reprieve. (*Wide World*)

Alert photographers discovered John F. Condon, the "Jafsie" of the Lindbergh kidnaping case, in the second row. Jafsie rushed to the stage to greet Lindbergh. He got a warm welcome. (*Culver*)

The Babe Ruth family photographed at Yankee Stadium in New York City, April 24, 1934, when the Babe started what was probably his last season with the Yankees as a regular player. Left to right: Mrs. Ruth, Julia Ruth, the Babe, and Dorothy Ruth. (*Wide World*)

Babe thundering in. Not only was Ruth safe, but the umpire called a balk. Ferrell is the Browns catcher, August 4, 1932. (*Wide World*)

Georgia—President Roosevelt, seated in a car, meets reporters for a press conference while resting here over the Thanksgiving holiday. Mrs. Roosevelt, seated in the rear seat, listens attentively, November 26, 1938. (*Wide World*)

Al Reich, a prizefighter friend of Dr. John F. Condon, 72-year-old Fordham University instructor, who accompanied the aged instructor on his last trip to meet an emissary of the Lindbergh kidnapers and hand over the $50,000 ransom money in a designated spot in St. Raymond's Cemetery, the Bronx, New York City. With Reich, according to reports, were also Col. Lindbergh and Col. Henry Breckenridge, lawyer. The three men were a short distance away as Dr. Condon handed over the money, receiving in exchange a note telling where the child could be found. Reich is shown on the porch of the Condon home in the Bronx, New York City, on April 12, 1932. (*Wide World*)

The Hunterdon County Court, Flemington, New Jersey, as sightseers swarm in to watch the Hauptmann trial. January 6. 1935. *(Wide World)*

Bruno Richard Hauptmann was executed for murdering the Lindbergh baby. Hauptmann is shown here during his trial at Flemington, New Jersey. *(Wide World)*

A sequence in Samuel Goldwyn's *The Pride of the Yankees* in which the Babe plays himself, April 14, 1942.   (*Wide World*)

Mr. and Mrs. Babe Ruth. Circa 1947.   (*Wide World*)

Mr. and Mrs. Ruth aboard the liner *Monarch of Bermuda,* sailing for a vacation in Bermuda, November 10, 1932. (*Wide World*)

Babe Ruth, flanked by nurse Agnes Kavanaugh and a friend, Charles Schwefel, walking from French Hospital, New York, February 15, 1947, where he had been a patient since November 26, 1946. He was greeted by a crowd of fans as he left the hospital for his Riverside Drive apartment. (*Wide World*)

President Roosevelt and British Prime Minister Winston Churchill speak to an unidentified British naval officer, while surrounded by some of their chief staff officers during their conference at sea August 10, 1941, aboard H.M.S. *Prince of Wales.* Standing in back of them are (left to right) Gen. George Marshall, U.S. Army Chief of Staff; Under-Secretary of State Sumner Welles; Admiral Harold R. Stark, Chief of Naval Operations, U.S.N.; Admiral Sir Dudley Pound, First Sea Lord of Britain; and Gen. John G. Dill, Chief of the Imperial British Staff. (*Wide World*)

Mrs. Cornelia Bryce Pinchot (wearing placard), wife of the former governor of Pennsylvania, is seen as she led the picket line of 2,000 National Biscuit Company strikers in New York City, April 17, 1935. (*Wide World*)

Picket signs contrast the lot of Barbara Hutton, Woolworth heiress, with that of Woolworth shopgirls as the company opened one of two units in New York occupied by sit-down strikers, March 18, 1937. (*Wide World*)

A young striker, off sentry duty, sleeping on an assembly line of auto seats in a factory in Flint, Michigan. *(Culver)*

Eastern farmers dumping milk in the 1930s. *(Culver)*

and Combs were all driving the ball into the scrubby Southern out-fields or over the nearby hills, while the Dodger pitchers began to wonder if baseball was such a great game after all.

When Babe got to Boston to open the regular season, however, he asked himself if perhaps that jinx was still perched on his back. For he had hardly driven across the city line when he was informed there was a warrant out for his arrest—for evasion of state income taxes in 1923 and 1924. Babe hastened to the State House and se-cured an immediate audience with the tax commissioner, who gave him some long long forms to fill out. Babe, who earnestly declared that despite his ownership of that farm in South Sudbury, he was not a Massachusetts resident, sweated over the questionnaires for three hours. Then he was granted a week to go home and fill out a declaration of nonresidence. Still scowling and glum, convinced he was being put upon, Babe hurried to get out to Fenway Park for the game. But when he returned to his auto, parked hurriedly in Court Square, he found an angry Irish policeman standing near it and a parking ticket hung on its door. What the hell, the cop wanted to know, did he think he was doing leaving a car where it snarled up traffic for hours, all locked up so a man couldn't move it? And who the hell did he think he was anyway?

Well, he was Babe Ruth, that's who. And he had to leave the god-dam car because he had to put in three or four hours in the goddam tax office answering questions about money he never owed. And goddam it, it was bad enough being rooked by the tax man. But now to get slapped with a ticket for something that wasn't even his fault, well by Jesus, that was going too goddam far! The policeman weighed this explanation, nodded his head, and took the ticket off the car. Photographers and reporters, who had gathered to get Babe's side of the tax story, tried to persuade Babe to pose with the policeman beside the car.

No, goddam it! Babe was not going to pose for any goddam pic-tures. And he was not going to answer any questions either! His visit to the State House had nothing to do with taxes! It was personal! And it was nobody's goddam business but his own. And he had to get out to the ball park right *now* and play some baseball and he had no time to fool around. So Babe jumped into the car, jammed it into gear, and went roaring out to Fenway Park, where in weather too cold to play anything but ice hockey he hit two doubles and a single, stole a base, and helped the Yanks outlast the Red Sox 12 to 11.

183

(The tax man eventually rejected Babe's plea, and Babe paid the taxes.)

The sports experts of the season were predicting that Washington or Philadelphia would win the pennant. Babe predicted the Yankees and kept on predicting them. The Yankees, after a slightly unsteady beginning, won eight games in a row and stood at the top of the league. Babe hit his first home run, plus four more hits, against a collection of Washington pitchers, including Walter Johnson. In the second month, the Yankees, with Ruth now swinging with all his 1923 authority, won sixteen games in a row and began to leave everyone behind.

Babe Ruth once more became the pet gorilla of the clubhouse. He nailed a photographer's shoes to the floor, he roughhoused with his mates, he chewed tobacco by the hundredweight, and he went out to Mitchel Field one day and caught a baseball dropped from a speeding airplane. ("No more of that!" Ruppert warned him. "Play ball in the ball park!") Then he accepted an offer to appear once again on the vaudeville stage when the season was over. These were the good times once more, for Babe and for all his teammates.

While Babe did not attain his goal of more than fifty home runs, he very nearly took the batting title (his .372 was second only to Heinie Manush's .378). He collected his final three home runs when the club needed them most—in a doubleheader against the St. Louis Browns after the club had fallen into a slight slump that made it look for a while as if Cleveland might catch them. Babe and the rest of the club had been awake most of the night before that double-header—not because they were out to "see a party" but because the St. Louis fans, celebrating the fact that the Cardinals had already won the pennant in the other league, had serenaded the Yankees outside the Chase Hotel by yelling, banging pot lids, setting off fire-crackers, and hurling every sort of casual garbage at the ballplayers' windows.

Ruth ended the 1926 regular season with forty-seven home runs, leading the league again and almost doubling his total for the year before. Then he hit three more in the World Series against the Cardinals, all of them in the same game. The third home run, made in the sixth inning of the fourth game, played in St. Louis, brought cheers even from the home-town crowd, who stood up and yelled for the Babe when they saw his blow streak on a rising line straight into the very top rows of the bleachers in centerfield. Why, that was six hundred feet from home plate! And no man alive had ever hit three home runs before in a single World Series game. So the St. Louis folk, who had been booing Babe heartily every time he showed himself at the plate, cheered and cheered him until he took his cap off in acknowledgment.

The rejuvenation of Ruth continued through the winter of 1926–27. Once more he committed himself to the ministrations of Artie McGovern, who sweated off all the pounds that Babe had put on during his merry twelve-week sabbatical on the Pantages vaudeville circuit. When spring training began, there was again a hint of triumph in the air. In the beginning, there was a new contract for Babe, whose "thousand dollars a week" contract had expired. Sportswriters suggested that the right figure for the new Babe Ruth would be about double the old—say a hundred thousand dollars a year. A *hundred* thousand? The fans could not see why not. Nor was there a major-league ballplayer alive who would have begrudged it, for all of them realized that Babe alone had lifted ballplayers' salaries up toward the heights that only industrial royalty and motion-picture stars had trod. (Even today, Frank Crosetti, the great Yankee shortstop whom Babe knew as "Dago Bananas," will occasionally stop before Babe's picture and utter silent thanks for all the good paydays that came his way in Babe Ruth's wake.)

But Babe lacked the gall to reach quite *that* far. When he came to New York to negotiate with Ruppert for his pay (Ruppert always liked to sign the Babe in person), he asked for seventy thousand. And Ruppert promptly put that figure in the new contract and handed it to Babe to sign. The contract was to run three years.

Rejoicing in his new wealth, Babe began to swing at moving baseballs with all the zest of the year before. *This* time, he was determined, he would bust fifty again!

This time he had a teammate to set the pace for him—Lou Gehrig, the Boy Scout type who had taken so long to make a place for himself in the crusty hearts of his hard-boiled teammates. But now Lou was one of them, finally at ease on first base and schooled at dealing with pitchers who threw hard and pitchers who threw crooked.

Babe opened the 1927 season with a missed step. Facing dour Lefty Grove, the meanest and fastest pitcher of the day (up to then he had been listed as "Groves" in the Philadelphia box scores), Babe struck out twice and once sent a sick-looking pop fly to the infield. On his fourth at bat, he remained sulking in his tent while Ben

Paschal, Ed Barrow's "new Babe Ruth," batted for him. Next day, however, Babe hit two singles, and on the day after that he hit his first home run. He hit three more in April. In May he hit twelve and in June nine more. That made twenty-five all together—halfway home. But Gehrig had hit twenty-five too and fans had begun to talk about Gehrig in the same breath with Babe. By mid-August, Gehrig was actually leading Babe Ruth in homers, 38 to 35, and newspapers were running daily tables showing the score as if it were a two-horse race. This may have prodded Ruth into concentrating a little harder, for before the month was out he had caught up with Gehrig and passed him, never to be headed again.

As for the Yankees, they were never headed at all in that wonderful year—that year when poverty was to be abolished, the stock market to be set on an ever-climbing course, movies to be made to talk, planes geared to fly nonstop the whole way across the Atlantic, and Babe was to set a record that everyone agreed would last forever. From the very first day of the season until the very last, the Yankees stood in first place in the American League, and on the last day they had won 110 games and lost but forty-four. They came in nineteen games ahead of the Philadelphia Athletics.

Babe Ruth set his new home-run record with an incredible surge at the very end of the season. With just a week to go, he had made fifty-six home runs, not even equaling his 1921 figure of fifty-nine, and there was hardly anyone ready to bet that he would reach it in the games remaining. There would be two games with Philadelphia at the stadium, and Lefty Grove, who was not above striking Babe out, would pitch one of them. Then there would be two blank days followed by three games in a row with Washington.

Babe took an extra-tight grip on his bat those days and fixed his eyes to the ball on every pitch. Against Lefty Grove he hit home run number fifty-seven. Then, when Washington came in, Babe hit two home runs in the first game, one off Hod Lisenbee and the other off a rookie right-hander named Paul Hopkins, who was pitching only the second of the eleven big-league games he worked in. That tied the record and proved the Babe was as good as ever. He had one game left in which to prove he was better. In the eighth inning of the final game, with the score tied 2 to 2 and Mark Koenig on base ahead of him, Babe saw a pitch from Tom Zachary that looked just right and he drove it whistling into the right-field seats.

With that final exhibition of his might, Babe once more became the most famous name in the land. Charles Lindbergh had flown the Atlantic with just a sandwich for company. Jack Dempsey, who had been scorned for several years as a slacker, became the most beloved fighter around when he lost his second fight to Gene Tunney—after the referee had given Tunney either twelve or fifteen seconds instead of ten seconds (no one was quite sure how long the long count was) to recover from a knockdown. But neither name ever earned quite the personal devotion Babe Ruth's did, for Babe was joy personified to most of the male citizens over six.

With more money than ever before to spend, with no need to pretend he lived anywhere but right in New York City, with the city itself freed from the irksome yoke of Police Commissioner Enright (his successor had cut arrests in half), and with a refreshed and renewed body to house his appetites, Babe swung into the World Series with relish.

The enemy this time was the Pittsburgh Pirates and the first games were to be played in Pittsburgh, at Forbes Field, which was almost too big a field to hit home runs in. The Yankees, some said, won that Series without ever coming to bat, for their top quartet of barn-wall busters—Ruth, Gehrig, Combs, and Meusel—scared the hell out of the Pirates at batting practice. Before the first game began, baseball after baseball had gone into the distant seats or out into unknown reaches beyond the fence. The Pirates all sat with their mouths half open, not quite believing.

But Babe did not hit any home runs in this Series until he got back to the stadium for the third game. And then his homer was not needed, for the Yanks took the game 8 to 1. But Babe did hit a home run in the final game that was necessary to bring the Yanks up even, after which they won on a wild pitch in the last of the ninth. The Pirates had not won a single game.

Now there was nothing to do but have fun, and there must have been a thousand places in New York or its close environs where young men and women could abolish an entire evening and half the day in joy and song. The baseball players who were drawing the top salaries could dine and drink and make time with their ladies at high-priced nightclubs like Connie's Inn in Harlem, another major speakeasy where blacks were welcome only as employees or entertainers.

No one concerned himself much with the blacks in that day, except the blacks themselves—and what advantages were to be won for Harlem folk were gained through the hungry Tammany machine that operated the whole borough as if it were a plantation. Not that voices were not raised in protest at the inability of black men and women to get hold of even the tail of the kite that seemed to be transporting the whole city to an everlasting worldly paradise. But when one heckler dared ask Jimmy Walker, at a public appearance in Harlem, what he had ever done for colored folk, Jimmy, one of the most gifted public speakers who ever entered politics, took his questioner's breath away by shouting back: "Nothing!" Then he milked the speechless audience of a tankful of happy applause when he elucidated: "I never did anything for colored people or for white people. I make no distinction between them. I do things for *all* people!"

It was a fact that Jimmy, for all his readiness to go along with the current system of lining one's own pockets at every turn in the road, had done many good things for all people. He had marched into Bellevue Hospital and won columns of newsprint by speaking on the horrors of that refuge where the penniless sick were ostensibly cared for, but where there was but one toilet for several dozen aged and infirm women, where the sick lay unattended in their own filth, and where a good portion of the machinery was permanently out of whack. Jimmy also insisted angrily that there should be better places for the working poor to live in—something other than the dreary "dumbbell" apartments that had adequate exposure only in front and back and all the rooms in a row. (The designer of this style of apartment had won a prize—not for coming up with a plan for housing families cheaply in comfort and health but in finding a way to create the most rentable space on a minimum of land.)

The articulate citizens of New York and most of its newspapers had more pressing matters to attend to than the lot of the city's losers. Even men and women in the middle of the middle class could afford hired help these days, often in exchange for only a few dollars a week and "a good home." Servants of every sort were expected to work from sunup until the boss went to bed. And every other Thursday was enough off time for such folk, who didn't know good when they tasted it.

One man in Long Island, however, a waiter in a speakeasy restaurant, staged a dramatic rebellion one day. He had long resented his boss's insistence that he should overcharge the customers for the drinks he served them. But one afternoon, when the boss's wife insisted that he wash her two Pomeranians, he said no. He had never done such work and was not about to begin. Whereupon the lady promptly fired him. The waiter, a tall, gaunt man who seldom smiled, brooded for a time upon his lot. Then, when boss and wife had gone to bed, he stalked up to the boss's office, took the boss's .38-caliber pistol out of the drawer, marched grimly down to the bedroom, and shot both boss and wife through the head. Then he went out on East Merrick Road, hailed a taxi, and took himself to the police station.

Had there been prophets abroad in that day, or even poets like William Blake, one might have read in this episode some fore-shadowing of the eventual ruin of the state. But it drew hardly any note at all. Far more attention was given to the hanging of Gerald Chapman, that slick little burglar who had often bragged that no jail could hold him but who was nailed away at last in a box from which there was no getting out. Those few authorities who were not simply congratulating themselves that they had got this little loudmouth out of the way for good observed quietly that he probably never commit-ted the murder for which he was sentenced to Connecticut's hang-ing machine. And that was what Chapman kept saying right up to the end.

The year 1928 was probably, for the nation, the very summit of the Roaring Twenties—or should it be the nadir? The government, with that tight little Yankee at its head, hardly poked a fingertip into the doings either of big business or organized crime. (Unorganized crime was still dealt with at the street level, by the nightstick, the clubbed fist, or the third degree.) Any man or woman who wanted a drink could buy it at the corner. Motion pictures had started to talk, so that the rollicking musical shows that lesser folk had learned of only by the songs they gave birth to, could now be staged for a million people to watch in a thousand different places on the same evening. Al Jolson sang for the whole country, made up in minstrel-show style, shamelessly burlesquing a black man, just as performers in an earlier age had decked themselves in green whiskers and ridi-culed the Irish laborers who were doing the dirty work in all the major cities.

Underpaid newspapermen and overpaid stockbrokers, along with stuffed-shirt salesmen, knocked off work these days in midafternoon and hastened to some blank steel door hard by the office behind which there was drink and revelry by both night and day. There were run-of-the-mill speakeasies where lavish free lunches were laid out.

The Palace Club on Forty-sixth Street provided hot roast-beef sandwiches without charge to any who asked for them. Other places kept meat balls and baby frankfurters sizzling on a hot plate and raw hamburger set out for the making of cannibal sandwiches. With dice and a dice cup to play with, or some mechanical gambling device to swallow nickels and dimes, there was no need to go anywhere but here for all the fun a man could cram behind his collarbone. There were no closing hours, no censors, no cops to clamp down on the dice games. What cops did show up appeared in uniform to absorb a few free drinks. There was nothing to fear except the rare visit from some flying squad of Federal agents who might padlock the place for a day or two, until the lawyers could manage a change of ownership and start the whole joint jumping again. And there was never any danger of waking up to find yourself, with pockets turned inside out, feeling for some comfort in a wet gutter. The midtown speakeasy owners took care of their own and let no harm befall a man who had outlasted his capacity.

Babe Ruth was backing up in the spring of 1928 to hit seventy-five home runs, he felt so strong and full of ambition. This time he started off at the same pace as he had come to the wire in 1927. By the middle of July he already had posted thirty-four home runs, so seventy seemed altogether within reach. The Yankees all kept hitting hard, although Gehrig this season could not stay close to Ruth. On the first of August Babe hit his forty-second home run of the season. That was just eighteen short of his record and he still had two months to break it. In 1927 he had driven out seventeen home runs in September. Newspapers now began to publish charts to show how Babe was faring against his marks of the season before. He had already left Gehrig far behind and there was no one to pace him but his old self.

His old self fell down on the job. Or it may have been that the Yankees, who had been thirteen games ahead of the second-place Athletics on the Fourth of July, suddenly began to stumble and needed help in getting men on base. So Babe, instead of swinging for the fences, as he felt he was ordinarily expected to do, began to shorten his swing and poke one-base hits into left field in order to get on base more often. Or he would tap a bunt down the unguarded third-base line and scamper to first, shaking with laughter. He made only five more home runs in August, though he was actually scoring more runs for the Yankees. In September Babe hit only seven fair balls out of the playing field, so that his home-run total was a mere fifty-four, the same number with which he had startled the world in his first year with the Yankees. It was the last time he ever hit more than fifty.

But it mattered not to Babe. The Yanks held off the Athletics, won the pennant by 2½ games, and earned a chance to square things with the Cardinals, who had beaten out the Giants in the curve-ball league. In the pennant struggle, Tony Lazzeri had strained his throwing arm, Babe Ruth had hurt his ankle, and Earl Combs had broken a finger, so New York fans were less than hopeful of getting even with St. Louis for the 1926 defeat.

Babe and his crew, however, never let injuries discourage them. It was not that Babe Ruth ever ignored an injury. On the contrary, he was inclined to make as much hay as he could out of whatever ailment currently afflicted him, and to take care, when he was not doing well, that everyone was aware that he was not his complete self. Once when he suffered from a dislocated finger he missed two pitches while batting against the Athletics. With each swinging strike, he would turn to old Cy Perkins, who caught for the Athletics in the years when Yankee Stadium was brand new, and offer his bad finger for Cy to yank back into its socket. With this tender office completed, Babe would turn back to face the pitch. Another strike, another pulling of the finger. On the third swing, Babe sent the pitch out far above the right-field seats. It whacked with a wondrous boom against the red-painted water barrel that stood in those days high above the right-field bleachers, and dropped into home-run land. After that Babe had no more trouble with the finger.

His wobbly ankle in 1928 set Babe to limping, but it did not keep him out of the World Series or muffle his guns in the slightest. In the first game, in which his playmate Waite Hoyt dealt but three hits to the Cardinals, Babe hit two doubles in helping the Yankees win the game 4 to 1. In the second game he hit a double and a single. In the third game, played in St. Louis after the Yanks had won the first two in New York, Babe scored a run by slamming his body in a reckless slide, bad ankle or no, into the Cardinal catcher and knocking him loose from the ball, thus turning an out into a run and putting the Cardinals too far behind to catch up. In this game, Babe hit two singles.

In the final game, played before an enemy crowd that was really thirsting for Yankee blood this year, Babe repeated his miracle of two seasons earlier. He first hit an overdue home run to tie the score at 1 to 1. In the seventh inning, with St. Louis leading, 2 to 1, Wee Willie Sherdel, five-foot-ten left-hander for the Cardinals, threw two strikes to Ruth. Babe, after the second strike, looked down at the grip he had taken on the bat. And while he was looking, Wee Willie, who had just taken a snap throw from the catcher, snapped the ball right back, straight across the middle of the plate, without Babe's seeing it until it was safe in the catcher's glove. Babe's mouth dropped open in dismay. This "quick pitch" was a standard device in the National League but illegal in the American.

Before the Series began, the rival clubs had agreed that the quick pitch would be outlawed. The umpire, Charlie Pfirman, knew that. But the players had forgotten. Willie Sherdel, followed by shortstop Rabbit Maranville and second baseman Frank Frisch, raced in toward the plate when Pfirman failed to call a strike. "He's out!" they murmured.

"Oh, no," suggested Pfirman. "That was an illegal pitch."

With that, the entire St. Louis club exploded and small debates sprang up everywhere as Yankee and St. Louis players set out to convince the enemy by screaming into each other's faces. Meanwhile Babe Ruth went about from group to group, offering smiling encouragement. No one, he knew, was going to alter Pfirman's mind. And no one did. Babe got another cut at the ball and he cut it straight into the right-field stand to tie up the game.

In the eighth inning, after Grover Cleveland Alexander had replaced Sherdel on the pitcher's mound, Babe wound up and hit his third home run—the second time he had worked this miracle in the World Series, and the second time he had worked it on the Cardinals. The St. Louis fans, already resigned to the loss of the championship, stood up and gave the grinning Babe a wilder ovation than they had offered him in 1926.

Earlier, the crowd had offered their own opinion of the quick-pitch decision by flinging empty bottles at Ruth when he moved out to the outfield. When one landed right at his feet, Babe picked the bottle up and cocked his arm as if to fire it back. Half the occupants of the bleachers cringed in dismay. But Babe just offered them his mile-wide grin, made as if to finish off the contents of the bottle, and tossed it gently over to the sidelines. He then picked up all the others and got them off the field of play, pretending to look at some

to measure how much was left. The crowd by now had responded to
his grin by laughing and yelling to him. No one could dislike Babe
Ruth. And Babe Ruth disliked no one, or almost no one.

It happened that on the Yankee roster this season was an acro-
batic young rookie shortstop from Springfield, Massachusetts,
whom Babe did learn to dislike, not just for now but for his whole
career. That was Leo Durocher, whom Babe accused of stealing his
watch.

No one ever saw Leo do any such thing. What happened was that
one earlier time in St. Louis, Babe, to whom St. Louis had become
his favorite playground (next to New York), had rolled into the hotel
wearing an aroma so rich that it was almost enough to stone the elevator operator. And Babe himself could hardly see three feet ahead
of him. Crowding into the elevator with most of his mates, Babe offered his bubbling laugh to the whole car.

"Whoozh?" he demanded. "Whoozh gonna pu' me t'bed?"

Durocher, the veriest freshman on the team and by no means accepted as a member of Babe Ruth's gang, hastened to volunteer,
and Babe subjected himself to Leo's guidance clear into his room. It
was not until next morning that Babe missed his watch. He forgot
most of what had befallen him the evening before or even what the
many places were where he might have left his watch behind him.
All he recalled was that this fresh-mouth rookie had helped him
climb out of his clothes. And that was proof enough for Babe. A
short time afterward, while the club was leaving Chicago in their
private Pullman, Babe came aboard, happily unsteady again, carrying, loosely wrapped in white tissue, a lady's wristwatch that he had
just bought from one of those "I-can-get-it-for-you-wholesale" lads
who seemed to specialize in bringing bargains to ballplayers. Babe
stopped at each berth, to display the watch, to show how the diamonds sparkled, then to bubble out in his booze-thickened chuckle
just how little it had cost him. "Gonna keep it under m'pillow!" he
declared as he neared his own roost. Then, catching the bulging eye
of young Durocher, he suddenly grew solemn. "An I wanna *find* it in
the morning!" he bellowed. Out of that grew the legend that Leo had
robbed old Jidge. And Jidge never forgave him.

The train trip home after that victory was the wildest in Yankee
history. Before the train pulled out, Babe had fetched some fifty
pounds of spare ribs from his St. Louis source, along with un-
counted buckets of beer, to give some heft to the hilarity. Then he

and the other young huskies set out to rip each other's shirts to shreds. Babe, laughing like a kid just turned loose in a playground, burst into the sacred drawing room of Colonel Ruppert and without a word of apology began to rip off the Colonel's priceless orchid-colored pajamas. The colonel, horrified at first, tried hard to laugh.

"Is this usual, Root?" he inquired plaintively. Babe assured him that it was and contributed the ripped-up pajama top to the collection of destroyed shirts that littered the car. Even Miller Huggins, who was not a man to see even fifty cents' worth of necktie wasted, contributed his share to the general holocaust, yipping and shrieking his own joy with the loudest of them.

At Mattoon, Illinois, where the train paused for a drink, there was a mob of fans awaiting, all screaming for Babe Ruth. Babe abandoned his succulent spare ribs and moved out to the platform to greet his fans, waving one large hand like a flag above his head.

"Everybody happy?" he called. And everybody instantly became delirious. Men reached out their hands and Babe shook them all. Boys and girls offered him everything to sign, from envelopes to baseballs, and Babe signed them all. Then he called for three cheers for the Yankees and the crowd rattled the train windows with their response. After that, it being the middle of the presidential campaign, in which Babe's friend, Governor Al Smith, was running against Herbert Hoover, Babe yelled for "Three cheers for another great guy! AL SMITH!" Whereupon Democrats and Republicans alike obeyed him with full throat. Then, Babe began "Three cheers for the Cardin . . . No! Those guys don't deserve it!" And the crowd bellowed agreement. It was not that Babe scorned losers. He just did not believe the Cardinals had really fought for the victory. Not the way the Cardinals had fought before. Not the way the Yankees fought.

At every stop along the way, no matter how weird the hour when the train pulled in, there were more swollen crowds of men and boys, with a scattering of ladies, all yelling for Babe as if it were he who was promising to heal the farmer's ills, end poverty forever, and see that every man had work. Babe tirelessly appeared each time, always grinning, always waving his big hand above his head, always crying out as if for the first time: "Everybody happy?" And all along the way it seemed as if everybody was.

Even though Babe had not set a new home-run record, the season was in some ways his best. Surely no one ever had a greater World

Series than Babe had just completed, with a batting average of .625, ten hits in sixteen at bats, nine runs scored, and three home runs in the same game—for the second time. As for the Yankees, they had just won their second World Series without losing a single game in either one. Where in the world was anyone going to find a better ball club than that?

The nation too, or that part of it that had managed to cut in on the general eruption of profits, prices, and newly invented comforts, had had its best year too. Republican campaign headquarters was busily dispensing gilt-colored "coins" bearing the legend "Good For Four More Years of Prosperity." Cautious little Calvin Coolidge, who had irritated our former Allies with his Yankee-shopkeeper demands that their debts be paid to the penny, dutifully issued statements from the White House, or from the mouth of a mythical spokesman, that were calculated to keep the boom booming. Not that he knew a damn thing about it, but he did allow, when asked, that he saw nothing to be alarmed about in the size of brokers' loans—even though their incredible total made it clear that most of those stocks that had hit prices of $200, $300, or $400 a share were being bought on borrowed money, and even though interest rates on "call" money, which was what brokers' loans were made of, had attained such incredible two-figure heights that cash was galloping in from overseas to share in this unheard-of increment.

A few calm voices, Miller Huggins's among them (but who the hell, outside of a few baseball players, listened to *him?*) did express puzzlement at some aspects of this blithesome prosperity. Why, they wondered, with corporate profits soaring like the Graf Zeppelin, were there so many many bankruptcies and business failures? Was it *just* because the big businesses were swallowing the small ones—chain stores driving out the independents and a coffee manufacturer even taking over the company that sold that scorched cereal that was supposed to replace coffee in the diet? Or was there some inexorable law at work they knew not of, something connected with sagging farm prices, the bitter strikes in the textile mills, the shoe factories, and the coal mines, and the hard times overseas?

Herbert Hoover, the Republican candidate, laid all such incipient fears to rest in his solemn campaign talks, all of which managed to achieve the singsong quality usually associated with a funeral chant. *Real* wages, Hoover intoned, had leapt far ahead of the climb in

195

prices and had never moved so far so fast as under the blessed reign of Calvin the First. (This was not true, but no one said so loudly enough to be heard. *Real* wages, measured by what a dollar bill would buy, which had climbed some 34 percent between the end of the war and 1924, had risen only another 1 percent in the Coolidge years.) All this was due, said Hoover, and most people believed him, to the sound governmental policies he and his chief and all the other stiff-collar types in the Cabinet had instituted over the last four years—a high tariff to keep those foreigners from competing with our good American businessmen, and stiff immigration policies to keep the wretched refuse of those teeming shores across the sea from crowding through our Golden Door. Why, that would mean mobs of applicants crowded about every employment office or lined up at every industrial gate. Apparently Candidate Hoover, as Al Smith always called him, had not visited any employment offices lately, nor stood long outside any industrial gate, nor even sat in the hiring hall of a large department store, else he would have seen that the crowds were already there, all speaking good American, too.

No, Hoover saw in continuation of these brilliant policies the ultimate abolition of poverty. No longer, said he, were we talking about the "full dinner pail" but about the "full garage." Many of Herbert's most ardent followers, however, were talking about other things altogether. Mrs. Willie W. Caldwell, for instance, who was Republican National Committeewoman from Virginia, had sent out a circular letter proclaiming that "we must save the United States from being Romanized and rum-ridden"— what *was* there about alliteration that Republicans could not eat their fill of it?—"and the call is to the women to do so."

All over the South and Midwest the "whispering campaign" was spread, despite valiant efforts by Hoover and other top Republicans to disown it. Ministers of the gospel warned their followers that Al Smith had made a compact with the Pope to move the Vatican out of the reach of Mussolini and set it up in the District of Columbia. White-haired lady shopkeepers whispered to their customers that they had it on good authority that arms were being stockpiled in every convent and monastery against the take-over when Catholic Al Smith moved in to the President's chair. And in Houston, a meeting of temperance ladies prayed that the nation might be saved for "Christian people"—i.e., Protestants.

The Ku Klux Klan raised its own voice to accuse Al Smith of having hired a "negro wench" as a stenographer. But Democratic head-quarters in Washington angrily disputed this libel. Governor Smith, they averred, does not have and never has had a Negro stenographer. Indeed, under Smith's enlightened rule, said the headquarters company, the state of New York has hired Negroes only for the sort of jobs they were awarded in the South, to wit, porters, janitors, char-women, etc. They might also have added, but they forgot, that Al had refused to appoint Major Charles Young, a West Point graduate, a regular army officer, and a black man, to command of the all-black regiment in the New York State Guard that had been authorized by William Sulzer, the last previous Democratic governor elected in the state. The State Guard refused to raise any black man to commissioned rank, and Al Smith went along with them. He appointed a white officer to lead the regiment.

But all this availed Al Smith nothing. He lost part of the solid South as he went down to humiliating defeat before Herbert Hoover. And the stock market immediately flew into a new upsurge, to provide a Hoover bull market to match the Coolidge bull market. And the intellectuals of the day, the Van Dorens, and the Villards, and the Kirchweys all declared that the Hoover victory could be ascribed to the "conservatism and stupidity" of the electorate. None of them concluded, apparently, that it had been folly for the Democrats to try to sell to the nation, still largely based on farms and villages, an archetypal big-city wise guy, with a brown derby cocked over one eye and a throaty New York accent proclaiming his sidewalk origin.

Nor did anyone note the portentous fact that the year had indeed been the Year of Ruth, with Babe Ruth even making the final out of the World Series by sprinting at top speed right to the fence to make a next-to-impossible one-handed catch of Frankie Frisch's long foul ball, and with three ladies, all named Ruth, being elected to their first terms in Congress. One was the daughter of William Jennings Bryan, Ruth Bryan Owen, and the others were Republicans—Ruth Hanna McCormick and Ruth Baker Pratt.

Will Rogers, who had been nominated for the Presidency by *Life* magazine (then a humorous weekly), observed that both Hoover and Smith were decent, able men—"but that ain't why they chose them."

When the new year started and the blessed reign of the Great Humanitarian was about to dawn, experts looked back over 1928 and found that it had indeed been a year when Heaven had showered bounty upon our land, almost past reckoning. What part of it could be counted was set forth in publications of all sorts, for the edification of those who might doubt. Compared with 1927, chain-store sales were up better than 17 percent. Automobile output had increased 24 percent, mail-order sales 15 percent, and business profits 11 percent. Had one been given to mucking about in ointment looking for dead flies, he might have found among the statistics a few that gave forth a stinking savor. Commodity prices, for instance, had advanced 2.5 percent or thereabouts, while wages had moved up less than half of 1 percent. And employment had decreased by more than 3 percent over the year before.

If it was percentages and figures you were interested in, there were still more frightening samples to be had when you put the numbers together properly. Most frightening of all was the fact that 90 percent of the nation's wealth was controlled by 13 percent of its populace. And the average wage of the nation's working people was a bare $1,280 a year, not nearly enough to support a family in anything but discomfort.

How a nation could be "prosperous" with more than two-thirds of its people living under the poverty line was one of those mysteries understood only in the very deepest recesses of the great banking fortresses that cuddled close to the Subtreasury Building in downtown New York. What nation, they must have asked themselves there, can fail to be prosperous when it has a Secretary of the Treasury who, without the tedium of seeking Congressional approval, could give tax refunds and credits of $57 million to United States Steel? Altogether, that made a total of almost a billion dollars refunded to big business in the eight Harding-Coolidge years. Best of all, nosy Congressman who questioned these deals could be told quite frankly that *they* had wanted income-tax figures kept secret— so this was part of the secret. (Congress had to come up with an emergency appropriation of $75 million to swing the refund to U.S. Steel and a few others, so that transaction did come out.)

Business experts of every stripe—both self-appointed and promoted from the ranks—at least agreed that there was nothing to indicate that 1929 could be anything but full of happy surprises. There were basic conditions, said the financial expert of the New York *Evening Post* (the paper that had urged New Yorkers to vote against Roosevelt for governor because he was a cripple), that would render prosperity self-perpetuating, chief among them being a record industrial output, inventive genius, and "high wages." Where the expert uncovered the high-wage figure was not revealed. Certainly not from his own paper's ledgers, for journalists of that day were supposed to grow fat on the romance of the job. Wall Street wages, in the middle and upper echelons, were high. Advertising wages, in the selling end of the business at least, were high too, considering how minimal were the mental requirements for the jobs. And with all those nice fellows so plump and smiling, how could the rest of the world not be happy as kings?

One reason they were not may have been that when wages were low, as they were for most of the folk far down on the ladder, they were low indeed. In New York, where Wall Street messengers earned $15 a week, girls who took dictation worked for about $17 a week; plain typists earned $14; file clerks made $12; drill-press operators made $13; and an assistant bookkeeper could be hired for $18. This at a time when a girl needed, just for room and board, $14.69 a week, not allowing anything for clothes and carfare.

Well, said the deep thinkers who wrote the editorials for the Brooklyn *Eagle,* "there are some persons, often estimable, who just cannot pull their weight as producers." Just as if anyone was ever kept on the job in New York, or even in Brooklyn, at *any* wage, who could not "pull his weight."

The best-paid ballplayers—and that meant the New York Yankees—were happy enough. A fellow who played baseball for New York found his days full of warm sun and the laughter of friends, bright company at night, a whole handful of ten-dollar bills to finger, and a royal array of entertainers ready to sing and play for him or tell him stories on his radio. Babe Ruth was addicted to radio, particularly the action serials like *Gang-Busters,* in which bad guys were put to rout with hammering fists and roaring guns. Babe might jump up from a business conference as if something had stuck him in the seat and run breathless to his waiting automobile to go roaring up Riverside Drive so as to be ready by his radio when the story began. Babe never read a book, or could not recall having read any, other than the one someone had written for him called *Babe Ruth's Own Book of Baseball.* He read that one twice. But largely he concerned himself, when not eating good steaks or spare ribs and drinking cold beer, with girls, or with golf, or billiards, or playing hearts, or singing to his own accompaniment, or listening to the radio. (His portable phonograph had been mothballed now.)

Babe also of course continued to say yes to men and women who asked him to come help them raise money for some kids' charity or some allegedly worthy cause. And he took more time off than anyone ever knew about to go visit children in hospitals and warm them with that ineffable and heartfelt grin that seemed to embrace the whole room. It was not Babe Ruth that James Whitcomb Riley had in mind when he wrote this rhyme, but had he ever known Babe it might have been, for Babe too was "a man who stands/ And just holds out in his two hands/ As warm a heart as ever beat/ 'Twixt this and the Judgment Seat."

It would not be right to look back over the Roaring Twenties without noting an undercurrent of bestiality, not entirely the contribution of the gangland philosophy that controlled so much of the common man's daily life. More likely it was simply a sidewalk expression of the animal urges that came to be identified as "rugged individualism." It was a fact, after all, that people everywhere sought success at the expense of their fellows. Big business wiped out small rivals by price cutting, sopping up the sources of supply, and even bribing local officials. Executives moved ahead by grimly elbowing out their associates. Workers could win preferment by taking care never to act in concert with their own kind.

And so it was that when the Brighton Express of the BMT pulled into the Times Square station and opened its doors, the waiting passengers would burst through like uncaged cats, surging without compunction against one another, flinging the weaker ones aside and sometimes bowling some small person over and stepping on him, without even taking note, so intent was each one on snatching for himself one of the too few places to sit down. Wherever any sort of prize was offered on a first-come, first-served basis, the scene was the same. The polite, the timid, and the self-effacing would be flattened against a wall, jammed against a door frame, or flung to the floor. Screams of pain and horror might cause some to hesitate, but they would soon be overwhelmed by those behind and hurled on like small stones in the way of an avalanche.

At the Yankee Stadium one afternoon in this era, when the club was playing before a full crowd, a sudden storm came up threatening to douse all the bleacher patrons in gallons of rain. In that day the right-field stands had no upper deck so there were thousands of seats open to the weather, and the builder had not considered that everyone might try to strike for the exits at the same instant. So when the rain came up, the bleacher crowd stampeded for the exit ramps, all bent on being first under the stands and hardly any looking out that he might do someone else an injury as he scrambled for the opening. As a result, two spectators were crushed to death, with one poor woman carried into the Yankee dressing room where she died on the training table, while the frightened ballplayers all stood by in silence, their eyes fixed on the face as it turned a terrifying shade of blue.

Traffic in the central city seemed moved by similar impulses, with the right of way always going to the driver who was boldest at cutting into an open space, and with professional drivers quick to scream curses at any amateur who beat them into an intersection. At the height of the twenties a traffic expert, after studying conditions in Manhattan for months, concluded that auto traffic would have to be barred from midtown altogether, else it would soon be impossible for cars to move from one side of the island to the other.

The end of the twenties saw an ending of a sort for Babe Ruth, or perhaps it was merely a turning point, for he had still may good days ahead. But never again would he climb even close to his home-run record. Nor would he for much longer sprint over the outfield sod as he did when he made that brilliant catch of the Frisch foul fly. He had fled to the clubhouse then, waving the ball high in triumph. There would be only one more such triumph, and it would not be quite the same.

Babe Ruth, when the 1929 season began, had caught cold again. He could not blame this one on Hot Springs and he tried for a while to pretend he wasn't even sick. But finally his breathing became so difficult that while the Yankees were playing an exhibition game in Chambersburg, Pennsylvania, the Babe taxied over to the local hospital to have himself looked at. The doctors at the hospital kept him there, for they found one lung so congested it was not drawing an ounce of breath.

Newspaper writers hastened to discover if Babe was once again at the near lip of the grave. But he wasn't at all. It was not his heart, as the writers had suspected. It was just a hell of a heavy chest cold. A week later he was back in uniform, bent on attaining at least thirty more home runs to bring his lifetime total up to five hundred. For the first time he found that he simply could not trot about the outfield or run the bases in the headlong manner he had been used to. His legs grew tired quickly. He had to let the other fielders move in on his part of the outfield. And sometimes he had to sit on the bench and let someone else do *all* the work.

He hit home runs enough to suit any other man alive. But he was not approaching his 1927 pace. On August 11, he finally hit his five hundredth home run, off Willis Hudlin of Cleveland, clean over the right-field fence. He wanted that ball and he asked the ushers to help him run it down. Before the game was an inning older, outside in the street they found the kid who had picked up the ball and they brought him in to Babe. Babe gave the kid a new ball, autographed, in exchange for the prize, and he handed the boy a twenty-dollar bill. Number 500, he felt, was going to be pretty near the top for him.

The Yankees had all grown older along with Babe. The pitchers tired more quickly. Gehrig's batting average had fallen many points. Curly-haired Bob Meusel, who had hurt his ankle the year before, dropped far below .300 at the plate and could no longer race out those three-base hits. Durocher at shortstop was a minor-league batsman, who would pile up a stack of base hits for a game or two and then post a string of zeros. Joe Dugan had been sent to the Braves and his replacement, Gene Robertson, was strictly a singles hitter. As a matter of fact, Babe Ruth was almost the only one, besides Earle Combs, who was batting near his best form, and he was about three-quarters of his former self on the field.

Even Miller Huggins had been ailing a good part of the year. By September, when the Athletics were some ten games ahead and gaining, Huggins had abandoned hope and had already begun to think of trading off some of his slightly spavined heroes. He was annoyed to have a pimple on his face turn out to be a boil that grew larger until it looked as if it might close an eye. He left the bench one day when the Yankees were playing Cleveland in the stadium, turned the managing job over to Coach Arthur Fletcher, and betook himself to the trainer's room, where he turned on a sun lamp to give his sore face a "treatment." Advertisements everywhere in that day urged everyone who suffered from any ailment at all to soak himself in the wondrous radiance of ultraviolet rays, which built "strong bones, sound teeth, and healthy bodies" and which were recommended for "sufferers from many ailments." That was good enough for little Miller, who had no money to throw around for medical fees, so he lay there and tried to imagine the lamp was making him feel better.

Huggins was alone in the locker room for only a few minutes when the door banged open and Waite Hoyt, who had been in the pitcher's box when Huggins left, strode unhappily into the room.

"What happened to you?" said Hug.

"I was knocked out of the box. Joe Hauser hit a home run off me. I don't know how. I could always handle that guy, pitching him high."

Huggins sat up and looked his weary pitcher over.

"How old are you, Waite?"

"I was thirty last week."

"Well, you have to make up your mind you can't do after thirty all the things you used to do. You don't bounce back the way you did. You have to spare your strength and get more rest."

That was the last bit of advice Miller Huggins gave to any player. The next day, the "boil" had grown so grotesquely, closing his eye, that he had to let himself be taken to the hospital, where they found he had erysipelas. No treatment seemed to check the disease. He was given blood transfusions every day. About ten days later he died, at the age of forty-nine, and there was no one at all to hold the Yankee machine together or even to know what few parts needed to be replaced.

Babe Ruth, like all the other players, was shaken by Huggins's death. He realized suddenly how devoted he had become to the little man he used to bedevil about the clubhouse. Ever afterward he told how much he wished that he had listened—that they *all* had listened—to what Miller had tried to tell them. He had been, said Babe, and all the other men agreed, the smartest manager in all baseball. Ten times smarter, said Waite Hoyt, than any other man who ever held the job.

There was another death in 1929 that shook poor Babe right to his soul. That was the shocking loss of his wife, Helen, burned to death in her sleep at the home of friends in Watertown, Mass. Babe, who had put Helen completely out of his mind except when he was in Boston, reacted to this tragedy as he had to the death of his father, whom he had seldom spoken of when he was alive. Perhaps this time the knowledge of all the sins he had committed against the plump little girl who had been his first deep love racked his conscience, for Babe was sincerely grief-stricken. He hastened to Boston to stand in the bitter cold with head bowed and tears on his cheeks, to see Helen into her grave.

There were other tragedies in the making and there were even a few seers, like Miller Huggins, who had been able to forecast them. But most of the country was taken utterly unaware by the depth and the breadth of the Wall Street debacle. There had been some slippages before and many a worried look as stock values fell off and did not promptly recover. But then there would be a slight forward surge, along with reams of published rhetoric explaining that there was no reason in God's world why stocks should be selling so "cheaply." (United States Steel was at 212.)

Irving Fisher, professor of economics at Yale and author of a regular message of "advice" on how to line your pockets in perfect safety, affirmed that these slight fallings-off in stock values were all to the good, in getting the "lunatic fringe" out of the market. Charles E. Mitchell, president of National City Bank, the largest in the universe, returned from Europe in mid-October full of cheerful observations. The drop in stock prices, said he, had already gone too far. There were stocks to be had right now for less than they were worth. And the fret about brokers' loans was rooted in a lack of understanding of their true significance. What if they did total near ten billion dollars? There had simply been a shift from long-term to short-term financing. If matters were left alone, they would correct themselves. As for there being "undigested stocks" not really sold but just held on collateral, that meant nothing. There was plenty of money around to sop them all up. (What Mr. Mitchell failed to impart to his audience was that he had up his sleeve the floating of stock in a new holding company, created by combining Hershey's Chocolate with Kraft Cheese and Colgate-Palmolive-Peet. An unsettled market would be no place to launch this untried craft.)

Most of these observations were uttered after the market had taken two rather severe tumbles—one on Saturday, October 19, from which the market did not immediately recover. On Monday, there was another downslide, with the most active stocks losing from five to fourteen points apiece. Wall Street folk looked at each other in slight bewilderment, not unmixed with fear. How could this be, with call money having dropped back to 5 percent? Already a good many accounts had been thrown overboard for lack of extra margin to secure the loans. Well, the sages told each other, there is simply bound to be an abrupt recovery. But that night, stockbrokers sat at their telephones urging customers to come up with added margin money, lest their heavily mortgaged stocks be sold out.

On Tuesday, however, what with all the cheer exuded by Mitchell (who had tossed carloads of cash into the market in March when there had been signs of unsteadiness) and by lesser wiseacres in the public prints, the market staged a strong rally. U.S. Steel climbed to 216½. Cotton prices were holding up. Bankers had indicated they were willing to "support the market until it gets on its feet." And there was talk that the Federal Reserve would drop the rediscount rate to make money easier to come by. Western Union, under these benign influences, soared eighteen points.

On Wednesday there were signs and portents that would have prompted an Indian to cash in his chips. The winds came up in the night and blew a fierce gale all day, with lashing rain that tore down signs, sent hats and umbrellas skittering, and soaked pedestrians to the knees. And inside the Stock Exchange next morning, where stocks had opened strong, there blew another fearsome storm. Of a sudden everybody in town seemed to want to unload what he owned and dodge into a cellar. Stocks did not merely decline, they collapsed. Adams Express plunged by 96 points. U.S. Steel dropped to a new low: 204. Losses in stock values totaled four billion dollars. Each new decline brought a thousand new orders to sell, so that in the last hour two and a half million shares were exchanged.

Where there had been doubt and bewilderment, now there was terror. And in many gleaming new homes there was despair. There was no counting the number of customers who had been in through the doors of the exchange to learn at firsthand what tragedy had befallen them. The gallery saw more visitors than ever before in history—725. Among them was a portly, cigar-chugging fellow from England who had been Chancellor of the Exchequer—a man named Winston Churchill.

The uproar in the well of the Stock Exchange never subsided throughout the day. People watching could not understand more than a wild word or two as men charged from one post to another, hands waving and faces contorted, while others stood besieged, trying to cope with a hundred petitioners at once, like men who had meat to distribute to a pack of ravening dogs. Then, at three o'clock, the gong sounded and there was instantaneous stillness, while the vibrations of the bell faded. After this breath of silence, a sudden spontaneous cry arose, of mingled cheers and boos, with an undercurrent of moans. Men everywhere threw up their hands, scattering bits of paper and small notebooks, and a few laughed in half-hysterical relief. Some men jumped off their feet a few times and beat their hands together, their shirt collars ripped and their ties dangling free. A few men stood dazed, with their hands filled with orders that had never been executed.

When the day was done, and men had found time to count over what had happened, the first "official" voices tried to scatter words of cheer. *Now* the worst was over! And there had been no major disasters. Brokers' loans had diminished by $167 million. Many stocks were selling below their true value. And bankers had pledged their continued support of the market.

The following day, there was a lessening of activity. Stocks moved cautiously upward. President Hoover reminded the nation that business was fundamentally sound. And Charles Mitchell of National City chose this moment to reveal the merger he had planned. Would he do *that* if there was any danger of further collapse? No, God was in his heaven. Hoover walked wakefully in the White House and watched over us all. And on Sunday, Babe Ruth and Lou Gehrig, playing for South Orange, New Jersey, against the New Brunswick team, hit five home runs between them, plus five other hits, and used up seventy-two baseballs while leading the South Orange semipros to victory. At half past eight the next morning, however, a young German chemist climbed out on the windowsill of the Savoy Plaza Hotel and jumped sixteen stories to his death.

The stock market opened on Monday, October 28, amid smiles of frozen cheer. There were some tentative upward motions, then the whole wagonload began again to slide down the tailboard. Before the day was done, stocks had lost another fourteen million dollars, with more than nine million shares sold, three million of them in the final hour. United States Steel plunged 17½ points. American Telephone and Telegraph fell thirty-four points and Eastman Kodak forty-one.

Hardly had the exchange closed, with the tardy ticker still chattering out fresh dismay for over an hour afterward, when anonymous "leaders" gave out to the newspapers more tidings of good cheer. Financiers were agreed, it was noted, that prices were now unusually attractive and money plentiful. Certain "informed members" predicted confidently that bankers would once again rush forth to shore up the market. And huge funds were expected to flow in as buyers picked up bargains at every post.

But the following day sixteen million shares were sold and prices dived again, seeking some incredible bottom. This time the voices of good cheer rose to a clamor. There had been, everyone noted, a slight rally before the gong sounded, proof that bargain hunters were on the loose. Thomas W. Lamont reassured investors that stocks were selling at well under their true value. Other leaders observed that fear was lessening. Banks agreed to reduce the margin requirements to a mere 25 percent, so that no one need have his holdings all sold out underneath him. John J. Raskob of Du Pont and General Motors announced that NOW was the time to buy!

In Providence, however, a customer dropped dead beside the stock ticker in his broker's office. And in Kansas City a man asked a friend to "tell the boys I can't pay what I owe them," then locked himself into his office and put a bullet through his head.

When the new day dawned, word came from John D. Rockefeller, Sr., that he and his son had begun to accumulate shares of common stock. The vision of this withered old man, his mouth sunken out of sight, leading his fifty-five-year-old boy by the hand down to the stock counter to pick out something pretty seemed to bring a thrill of good cheer to the whole financial district. Stocks climbed up a few points once more. Brokers found time to smile. Some of them waived margin requirements and refused to "sell out" their good customers. And the exchange announced that it would close for two days so that clerks might catch up on paper work.

When the exchange did open, stocks shot upward again. Brokers' loans had dropped by more than a billion dollars. The rediscount rate had been cut to 5 percent. Brokers all over town observed "an end to hysteria." And someone noted out loud that "no brokerage houses had gone under." This was not strictly true. None of the famous names had closed their doors. But a scattering of minor firms throughout the Equitable Building and in other structures where freshman brokers had been able to find a footing had closed up and gone home, unable to pay their bills or settle with their customers.

And when the paper-work holiday was over, stock prices sagged again, like a drunken man who had just been set on his feet. And this time, as the closing hour neared, a whole wave of sell orders rolled in and promised new collapses for the morrow. And so it went. United States Steel, which some men had sworn could never break 200, was selling now at 165 and looked likely to go below 150. Charles Mitchell, without making too much noise about it, decided that now was *not* the time to put together that merger. And a fifty-one-year-old lady who worked in a stockbrokerage house rode twice to the top floor of 120 Broadway, coming down once in a distraught state, then riding back up again. On her second trip she went up to the roof, walked around and around for a few minutes, then climbed the parapet and jumped. Her body struck the building across Cedar Street and rebounded to the sidewalk, almost landing on the people who walked there. For hours after her poor shattered body had been taken away, crowds watched solemnly as men with buckets and long brooms washed her blood off the side of the building where she had struck. And someone found in the gutter far down the street, where the terrible shock had sent it, one of the small shoes she had been wearing when she fell. A few days after that, when the market, it was reported, had returned to "normal," J. J. Riordan, president of the County Trust, in which Raskob was a leading figure, shot himself to death.

Cheerful predictions grew less fervent after this. Stocks would climb feebly one day and plunge the next, until finally United States Steel closed below 150. Wall Street now, expert observers reported, was "puzzled." *Could* there be something really wrong? Secretary of the Treasury Mellon, in a munificent gesture, announced that income taxes would be immediately reduced, for corporations as well as individuals. This would be proof, everyone agreed, that the kindly gentlemen in Washington who spent their days ordering our lives had utmost faith in business. The cut granted would save $3.75 a year to a man earning $4,000 and a hundred dollars to a man earning $15,000. R. M. Searle, a Rochester utility man who had lost more than a million dollars in the stock market in the preceding month, found no comfort in this news. He locked himself into a room and turned on the gas and never came out alive.

But there were more upturns in the market and smiles again on Wall Street. One day stocks rose as much as thirty points and the traders on the exchange floor broke into cheers. Thomas Lamont found the market "normal" once more and could locate "no weak situation anywhere" to justify another decline. Herbert Hoover assured businessmen that he would hasten to "coordinate" government agencies with business. Babe Ruth announced that he was going to seek an $85,000 salary for 1930.

And freshmen at Columbia, having won a tug of war with the sophomores, carried the rope out to Broadway and strung it back and forth across the street, halting all traffic, and smashing all the windows in a streetcar that tried to push through. When police arrived, the freshmen, now joined by the sophomores, fought them too, asserting their right to celebrate as they pleased. One student was beaten over the head and taken off to jail.

Then stocks fell still another time and Wall Street became more puzzled than ever. More brokers closed their doors for good. Customers looked ruefully at the new prices of the "bargains" they had been urged to buy. John J. Raskob, after assuring everyone that the County Trust Company was perfectly sound, with assets aplenty, uttered no more words of cheer. If the Rockefellers, father and son, were out shopping for stocks again, they failed to tell about it. And not even Thomas Lamont, with all his acumen, could explain what had taken place.

There was one man, however, who was not puzzled in the least by the stock market disaster. Ralph B. Wilson, vice-president of the Babson Statistical Service in Boston, observed that stock prices had collapsed because the state of business did not warrant the prices. Wall Street folk, he declared, had failed to forecast the crash, first of all because they had forgotten their multiplication tables and, secondly, because they had ignored the commandment against bearing false witness. Many stocks, Wilson pointed out, were earning less than a 1 percent return. And anyone who said that stock prices, under those circumstances, were "justified" had lost his reverence for the truth.

Truth, however, as later investigation showed, was little regarded by any of the men most active in scattering cheer over Wall Street. Charles Mitchell and his cohorts, even while they were uttering, from their castle keep at the National City Bank, bulletins that announced an early upturn in the market, were busily selling their own stock short. That is, they were offering National City stock, often in greater quantities than they had on hand, at prices lower than the current market, confident that when the time came to make delivery, they could fill the orders with stock bought far more cheaply than the current price.

But these sleek gentlemen, whose every word was being courted, worshipfully listened to, and dutifully printed by all the newspapers in New York, were also taking care that the market crash should leave no bruises on their own bank accounts. After the market had taken its worst tumble, they all voted to lend themselves, on notes that bore no interest and in meetings that were never reported to depositors or stockholders, upwards of $2 million, to be used to keep their private stock accounts from being sold out for lack of margin. Meanwhile, they not only sold out in wholesale manner the accounts of their own stock customers; they also forced full payment from all the tellers and clerks of the bank who had been "persuaded" to buy the bank stock on installment. These underpaid fellow workers of theirs had the choice of continuing to pay at the rate of some $200 a share for stock now quoted at $30, or they could join the hordes of others who were walking the streets in search of their lost paydays.

Mr. Mitchell himself, in a fine exercise of thrift, sliced himself a share of the bank's profit so generous that it came to over $3 million in three years. And by "selling" some of his stock to a relative at a bargain price (with a private agreement to let him have it back at the same price when he wanted it), Charlie managed to show a big loss on his tax return and avoid paying any tax at all in 1929. No wonder he was able to turn a brave and bright countenance to the panic that seized the Street that year.

There were almost daily brokerage failures and there were suicides every week of men and women who could not face the world without being rich. Midtown hotels learned to be wary of guests who sought rooms on upper floors. One new skyscraper refused to allow visitors to go to the top floor without an attendant to accompany them. Customers' men (i.e., salesmen) from defunct or tottering brokerage houses were suddenly without salary or commissions. Some advertising account executives, whose accounts had shrunk or evaporated, had no offices to report to. Advertising salesmen, particularly those who worked in Wall Street, were put on indefinite furlough. Writers for a number of weeklies that specialized in cheery words from Wall Street had to go to free-lancing in other fields. The great crash, however, was not really, as some folk seem to recall, the beginning of the Depression.

PART VI

Hard Times

THERE was no great dumping of working people into the streets. And spokesmen for the farmers still saw hope that one scheme or another might be devised to raise farm income without costing the Eastern bankers an extra dime.

Even those who found themselves immediately out of work, mostly upper middle-class types who dwelt in the new suburbs that had been built without sidewalks, did not immediately despair. They continued to commute to the city and to frequent the breakfast bars and the speakeasy lunchrooms where their more fortunate fellows still foregathered, confident that the world could not long turn itself about without their well-tailored shoulders to keep it going. Some mortgaged their expensive houses so that they might continue to pay dues in their downtown club, or borrowed from Mom and Pop, or began quietly to cash in some of their private treasures.

The *Wall Street Journal,* moreover, saw no cause for despair. This was, its editors declared, a "prosperity panic" with nothing at all basically wrong with business, with agriculture, or with foreign trade. Or it was a "psychological panic" rather than a disaster that could be laid to some flaw in the economy. Only the speculators were hurt, after all, and most of those who had now got hold of the speculators' money agreed that those guys had it coming to them anyway. Cartoonists pictured a healthy "Industry" striding through the storm while a shabby speculator was bowled right over, or showed a plain Joe giving up his pursuit of a busted bubble and taking up pick and shovel again at the "gold mine."

The gaunt Depression itself, that would mark the ultimate unloading of the burden of the crash upon the working poor, approached on little cat feet, with most of the well-fed citizens not even aware of its coming. The nightclubs of New York made jokes about the stock-market crash and all their customers laughed fit to kill. Eddie Cantor, the most famous radio comedian in the land, wrote a book about his own stock-market losses and helped thousands of ordinary folk see the laughable side of the market panic. A number of impecunious men and women, it must be granted, had already taken to laughing out loud to see so many of the purse-proud brought low, to watch young new-rich alcoholics gone white about the eyes and ears as they looked at the bare bottoms of their bank accounts, to watch stiff-necked young men who had been used to talking over the heads of their inferiors suddenly turned friendly and humble, even obsequious. "Now they know," said Will Rogers, "what the farmer has been going through for eight years."

Baseball was hardly affected at all, except as some players were distracted by the sudden dissipation of the millions they had seen at hand. Attendance at ball games grew larger as more and more men found they had to go *someplace* during the day and dared not go home. In the minor leagues, ball games were sometimes played at night, to the immediate enhancement of the gate receipts. Babe Ruth did not get his $85,000 salary in 1930. But he did sign for $80,000 a year for two years and set out immediately to earn it by hitting home runs at near his earlier pace. No other baseball player in history had ever earned such a sum. It was more than the President of the United States put in his pocket. And it was not the total of Babe's income by any means. He still had endorsements and exhibition games and stage appearances and his weekly Hearst-chain column (written by a youngster named Ford Frick) to augment his take.

By the time the World Series came up, hard times had begun to cast their long black shadow ahead. Private banks—too many of which had been tossing their depositors' money into speculative stocks—began to fold up like fortune-tellers' tents, leaving men and women of every station with not a penny saved to see them past a payless payday. But the World Series was played amidst all its old splendor, with parks in Philadelphia and St. Louis filled to the walls and President Hoover, who had heard a few boos when he came to the World Series in 1929, still willing to show himself to the people to whom he had promised prosperity. (In 1929, a number of raucous voices had called out at the sight of the President: "We want beer!")

It was not a good season for the New York ball clubs. But it had been a great year for Babe Ruth. He came within one of hitting fifty home runs again and earned a batting average of .359. He had actually *pitched* the final game in Boston and beat the Red Sox. Life tasted sweet indeed to him still and good food tasted better. Babe still subscribed to the poor boy's notion that a rich man's meal was a chicken dinner. But to Babe that meant the whole chicken, along with all the vegetables the platter would hold and several hillocks of mashed potatoes adorned with thick gravy. And ice cream, of which he could eat a full quart at any time, was Babe's idea of the perfect dessert. There were still some goals in sight in baseball, and the immediate one to Babe seemed to be managership of the Yankees. Bob Shawkey had taken over the job and could do no better than bring the club in third. And Babe told himself that in all logic he should be next in line.

Colonel Ruppert and Ed Barrow, however, did not agree. They hired Joe McCarthy, the man just fired by the Chicago Cubs, and left Babe to complete his career as a private in the ranks. Babe did not really sulk or sorrow. He was enjoying his new playmates, notably young Jimmy Reese, a second baseman from the Pacific Coast League whom Babe selected as his favorite guy to stay up late with.

Babe remarried in 1929, to someone he had met when he was still new with the Yankees. He had gone to a show in Washington called *Tumble In,* with the hope of meeting the star, James Barton. But after Babe got there he had no eye for Barton. He focused on a young soubrette who had a minor speaking part, a girl named Claire Hodgson, and he kept company with her off and on (as he did with a few other ladies too) over the next five or six years. After his wife died, Babe married her, and Claire, who was wise in the ways of ballplayers and other footloose types, made sure she accompanied the Babe when the club went on the road. Still, she never drew the reins too tight, so Babe and Jimmy often found time to blink at the bright lights throughout the circuit. Unhappily, poor Jimmy lasted only two seasons with the Yankees, helping underscore the superstition that any man who tried to ride tandem with Ruth was destined for a brief career with the New York club. Babe always enjoyed the company of younger players, whom he would tease as if he were still the biggest boy in the industrial school, and whom he could overwhelm with his openhandedness and whose wide-eyed wonder at the marvels of the after-midnight world Babe could relish, recalling the days when he first had extra money in his pocket. He made a favorite too of young Arndt Jorgens, whose name he never *did* get the straight of and whom he loved to stick with the queen of spades in a hearts game.

In the thirties, although he continued to hit handsomely and make more home runs than most other men in the game, Babe, like the national economy, began to grow weak in the knees. He had owned one trick knee since his very early days with the Red Sox, when he sometimes had to call time out on the field after throwing his knee out on the left-field "cliff." But now his knee was likely to buckle when he completed a full swing at the plate. And so Babe began to cut down on his swing. He no longer took hold of the bat so he had the knob in his palm, nor did he follow through with a complete about-turn of his body. He held the bat up a few inches from the end and began to hit the ball where it was pitched—outside pitches to left field, inside pitches to right. Other great sluggers had scorned to surrender to the years in that way and had gone out of organized baseball still flailing vainly at the circumambient air, determined to summon back their youth by main strength and bitter determination.

But all Babe wanted to do was keep on playing baseball, and keep on winning games. And when he could not do that any longer, he felt sure he would make someone a good manager. There wasn't anyone *he* knew of who knew any more about baseball than he did or who owned the respect, and even the gratitude, of more major-league ballplayers.

The gradual deepening of the Depression made hardly any impress on Ruth or any of the better-paid players. A few more Yankee stars were traded off and went into their own private depression when they noted how different it was to be a Yankee, where every man had to sit clean and spruce and attentive on the bench (lest

Colonel Ruppert, who almost refused to hire Miller Huggins when he observed that Huggins wore a cap rather than a hat, take note and send word that the reins should be tightened)—different from being a Detroit Tiger, for instance, whose men could sit around on the backs of their necks and even talk about girls or music or stocks and bonds while the game was being played in front of them. But most ballplayers were getting by better than their neighbors. And possibly the general run of professional players, many of whom were earning no more than $3,000 a year, found living a little easier as prices began to shrink like stock values.

By the middle of 1930, men started to set up little stands on street corners in the major cities to sell apples from. This move was hailed by the well-fed folk in Washington as a splendid example of the devotion of America's plain people to the glorious traditions of free enterprise. There were soon not corners enough in all the nation to accommodate the free-enterprisers who would have liked to bring home an extra dollar or two each day, nor were there nickels enough available to pay for all the apples. Some men, whose souls would have shrunk a year earlier from the very vision of peddling from a pack, found themselves carting small fiber cases from door to door soliciting ten-cent sales of razor blades, first-aid kits, styptic pencils ("stops the blood while shaving!"), and papers of pins. When a chance was offered to earn $2.50 a day tucking advertising fliers under doors and into mailboxes, men would line up by the hundreds to apply. And of course the streets were alive with men and women who asked for nickels or dimes—not because they were blind or disabled but because they were simply "unemployed." Indeed, unemployment came to be accepted as a chronic disease that entitled its victim to treatment as tender as if he had been born blind or had lost both legs in an accident.

President Hoover, however, was determined that, whatever might be done to ease the lot of the unemployed, they should not be "robbed of initiative" by having money put into their hands. Caring for these "jobless through no fault of their own," according to Hoover, was a matter for private charity or local governments. Many local governments, however, from long-established habit in dealing with street folk who had no visible means of support, were not adjusted to treating joblessness as anything other than a petty crime. In Baltimore, as in many other cities, the unemployed who sought relief were required to apply at the police station, where they could be fixed by some cold eye that would determine if their need was real.

At the behest of Hoover and his henchmen, working people everywhere were urged to dump the Depression off their backs through united and unselfish action. A White House formula for getting all the jobless back to work called for all those currently employed to pay up all their debts and then rush out and buy some product they needed and could afford. (In more recent times, President Eisenhower suggested that a recession might be sent scattering if we would all go out and "Buy something!") Posters appeared on billboards everywhere showing an overalled figure ten times life size, digging into his pocket and exclaiming "I will share!" (Perhaps hearing of this campaign from a missionary, a group of impecunious African natives sent $3.77 to this country "for the starving Americans.")

New York had a new governor now who was insisting that his state establish a system of unemployment insurance—a scheme which most of the newspaper owners in the state, speaking as always as if each of them were a dozen, scorned as a rather thin disguise for a dole. And stories of the dread impact of the dole on the souls and bodies of poor folk overseas had made "dole" into a dirty word. So it was agreed in most of the rich men's clubs in the city that this minor Roosevelt (the big one then was still T.R.) simply didn't know what it was all about. But of course *they* did. They knew that all depressions ended sometime. They knew that it was loose talk, and not loose fiscal practices, that sank banks. And they knew that the country stood in dire need of a bull market.

Even without talk, however, banks continued to sink. As a matter of fact, the bank failure that damaged more plain people in New York City than any other was the collapse of the Bank of the United States—not a government bank, as many innocent immigrants imagined, but simply the private preserve of two operators who thought that whatever depositors put into the bank belonged to the bankers. When the imminent collapse of this institution was common knowledge among all those who had even a backdoor acquaintance with anyone in the money business, newspapers took care not to print a whisper of the truth—that Bernard Marcus and Saul Singer, president and vice-president of the bank, had been freely misusing depositors' funds and had been unable to find any bank to bail them out. So when the 160 offices of the bank, all through the five boroughs, locked their doors, they left some four hundred thousand depositors—most of them with balances of a few hundred dollars each—out in the rain. Although the Bank of the United States was not a savings bank, it had urged working people to store up their cash in "thrift accounts" that gathered interest hand over fist. They made no such claims as Ponzi had, but they left their customers just as broke. The New York Clearing House took pity on the victims, however, and immediately offered to lend any depositor (at 5 percent interest) up to half of what he had had in the bank when it closed.

Baseball money, along with plain folks' money, found its way into the Harriman National Bank, whose president, Joseph W. Harriman, a man of very limited endowment, had used depositors' money just as freely as Marcus and Singer had. Like those two well-starched fellows, Harriman was eventually arrested and ticketed for the Tombs. While in the custody of the arresting officers he made several feeble efforts to do away with himself, or at least to get credit for trying. While men held him firmly by either arm, he made as if to hurl himself in front of a subway train. Outdoors, when no one was holding him, he walked out into the lake at Central Park until the water covered his knees. Then he allowed himself to be "rescued." A third time, with men right at his elbow to save him from himself, he made a few digs at one wrist with a dull pocket knife. Having thus demonstrated how deep was his remorse and how sincere his repentance, he was ready to fling himself on the mercy of the court. (The court sent him to jail.)

There had been a deep depletion of savings accounts all over the country. But the sudden evaporation of the life savings of thousands upon thousands of poor people in New York City meant immediate misery, for many of these had been counting on the cash they had thus squirreled away to keep themselves solvent while they looked for new jobs. One might have thought that under these conditions there would have been relatively little interest in which team beat what other team on a summer afternoon at the baseball park. Yet interest in baseball seemed if anything more emotional and more intense. There must have been a sudden deep yearning on the part of thousands of the nation's losers to participate in some degree in victories over a vaunted enemy. There was also soul-deep satisfaction in owning membership in the brotherhood of fans, or a brotherhood of any name, no matter how loosely strung and ephemeral.

When the St. Louis Cardinals, led by a dirty-faced young outfielder called Pepper Martin (named after a forgotten heavyweight fighter), beat the princely Philadelphia Athletics in the 1931 World Series, the employed and unemployed, worried banker and dispossessed laborer, panhandler and priest, all over the city of New York gathered by loudspeakers to cheer the tatterdemalion Cardinals on.

There could not have been a choicer champion for a people who all felt more than a little down at the heel. Pepper Martin had arrived in organized baseball on the rods of a freight car and had been held in jail for vagrancy along the way to training camp. He habitually slid to bases on his belly in the manner of Mike Kelly of yore (Slide, Kelly! On your belly!) so that his uniform front was nearly always soiled. He worked for one of the smallest salaries in the league, $4,500 a year. He had no knowledge of finance, had hoboed long miles with cinders in his hair, had sat on the Cardinals bench as a utility man until he angrily insisted that he get a chance to play or be sent somewhere else, and had startled the home fans when, as a pinch-runner in the ninth inning of the final game of the 1928 World Series, he had stolen his way from first to third, then scored on an infield out.

The financial collapse had rather more to do with the St. Louis victory than most people ever realized. The Athletics, who fielded the most awesome lineup in professional baseball, were handicapped by the fact that mighty Mickey Cochrane had been devastated by frantic margin calls that left him without funds—and with an enormous debt to pay from having endorsed a note for $25,000 for his old catcher, Cy Perkins, who was now dead broke. On game days, Cochrane would often sit in the clubhouse with his head in his hands before going to the dugout, staring distractedly at the floor, not always aware of what was being said to him, and sometimes being interrupted by his broker. In the game too, his mind did not always focus as sharply on the play as before, and sometimes he reacted with something less than the chain-lightning reflexes that had brought so many base runners down. In the final game, with a man on third, the Athletics pitcher, George Earnshaw, ostentatiously spat into the dirt near the mound—his signal to Cochrane that a spitball (then illegal) was coming. But Mickey missed the sign and never expected the pitch to break as wildly as it did. It flew over Mickey's shoulder to be recorded as a wild pitch. And the St. Louis runner scored.

Margin calls were no matter to a great many of the wage-earning stockholders in the land. They had purchased common stocks as an investment that was to render them immune to the vicissitudes of old age and failing fortune. Many of them, convinced that the most solid properties in the world were the great utilities—the gas, electricity, power, and water companies upon which the entire economy depended—had put all their under-the-mattress cash into the stock of Electric Bond and Share, Associated Gas and Electric, or Midwest Utilities.

These staidly promoted issues seemed as secure as banknotes, for what small stockholder had the patience to inquire into the methods by which the parent holding companies were making the profits grow? It was enough to find that Electric Bond and Share, for instance, as just *one* of its holdings, owned a subholding company called American and Foreign Power that controlled power and light companies through Central and South America, and which, through still other subholding companies, controlled utility networks in Arkansas, Louisiana, New Jersey, and Virginia. Actually, with an investment of only about $20 million, Electric Bond and Share controlled many billions of dollars in utility assets and practically printed its own money, uttering debentures, preferred and common stock, and other paper, with which it bought control of more and more companies to add to its pyramid. When it had stretched out to its ultimate reach, Electric Bond and Share controlled from 15 to 20 percent of the entire utility assets in the United States. How could an investor lose in an organization as solidly based as that?

Well, the money-hungry promoters were quick to illustrate how neatly just about everyone but their good selves could be robbed of all they owned except the bits of silver amalgam in their teeth. First of all, having taken control of a utility operating company, they would employ an accommodating appraiser to "write up" the firm's value—that is, inflate it by as much as a third, so that assets worth $100 million would be valued at $133 million, with a resultant watering effect on the company's common stock. Thus, the man who seemed to be buying a one-ten-thousandth share of a company, really worth $100, would pay $133, for it, with the extra $33 being backed by "water" or pure fancy.

Next, the holding company that had bought control would strip the operating company of all its brains, taking accountants, engineers, and technicians into the employ of the holding company and then renting back their services to the operating company at fantastic fees. Most of this income would go to swell the profits of the holding company, fattening the bank accounts of the insiders and adding luster to the stocks and other papers the firm was peddling. But this move would also increase the operating expenses of the utility, and these expenses would be used to justify an upward swoop in the rates the consumers would have to pay.

The top companies in the pyramid, which were in the business of making money and not of making electricity or energy of any sort, would raise money through public offerings of stock to buy control of still more operating companies—exchanging crackly pieces of paper for hard cash, and often selling these bits of paper on the installment plan and counting the money owed for unpaid installments as "Accounts Receivable," as if it was owed for food and drink, or furniture, or automobiles.

Of course hard times meant dwindling income from the operating companies, whose consumers were losing their jobs or closing their plants down. And local governments began to examine rate structures more persistently as the electorate made its irritation felt. So the operating companies were unable to pay the exorbitant "service" fees to the holding company; the holding company had to default on its payment to holders of debentures and preferred stock. As a result, even though the companies were serving more customers than ever, the parent company wasted away from starvation. And the hundreds of thousands who had thought they were buying bits of the very bedrock of our national economy were left holding intricately engraved certificates that were worth hardly more than the paper they were made of. Electric Bond and Share, which was one of those "bargain" stocks in 1929, selling for about $200 a share, fell to one dollar. Thus the man who had tucked his lovingly gathered $10,000 there to keep him warm when the chill winds blew, found, when he looked inside the vault, that he had but fifty dollars left.

Middle West Utilities, the structure pasted together by Samuel Insull, operated in similar fashion. And so did Associated Gas and Electric, the creation of a former government accountant named Howard Hopson. Even J. P. Morgan set up his own set of holding and subholding companies, called the United Corporation, to keep Insull and Hopson out of his chicken yard.

The barefaced manner in which these sleek and plausible gentlemen lured small investors to trade in their real money for counterfeit was exemplified by a confession finally offered by Samuel Insull, Jr., who was left behind when his father fled to Greece to avoid prosecution. In 1930, Insull admitted, the firm had publicly reported earnings of more than $10 million. But that same year, the firm filed a corporate income-tax report showing a *loss* of more than $6 million. As for Halsey, Stuart—that right-hand temple column of the Wall Street world—it even hired, to push Insull stocks and others of equal worth, a velvet-voiced radio salesman, posing as "The Old Counselor," whose advice was broadcast weekly on stations from Maine to Oregon. One of his talks was entitled "How a Widow Should Invest $10,000." But one of the facts he forgot to impart to the widow was Halsey, Stuart's own involvement in the Insull enterprise. For Halsey, Stuart was not simply earning commissions and underwriting fees but owned a large chunk of Insull securities on its own, which it was trying fervently to create a market for. That may have been why The Old Counselor, confiding his wisdom in the manner of a family physician, urged widows everywhere to sell their United States government bonds and buy the trash that rolled off the Insull presses.

Nor did The Old Counselor and his employers represent by any means the entire complement of respectable folk who lied or violated banking laws or betrayed their own stockholders in order to keep old Samuel Insull afloat, so that he might continue to extract indecent profits from the utility companies he controlled, and which he forced to pay him fees for service they might have had for less than one-third the price. Owen D. Young, boss of General Electric and negotiator of the 1929 Young Plan for German reparations payments, a man so sanctified in the press that he was talked of as a possible Secretary of the Treasury or even President, granted Samuel Insull a loan of $2 million from General Electric's treasury without upsetting his stockholders by telling them about it. At the time Young reached out this helping hand, the Insull Investing Company was tiptoeing along the brink of bankruptcy, had put up all its available securities as collateral for loans from several banks (all of which had refused to come up with the extra $2 million), and was just about to default on interest payments on some $60 million of debentures. The loan from General Electric was to still the cries of the debenture holders and buy a little more time for the Insulls, father and son, to work the bailing bucket. (The holders of the debentures had already been swindled, for they had bought the paper on the guarantee that the Insull company would not incur any added debts that would raise the total indebtedness beyond 50 percent of the value of its assets. The banks already held *all* the assets as security.)

When nosy lawyers at the bankruptcy proceedings inquired if Mr. Young had not observed that the "accounts receivable" of $12 million that he argued made the loan safe represented only the commitments of purchasers who were paying on the installment plan for stock in an insolvent company, Mr. Young replied that no, he had never noticed that. He had dealt, he said, with the Insull situation "in a large way." How many hundreds of thousands of small-time bankrupts must have wished that they could have coped with their own creditors in an equally large way, ignoring simple dollars-and-cents matters to deal in confidence, faith, and devotion to the American system!

Most of the simple folk who bought small bundles of the common stock of these great holding companies really imagined that they were putting their wrinkled dollar bills to work at harnessing waterpower to make electricity or building new plants where nightmare-size dynamos would start howling to bring the blessing of electricity to more and more and more plain people throughout the nation. But they weren't doing any such thing. The money the companies needed for improving or extending their service had already been supplied by bankers and other "insiders" who had purchased the bonds—the official IOUs that were backed by the assets of the company. The common stock had been handed to these insiders either outright as a bonus for buying the bonds or at nominal prices (say $7.50 a share) that they did not even have to pay until the stock had been sold.

These slicksters then engaged in the traditional game of "creating a market" for the stock by playing catch with it—tossing it back and forth from one brokerage house to another, selling it here and buying it right back there, at a price perhaps six times what they had paid for it. They were engaged, through the major stock exchanges, in exactly the same sort of legerdemain that the peddler of fake watches used as he strode down Broadway "selling" his wares to himself, through a squad of phonies, who kept handing him money and taking watches as fast as he could fork them out. Naturally, as this went on, an occasional "live one" came along who would *really* buy a watch, or a hundred shares of stock, at the "market" price, with money that did not have to be given back. As the watch peddler might dish out twenty watches to sell ten, the stock insider or underwriter might buy (from himself) thirteen thousand shares to sell four thousand. But he could keep tossing the ball back and forth in this private game of catch until it had all been nibbled away by the public, who may have been put on to a good thing by some such grandfatherly figure as The Old Counselor himself (who had got his own piece of the $50 stock at $7.50).

Thus savings of the investor did not go into power plants but into the pockets and piggy banks of the wealthy men who had established the rules of the game. This represented, according to John J. Raskob (who had backed Al Smith against Hoover in 1928) "the profit side of wealth." In other words, it was one of the prizes awarded you for owning a whole lot of money. It added not a dime's worth to the nation's assets. But it did make life a deal more comfortable for Samuel Insull and the fine folk who created Electric Bond and Share.

What a delicious joke that was! And how the Wall Street gods must have laughed—even as J. P. Morgan, at the congressional hearing that inquired into the manner in which he influenced legislation, laughed out loud when the existence of his "preferred" (i.e., bribery) list was laid out in public.

Laughter was not quite so hearty in the streets where lived the men and women who had been employed in haling the nation out of its stable in the morning, teaming it through its chores, and getting it to bed all properly fed and watered at night. New York pavements were alive with long-faced men of middle age who were finally facing the fact that there might never be another job for them. They plodded from door to door, in a doleful dance figure, with hardly a flicker of hope in their hearts but trying each time to summon up an imitation of the old offhand heartiness, pretending not to notice when true friends dodged out of sight, and yielding at last to the urge to cluster somewhere with others in a like fix, to wring a drop or two of wry comfort out of confessing their miseries to each other.

More than one or two such men rode home in the subway, climbed to the very top of the stairs in their apartments, and plunged head-first to the ground, to set a final period to their woes.

Younger families, after seeing the final dollar drained from their savings, either by a bank closing or through the need to make some payment on the grocery bill, began to move in with the old folks, crowding themselves within a small flat, sometimes vainly seeking a corner to whisper in private, guiltily sharing a stingy pension and a dwindling bank account, trying not to help themselves too heartily at mealtimes, vowing every day to find *some* honest labor, when everyone knew there was none to be had. Boys and girls too old to be home still turned back to Mama and let her feed and clothe them, half ashamed to let the neighbors know they had come back to stay. Some jobless men found a wretched haven with friends for whom they might act the part of house servant, until the friendship was worn to the bare bone and resentment festered on both sides.

Yet hard times brought the poor some benefits too. A woman with a husband and a baby to feed could sometimes, by waiting until the store was about to close, buy for five cents a brown bag full of "soup greens"—carrots, beet tops, a turnip, a few stalks of celery, even a potato—to carry happily home and turn into a hot meal that could send everyone smiling to bed. Beef sank to fifteen cents a pound in some of the new self-service markets; bread and frosted cakes could be had at the "stale store" for dimes. Neighborhood movie houses often charged only twenty cents admission on week nights. There were softhearted landlords in New York who would turn back from evicting a family that had occupied the same apartment for years. Doctors occasionally "forgot" to send a bill for delivering a new baby into a barren household where all the husband might scrape up in a week would go to buy the formula and the vitamin D.

There were many small-town aspects to New York in that time, even though the denizens all deemed themselves case-hardened, wary, and mature beyond reckoning. There were neighborhood services of all sorts that still lay in the hands of individuals who sought only to live in moderate comfort among their kind and were not constrained to maximize profits with each turn of the hand. The tailor did his pressing with a flatiron and took spots out of coats with a can of cleaner. The druggist prescribed freely for headaches, nausea, missed periods, and aching teeth. On almost every corner in the semicommercial neighborhoods there was a feeding spot, done up in white enamel, that bore the name Coffee Pot. Although Coffee Pots all looked alike, they were not parts of a chain, and did not even purchase from the same supplier. They were rather like temperance taverns, where neighbors could collect over coffee and call back and forth to each other and to the cook-waiter-proprietor, or even sing together sometimes, or get a small meal on the cuff; or like cubbyholes they might repair to when an evening grew too long and lonesome, and sit over coffee and Danish without any pressure to buy more or yield up the seat.

In the residential reaches, in the Bronx and Queens and Brooklyn and uptown Manhattan, street singers wandered onto the courtyards and yelled out, with one hand to an ear, ballads of an earlier day, or some sentimental "theme song" from a movie, then bowed and waved their thanks when nickels and dimes rattled down to them. Small bent men walked patiently through all the concrete courts and side alleys, chanting the traditional lay: "I cash clothes! Buy old clothes! I cash!" Where the Italians lived there were loud games of *padrone e sotte,* with hands flung half-angrily down at each other with one fingor, two fingers, all fingers or no fingers extended, while one tried to call out in advance the upcoming total: *"Uno! Cinque! Quattro!"*

One game was played everywhere in corner lots where space might in a later day be marked out for a parking lot. (In that era, every new "development" built garages by the score, on the theory that no man would want his car left in the weather.) The new game was called Tom Thumb golf, and later simply miniature golf, and it was played on a course of wooden fairways and papier-mâché bunkers and hazards, with golf balls and putters—a course that would be no larger than a tennis court, perhaps a third of an acre or less. For a while it seemed as if this simpleminded pastime might so subvert the public tastes as to turn boys away from baseball and keep fans out of the parks. One or two baseball executives warned solemnly that such decadent pastimes would rot the National Game at its roots, soften the fiber of our youth, and put hot-dog concessionaries on the town. But big-league baseball, like the movies, actually prospered from hard times, and for the same reason that miniature golf developed into a minor madness. Men and women with only quarters to spend where before they had ten-dollar bills relished any entertainment that would woo their minds away from the woes that lay in wait. Talking pictures, largely uncensored, so that double entendres of a rather tame sort ("Go out and get the lay of the land." "Never mind the lay of the land, get Marie!") and even occasional topside nudity could be savored, proved far more enthralling than the old silents with their tinny piano accompaniment. And when there was no money for movies, there was Amos 'n Andy on the radio at 7 P.M.—a never-ending serial that helped perpetuate the notion that black men and women were put into the world to make white people laugh. In every shop and office, on street corners and in speakeasies, the catch phrases of the Amos 'n Andy characters were freely mimicked and laughed at as if they had just been thought up new: "Ah's regusted! A-wah! A-wah! Buzz me, Miss Blue!"

To the jobless and the homeless, of whom there were many thousands on the streets and in the subways, there was often no better recreation than gathering in Union Square or in Columbus Circle to hearken to speakers, one of whom might beseech them to flee to the arms of Jesus, while at the same moment and not fifty feet away, another might charge them to organize themselves into a mighty army and go storm the citadels of power at City Hall or in Albany, following the guerdon of Lenin, Trotsky, Jay Lovestone, or some splinter radical whose name was promptly forgotten.

Sometimes a youth in a blue shirt, flaunting the Share the Wealth slogans of Senator Huey Long of Louisiana, would call upon a gathering of half-attentive listeners to endorse the program that would make Every Man a King. After the speakers had folded up their synthetic soapboxes and gone their ways, then would come the most parlous hour, when the idlers would break up into knots to indulge in man-to-man polemics, with the listeners occasionally injecting words of agreement or dissent. On a warm night, to move about among a thousand as shabby and disaffected as yourself, to find in every small circle a man who would become an instant friend when you unexpectedly shared an opinion, was balm to the heart.

The government, in the early thirties, was largely concerned with wishing all discontent away. When the President returned from a trip to the West he would rejoice openly at the "disappearance of bread lines." When a group of business and religious leaders gathered in Washington to importune him for action in the face of growing unemployment, Hoover responded with beaming countenance that all the bureaus of the government had already been set to "working day and night" to solve these besetting problems. "Gentlemen," he assured them, "you have come too late!"

They had indeed. But Hoover did not mean it in the sense that later observers would take it. He just *knew* that with all these great minds bent together on a single task, glad and golden hours must surely be coming swiftly on the wing. The government, he explained to some students one day, is merely an "umpire of fairness." Once it had trained all the contestants and seen to it that all had an equal start, government just stood by and watched that there be no elbowing on the turns or dirty work on the stretches. And the winner, Hoover declared, was invariably the man who showed "the most conscientious training, the greatest ability, the strongest character."

By those standards, the strongest character in the nation must have been Andrew Mellon, former Secretary of the Treasury and named ambassador to the Court of St. James's in 1932. For lean Andy, obviously trained down to the quick, further enriched his already rich self, his family, and his friends, by using his job as boss of the nation's cash vault to turn back millions upon millions of the "excess profits" that had been confiscated by the tax man during the war. The tax man after all had been a Democrat and his decisions had, one concluded, all been repealed by the election of Warren Harding.

One point Hoover and his spokesmen did not dwell on was the obvious fact that, in a system that was set up like a long-distance race, it was necessary to have losers, outnumbering winners by a thousand to one. As the Depression deepened, the losers began to register their dismay more aggressively. Congress thought to still their cries by approving the creation of the Reconstruction Finance Corporation, which would be charged with funneling tax money into businesses that would then start producing again, and of course calling back their employees and paying them. But it was not lack of money that had slowed the business pulse, it was lack of customers. So the businesses that enjoyed this government largesse, instead of returning to the manufacture of goods no one could buy, simply used the cash to pay off the banks or to boost the executives' salaries.

It is worth noting that throughout the Depression, there was no diminution in dividend and interest income. And among the insurance companies, it was a golden time indeed for the men who held the top jobs. Thomas I. Parkinson, president of the Equitable Life

227

Assurance Society, was granted a raise in salary in 1931 to $100,000 a year. He had been making $75,000 in 1929. Frederick H. Ecker, president of Metropolitan, promptly sought and received a raise from $175,000 to $200,000, and all his vice-presidents were granted increases over their 1929 salaries too. Meanwhile the companies were thriftily refusing to take the risk of granting to policyholders loans upon their policies. How could they afford to, when the president had so many bills to pay?

Other well-fortified men and women were watching over their personal fortunes with equal diligence. Despite all public exhortations to share, the very very rich were letting go of hardly more than 6 percent of their gross income, even though they could deduct all charitable contributions from their taxable take. But the working people of the land, whose average income now was $1,000 a year, were urged, nay even required, to hand out wholesale shares of their wages to help their brethren. President Hoover even set up a committee to encourage the sharing of work through cutting the workweek down so that two men could work part-time at a job that had been full-time before. There was much public rejoicing at the "success" of this experiment, which some business leaders saw as the perfect method of curing the Depression without dipping into profits at all.

Hoover was indignant, however, when Congress handed him an appropriation of $300 million for "direct relief." This, Hoover declared, would be parceled out only with the approval of the Reconstruction Finance Corporation, and any states that hoped for a helping would have to prove that their own resources were utterly exhausted. As a result, only about $20 million was ever allotted, and if any of that trickled down to the unemployed it was hardly noted. It should not have been surprising that hungry people began to grow restless.

Even though the banker Charles G. Dawes, Vice-President under Coolidge, observed in July 1932 that "we have reached the turning point in the depression," there were hundreds of thousands of men and women who were not persuaded and more who did not even listen. If there was going to be a turning point in their lives, they began to suspect they were going to have to lay their own hands on the tiller. Bread lines indeed had disappeared, for state funds and private charities had gone broke. Apple sellers had dwindled to a very hardy few, for there were not customers enough for even the shiniest fruit. When some jobless men set out to sell ice cream on city sidewalks, they were soon run out of business because the nearby retailers complained that they were being undersold.

In Oklahoma, a gang of jobless men, numbering more than three hundred, marched on food stores and demanded food—else they would simply take it. They were granted direct relief by the store-keepers. In New York City, when a crowd of unemployed, having met in Union Square to listen to Communist speakers call for immediate handouts, marched on City Hall, they were met by foot patrolmen and mounted police, who endeavored to punish them for daring to wish out loud for a change in the American system. Women were grabbed by the hair and dragged screaming along as the mounted cops urged their steeds to a trot. Policemen who lacked nightsticks cornered individual protesters and beat them bloody with their fists. Many an innocent spectator, caught in the surging mob, found his hat beaten down over his ears and his skull dented by a flailing nightstick. One marcher was chased right up into an El station and mercilessly clouted and kicked until he was past feeling.

Patience everywhere seemed wearing through. Even on the base-ball diamond, players took to whacking each other with unprece-dented ferocity. In Washington, Yankee catcher Bill Dickey was knocked off his pins when he tried to tag out Carl Reynolds of the Senators at the plate. Bill got up, charged after Reynolds, and fetched him a full-blown crack in the face that broke Carl's jaw. In Chicago, White Sox pitcher Milt Gaston, distressed over a decision by umpire George Moriarty, knocked the umpire flat. Poor George was then beaten and kicked by other White Sox players who had gathered to see fair play. Bill Jurges of the Cubs, that same season of 1932, staged an impromptu fist fight with Neal Finn of the Dodgers. Marv Gudat, part-time outfielder of the Chicago Cubs, also engaged in a bare-fisted, no-decision encounter one afternoon with Arky Vaughan, the slugging shortstop of the Pittsburgh Pirates. And on the Fourth of July in that same year, Manager Charley Moore of the Jersey City Skeeters laid out Manager Al Mamaux of Newark with one hearty blow.

Most people, however, had to deal with an enemy they could never even identify, much less drive into a corner. Baseball itself, which had prospered in the first two Depression years, at last began to feel the grip of hard times. A number of minor leagues, including the Eastern, the Three-I, the Cotton States, and the Interstate, all shut down their parks forever. The New York Giants, on one trip to St. Louis, brought home $187 as their share of the gate—$11 less than their hotel bill.

In the Colorado beet fields, where farsighted employers evaded the child-labor laws by making labor contracts with the head of each family, the workers were kept alive only by supplementary relief payments from the state. The "earnings" of an average worker, including the kids, who all worked from sunup until pitch dark, were $108 a year. And every major city sprouted Hoovervilles, under bridges and viaducts or on the public dumps, where men, sometimes with their families, tried to make homes in houses built of packing cases and abandoned strips of lumber.

The most notorious Hooverville of all was built in this election year of 1932 on the outskirts of the capital, to house the twenty thousand troops of the Bonus Army who had gathered to petition Congress for the immediate redemption of the "bonus certificates" or "adjusted compensation" (payable in 1945) offered to veterans of World War I to make up for the fact that they fought for starvation wages while the men at home grew rich. The veterans, some in rags and some in tags but none in velvet gowns, gathered from every corner of the nation. They came five and six in an aging touring car, or a whole squadron in an open truck, hundreds through bumming rides with travelers or truckers or hitching them on freight trains, some by the steam cars, wearing their American Legion regalia, and some in jitney buses from towns not far away. The advance guard sought housing immediately right on Pennsylvania Avenue where two or three abandoned buildings, partly torn down, still wore roof and walls tight enough to withstand a sudden rainstorm. Some two hundred men chose this bivouac. Others found vacant lots elsewhere in the city. But the main body of the army camped on the Anacostia flats, across the Potomac from the Capitol, where they set up tents and dug latrines and built wooden shacks, some of which seemed strong enough to stand until the certificates came due in thirteen years.

The reaction of the Hoover Administration to this peaceful invasion was one of terror. No matter that the army bore no arms, or that when the word came that the bonus bill had been rejected, the troops gathered in good order and sang "America" at the top of their tired lungs. To Hoover and his minions, these men and the few

230

women and children who came with them constituted a mob, met to disrupt the orderly processes of government and—who knows?— maybe even hurl eggs and tomatoes at the sacred carcass of the President himself.

The Bonus Army had been encamped for two months when Hoover moved to disperse it. The first official move against the "Army of No Occupation" was a sudden decision to clear away the remains of the buildings the advance guard had occupied. This was necessary, the authorities declared, so that new buildings might be erected to "provide work for the unemployed." This, if it had turned out to be true (as it did not), would have marked the first time in the history of the parish that the Hoover Administration had acted directly to set men to working again. There had been $2 billion or more of Federal funds already laid out in loans by the RFC. But Hoover refused to tell where they had gone. All any private person could discover for sure was that not a single man had been hired for wages as a result of this largesse.

The Washington police, commanded by a sensible, conscientious, and kindly man named Pelham D. Glassford, a retired U.S. Army general who never concealed his sympathies for the jobless veterans, were given the job of dispossessing the dispossessed who had moved in among the half-demolished buildings on Pennsylvania Avenue. There were 120 members of the Bonus Army encamped there when the police arrived to order them out. Commanding the veterans was a curly-haired young man in leather puttees, khaki jacket, and bow tie who carried the title Commander-in-Chief of the BEF (Bonus Expeditionary Forces). This was Walter W. Waters, who had led the march of the ten thousand who had made it to the steps of the Capitol to await word of the vote. He had led them too in singing "America" in response to their betrayal by Congress. And now he tried to draw this ragtail hundred or so out of the buildings they had camped in. But one oversize veteran rushed up to the partly demolished second floor of one of the buildings, yelling, "Come on, veterans!" Eighty men promptly followed him and squatted there, in defiance of the cops. An undersized veteran then picked up an American flag and climbed a rickety ladder to the roof, where he began to march about waving the flag as if he were patrolling the ramparts of a fort.

Within minutes three hundred more veterans appeared on the avenue, led by a husky with a club but marching peacefully in ranks toward the embattled building. Two thousand veterans who wandered the nearby sidewalks cheered as the ragged contingent stepped by to join the group already encamped there. Superintendent Glassford and Commander Waters took counsel together on what might be done, with Waters admitting that he had lost control of this wing of his army. The police then began to close in on the buildings, and the veterans entrenched there met them with flung bricks and chunks of concrete. One cop was felled and led off bleeding from a jagged cut. Glassford, who had waded right into the center of the area, was also hit. Then someone fired a pistol four or five times There was sudden silence. The shots were repeated—bang! bang! bang! The cops moved close and dragged the men out bodily. One veteran, William Hushka of Chicago, lay dead.

The whole gathering now fell still and there was no more resistance as Glassford's forces completed the task that had been wished on them of making the building safe for the wreckers. Hushka's body was consigned to a patrol wagon. One after the other, the ragged men, black and white, were rudely hustled off to the waiting police carts, while the veterans from other areas watched gloomily.

At the White House there was panic. The night before, President Hoover, his heart aflutter, one presumes, with fear that the ragged host might overwhelm the cavalrymen already encamped about the White House, had called into private conclave Attorney General William D. Mitchell, Secretary of War Patrick J. Hurley, and Treasury Secretary Ogden L. Mills, and taken solemn counsel with them as to how the Republic might be saved. They decided it was time to send the cavalry against the invaders. So the word went out that the White House was considering martial law; and the Great White Father sat back to see if the savages would take heed and skulk off under cover of darkness. Action must be taken, Hoover told the press, because the bonus campers were delaying the demolition "necessary to extend employment in the district."

General Glassford assumed that he was to be given a chance first to urge the bonus marchers out, and he reported after the first affray that he had the situation well in hand. Meanwhile, however, Pat Hurley had sat down with the Army Chief of Staff, General Douglas MacArthur, and between them they had decided to wipe out the entire force of the enemy with one fell blow. So the bugler sounded boots and saddles, the Third Cavalry assembled in battle array, and five slightly rusty tanks were rolled out to strike the necessary terror into the hearts of the foe.

When the cavalry appeared, riding along the full width of the avenue with a steady clop-clop-clop, steel helmets on their heads, guerdon flying, and sabers ready, the veterans on both sidewalks cheered. But when the clanking tanks came into view, there was loud laughter and hoots of derision. This, apparently, was all the signal that bold MacArthur required to send his men into action. Promptly tear-gas grenades began to fly and veterans and civilians alike fled choking and coughing into the byways. The camp site was almost immediately cleared of that handful of stubborn men who were holding up the Hoover public-works program. But Hurley and MacArthur had decided that the rabble must be rooted out wherever it had established a footing. When the BEF had first gathered, ten thousand strong, on the steps of the Capitol, the bridges that gave access from Anacostia were raised and guards set on them, to prevent the entire horde from entering the city. Now the bridges were in place again, and over them rode the intrepid Third Cavalry, along with an infantry contingent, ready to wipe out the entire village on the flats and to brave the sticks and stones and dirty names that comprised the entire BEF arsenal. As the action began, MacArthur took time out to pose for news photographers.

The troops under MacArthur (who would later proclaim that "another week might have meant that the government was in peril!") set fire first to a shack at the edge of the encampment. The veterans promptly began to retreat, some of them firing their own shacks as they pulled back. But the troops would not be stayed. They hurled the tear-gas grenades freely, right and left, and laid about them with their sabers and bayonets. The ugly tanks hung back, ready to let go with their own guns should the veterans show fight.

Many a veteran, and especially those with their families, took refuge in the back yards of some of the sympathetic citizens whose homes bordered the flats; they and their neighbors stood watching in dismay as the troops closed in with sabers swinging. The sight of 750 fully armed soldiers thirsting for battle charging into this unarmed, badly clothed, half-starved remnant, putting little children and frightened mothers to rout as well as gaunt veterans, moved many of the citizens of Anacostia to wrath. They expressed that wrath in the only way they had ever learned, by hissing and booing as the troops rode by. The troops thereupon hurled tear-gas grenades at the bystanders, too, to offer them a taste of what might lie in store if they dared imagine they could find public fault with the Throne.

In one back yard, a mother named Myers, with her husband, who held their eleven-week-old infant in his arms, stood watching the holocaust, as her wretched home, along with hundreds of others, went up in smoke. A gallant cavalryman, seeing the enemy there all uncowed, flung a tear-gas bomb their way. The searing gas nearly choked them all and set little Bernard Myers to strangling. Already ill with diarrhea, he seemed so near death that another family that lived there sent for an ambulance and he was rushed to a municipal hospital, where he died one week later.

The military authorities, having heard of this mishap and foreseeing a burst of unpleasant publicity, had rushed a Chemical Warfare officer to the hospital, not to succor the infant, God knows, but to be ready with an "explanation" if the worst should come. The worst did come, and the coroner vowed that the gas had not affected the child at all. How did he know that? Well, the officer had explained that there was no sign on the baby of any contact with gas whatever. The doctor was questioned and all he would say was that the tear gas certainly had "not done the baby any good."

A small boy was hurt too, when he rushed back to his shack to rescue a pet dog and got a bayonet in the thigh for his trouble. But that, after all, was merely the fortunes of war. If his family had wanted to keep him safe, the proper folk insisted, they should never have brought him to Washington. Still, the odor that arose from this affair caused a stench more noisome than that of tear gas in the public nostrils. Hoover, solemn and portentous as a hanging judge, then saw fit to offer a number of explanations of his conduct. There were, he vowed, a great many Communists among the marchers and hardly any bona fide veterans at all. Hurley and MacArthur fervently endorsed this explanation. They paid no heed at all to General Frank T. Hines, director of the Veterans' Bureau, who attested that his agency had examined the histories of eight thousand of the marchers, had found that two-thirds of those had seen action overseas, and had uncovered only five hundred who had no papers to prove they had served in the war.

Hoover urged his Attorney-General, the egregious John DeWitt Mitchell, to push for a grand-jury investigation of the BEF so that the world might know of the deadly peril his government had stood in during the summer of 1932. One of Mitchell's assistants took charge of the inquiry to see that the right answers were produced, and the municipal justice who charged the jury took some observers' breath away by expressing a fervent hope that the jury would come up with the finding that the mob that had been conquered by MacArthur's Myrmidons had contained relatively few veterans and a great many "Communists and other disorderly elements."

The grand jury found no such thing. Although they were given no chance to listen to the Washington citizens who were ready to testify to the brutality of the troops, and they paid no heed to the affidavit from one BEF leader charging that government agents disguised as veterans had instigated some of the violence, they never found a single Communist. They returned but three indictments, charging with rioting three wounded veterans, one of whom had been awarded the Distinguished Service Cross for rescuing wounded comrades under fire.

None of this deterred the President, who was bound he would come out of the affair as white as snow. With his blessing, Attorney General Mitchell issued a "report" (timed to coincide with the annual convention of the American Legion) that the bonus marchers, made up as they were of an "extraordinary proportion of criminal, Communist, and non-veteran elements," had brought into the Holy City "the largest aggregation of criminals that had ever been assembled there at one time." This finding might have raised the hair on many more scalps had it not been for the Administration's failure to place some prior restraint on Washington's Chief of Police, Pelham D. Glassford. Glassford, who had dealt directly with the marchers and with their own elected "military police" from the first day they entered the city, picked up the police records for the two months of 1932 when the BEF was in uneasy residence and showed that there was less crime while the army was there than there was after they left. He recalled the many patriotic demonstrations held by the marchers and reported that he had found just 210 Reds among them, who had been dealt with by the marchers themselves. He also repeated what he had said before, that he had told the commissioners of the District of Columbia that he needed no Federal troops, and that the commissioners had lied when they told the President a few minutes later that Glassford had asked for martial law.

The commissioners were not the only ones who lied about this episode, which the marchers named Bloody Thursday. Presidential mouthpiece Ted Joslin unblushingly announced that "no one was injured after the troops came." This despite the fact that every Washington newspaper had printed on its front page the names of the injured and the hospitals where they were confined.

Of course that was a more innocent day, when men in high position could count on the fact that the humble electorate would never question a statement that issued from the sacred Oval Room, and when newspaper editors all knew that truth was whatever advanced the cause of decent, white, Christian, Protestant, business rule.

The marchers, having learned the bitter truth five times over as they were harried out of Washington and on along the roadways, all bore with them a driving hatred of that well-upholstered, self-righteous, and solemnly introverted man who puffed with satisfaction when he heard an admirer declare: "Thank heaven we have a government in Washington that knows how to deal with a mob!"

Mob or no, the bonus marchers loved their country still and sang its songs with fervor as they wandered aimlessly toward the highways that led away from the city. Only two veterans had been killed by gunfire. One had had an ear sliced off by a cavalry saber. But thousands had been gassed and now staggered about, their eyes streaming, their throats on fire. A few had been separated from their wives and families and had no notion where to look. The roads into Maryland and Virginia were all closed tight against them by state police with pistols at their belts. God, where could a man even sit down? Well, nowhere in his nation's capital, unless he had a job, or a pocket full of cash, or had disowned his comrades.

Eventually the Maryland state police agreed to let the marchers through, provided there was no straggling nor stopping within their borders. Word came that Mayor Eddie McCloskey of Johnstown, Pennsylvania, enraged at the attack upon the marchers, had invited them all to come to his town where there was at least room to rest awhile in an abandoned amusement park.

Cheering, moaning with relief, with some of the men just about strong enough to get aboard, the marchers climbed into open trucks and chugged away, crying, "On to Johnstown!" More than a dozen of them, seeing no advantage in having the name without the game, vowed that they would gather up guns and come back to meet the "tin soldiers" face to face once more, on better terms.

At Johnstown, Eddie McCloskey had to withdraw his invitation, for Hoover's talk of Communists and criminals had frightened the good citizens into demanding that the BEF be driven away again, lest they take to looting and raping in the open streets. State troopers on motorcycles posted themselves then at the crossroads near Jennerstown and waved the trucks all straight through past the Johnstown road. It was hours before the veterans learned they had been tricked. Then only part of the army turned back and made for Johnstown, many of them almost too weary to stand. In Ideal Park, on the sweet grass, between fragrant grain fields, with a thick growth of trees beyond, the starving men merely flopped on the sod, heedless of who lay beside them. Many fell instantly asleep. A few sat up and wept.

One man had seen a "tin soldier" burn the American flag that had adorned a bonus marcher's hut. "God damn it," he vowed, "we're going back!"

But it was another year before they did, and there was another President in Washington by then, who granted them food and medical care, shelter for the sick, and money for their fares home. Nor did Commander Walter Waters, who had dreamed of leading an army of Khaki Shirts, like the Black Shirts and Brown Shirts of Mussolini and Hitler, ever see his dream come true. (Two years later, Waters returned to Washington to ask General MacArthur to get him a job as foreman of a Civilian Conservation Corps camp. MacArthur could not arrange that. But he did give Waters a desk job in the War Department at $1,500 a year.)

But 1932 seemed full of portents. There were scandals brewing in New York City, where Jimmy Walker, long the darling of speakeasy society and beloved of baseball men for his sponsoring the bill that permitted ball games on Sunday, had given over his smart cracks and begun to snarl back at his enemies. "I will match my private life," he declared, "with that of any of my accusers!" Fortunately he did not need to, for he would have come out far ahead in freehand breaking of the Ten Commandments. Babe Ruth, now thirty-seven years old, took sick in mid-April, after he had begun the year as if he meant to outdo his younger self, even in stealing bases. Beniamino Gigli quit the Metropolitan Opera rather than submit to a cut in salary. Al Smith and Franklin Roosevelt, who had long admired and supported each other, turned into bitter rivals, with Al offering to "take off my coat and fight any candidate who persists in a demagogic appeal to the working classes to destroy themselves by setting class against class." And that, according to the Republican newspapers, was exactly what Roosevelt, and only Roosevelt, had been up to.

Ex-President Coolidge had to send an apology and a $2,500 check to an insurance man in St. Louis for maligning insurance brokers on the radio. At Columbia, the student body, or most of it, threw eggs and apples at buildings and faculty members, and dropped water-bags on passersby to protest the expulsion of Reed Harris, editor of the *Columbia Spectator,* who had dared to suggest that college foot-ball was a semiprofessional racket and that the student cafeteria was run for profit. Killings in New York had increased by 16 percent and holdups were up 23 percent. And Andrew Mellon, now ambas-sador to the Court of St. James's, where he had fled when congress-men talked of impeaching him, was threatening to sue the United States government for excess-profit taxes "unlawfully collected"—just as if he had not already drained the U.S. Treasury to the halfway mark with refunds and abatements to his family and friends.

PART VII

Roosevelt or Ruin

THE most shattering event of 1932, at least to the citizens of New York and its environs, was the kidnapping of Charles Lindbergh's baby. Late in the wet evening of March 1, a man in a green Dodge sedan drove quietly up to the newly built Lindbergh home in Hopewell, New Jersey. He stopped out of sight of the house, which was hidden in the woods, lifted a homemade ladder out of his car, and made his way through the shadows and the rain until he could see into the windows. He watched a light in the second floor go on and saw a nursemaid making the baby ready for bed. Then he set his ladder down and waited. When the light had gone out, the man sat still long enough for the child to fall asleep. Then he raised his ladder to the window, climbed quickly up, gently lifted the partially opened window all the way, stepped into the room, took the baby, pinned blankets and all, into his arms, and set a small piece of paper on the crib. He climbed out on to the ladder. His foot did not make square contact. The ladder slipped in the mud, then cracked; man and baby plunged to the ground.

In the living room of the house Colonel Lindbergh, sitting with his wife, heard the sound of wood cracking.

"What was that?" he said. He and his wife sat listening but there was no other sound.

"It must have been an orange crate breaking in the kitchen," said Anne Lindbergh. "That's what it sounded like."

Lindbergh nodded and went back to his reading. Outside, the man pulled himself to his feet. He had hurt his leg so he could hardly hobble. The baby, still in his sleeping suit, with a guard fitted over one thumb to keep him from sucking it, lay absolutely still at his feet. The man lifted the baby and knew at once it was dead. The thumb guard fell off into the wet grass. His breath whistling through his nostrils, the man, grimacing with pain, limped back to his car, holding tight to the dead baby. He set the child's body on the front seat, started the car, and sped off to the highway. There were no other cars moving. About five miles down the road, where the woods were deep, the man pulled his car off the road and lifted the baby's body out. He stripped off the blankets and sleeping suit the child was wearing, pocketed the safety pins, put the garments into the car, and carried the small cold body into the dripping woods. When he felt he was well out of sight of the road, he scratched a sort of hole in the leaves and trash and set the small body down. He covered it quickly with leaves, twigs, mud, and whatever else his hands could dig up. Then he hastened back to the car and drove swiftly off toward New York.

He was many miles away before the Lindbergh maid peeked into the baby's room, heard no sound, then saw the empty bed. The wide-open window, yawning starkly, told the whole story. Betty Gow, the maid, screamed and ran downstairs.

"The baby's gone! " she cried.

The Lindberghs would not believe it until they had seen the room themselves and peered, aghast, out the open window. Then Colonel Lindbergh rushed downstairs, grabbed up his hunting rifle, and charged into the dark yard. Out there all he found was the broken ladder, which he brought into the house and grimly examined, while his wife and the maids wept helplessly.

The note was found much later. In crudely penciled letters it asked for "70,000$" in small bills and promised there would be further contact. It gave the comfort at least that the child was alive and would be returned unharmed.

But there was no contact for the first several days. The parents broadcast the baby's diet, including the number of drops of Viosterol that had to be added to the milk, and begged for some word. Simple hearts everywhere were filled with woe as they told and re-told the story. It was assumed that surely the underworld—the sort of villains who had stolen the sons of other wealthy men and spirited them off in high-powered cars—must be involved in a crime as ambitious as this. Colonel Lindbergh even named two notorious underworld figures named Spitale and Bitz to act as his representatives in dealing with whatever satraps of organized crime had stolen his baby. But no response was made.

Flighty folk almost everywhere had tales to tell of men or women who had "acted suspiciously" on the night of the kidnapping. An excited woman in Philadelphia called police to report a man who had purchased all the items listed on the radio as parts of the baby's diet and had returned to his own home "acting guilty." Just what he may have been guilty of, the police could not determine. But it had not been kidnapping.

There were even creatures so bereft of decency as to find, in this tragedy, a chance to turn a quick dollar. Gaston B. Means, a jailbird who had won notoriety at the time of the Teapot Dome scandals, talked Evelyn Walsh McLean, wife of Washington *Post* proprietor Ned, into providing him with $100,000 with which to ransom the baby from criminals with whom he could make connections.

In Norfolk, a shipbuilder named John Hughes Curtis volunteered to act as intermediary for the Lindberghs, promising that he could get in touch with "bootleggers" who were involved in the crime. Lindbergh authorized him, along with the Reverend N. Dobson Peacock and Rear Admiral Guy Burrage, to enter into negotiations. Major Alan Schoeffel of the New Jersey state police also hastened to Norfolk to see if he could pick up a scent. From Norfolk he set out for Glasgow, amid rumors that he was on the trail of an international conspiracy. He stopped in London, however, and never reached Scotland at all.

Curtis soon reported contact with the kidnappers and sent the Lindberghs assurances that the baby was well. But no details of ransoming arrangements were revealed. God help us, the Lindberghs must have wondered, is this another hoax?

Then the Lindberghs received an offer from a semiprofessional busybody in the Bronx, a mildly eccentric college teacher named

John F. Condon, who called himself, after his initials "Jafsie." (He pronounced it "Jayfsie" but few others did.)

Colonel Lindbergh invited Jafsie to come visit him in Hopewell, but he told no one outside the family about it. He then gave Jafsie permission, as he had granted others, to try to "make contact" in his own way. Jafsie's way was to run a classified "personal" ad in the *Bronx Home News,* the favorite daily reading of all unreconstructed Bronxites, offering to deal with the kidnapper. The speed with which he received a reply must have sent a chill down Jafsie's spine, for a letter came almost at once, containing some strange markings and asking for a meeting. Jafsie brought the letter to Lindbergh, where he found that the markings matched the "code" on the kidnap note that had been left in the crib. There was no question now in Lindbergh's mind that he had reached the kidnapper at last. He said nothing to the police and told Jafsie to proceed.

Jafsie, following the directions in the letter, set out to meet a contact at midnight at Woodlawn Cemetery, at 233rd Street in the Bronx—the very final outpost of the city and an area so forsaken even in broad daylight that honest folk kept clear of it in the dark. Jafsie rode up there in a car with one of his intimates, a fellow named Reich, and they sat there near the cemetery gate and waited in utter silence for a while. Then Jafsie got out of the car and walked a short way along the edge of the cemetery.

"John!" he called out. "John!"

That was the name that had been signed to the note. No answer. There was the sound of an elevated train moving far away. Jafsie, after stopping for a moment, turned back. As he did so, he caught a glimpse of something white that fluttered near the wall. He looked toward the gate of the cemetery and saw a white handkerchief waving there, slowly moving up and down. Jafsie walked back until he was able to make out a dark figure inside the gate.

"Did you bring it? The money?" a throaty voice demanded.

"No, I couldn't bring it. I must see the package first."

There was a rustle in the brush nearby, as of a small animal. The dark figure behind the gate suddenly came to life. "There's a cop!" the voice cried. Agile as an ape, the man scaled the gate and vaulted to the other side, landing face to face with Jafsie. It was too dark to make out features, but the man was slightly taller than Jafsie, of sturdy build but not stout or unduly large. A young man. His accent was strong and Jafsie decided he was a German.

"Did you bring de police?" the man snarled. Before Jafsie could answer, the man started to run. Jafsie started after him, shouting: "Hey! Come back here! I promised not to call the police! I kept my promise! I'm just an old schoolteacher and you're leaving me here to be drilled!"

The man, still moving away, had slowed his pace a little and Jafsie caught him by the arm.

"It's too tam dangerous! " the man growled. "I could get twenty years! I could burn!"

"No. No," Jafsie soothed him and started to lead him back to where they could sit together on a bench. "I *promised* I would not bring the police."

"Could they burn me if the baby iss dead?"

"Not unless you had a hand in it."

"I am only go-between," said the man. They sat together then and Jafsie scolded the man on his evil ways. He seemed like a decent young fellow. A clean fellow. What would his mother think?

His mother was dead.

Still, what would she think if she knew he was mixed up in something like this?

She vouldn't like it. She vould cry.

Well, then. Why didn't he break away from this gang? Come over on the side of the law?

"Der leader vould schmack me!" said John morosely.

So they talked on in low tones and John agreed to send some evidence that his associates had the baby. Then he would arrange another meeting place for the ransom to be paid.

"Do not vorry," said John. "You vill put the baby in his mutter's arms!"

Within two days, the pathetic little sleeping suit came to Jafsie in the mail and he brought it to the Lindberghs. It was without question the garment little Charles had worn. Next Jafsie received a note directing him to a Bronx greenhouse, where he would find, under a certain stone, a further note to tell him what move to make next. And this time he *must* bring the money. In twenties and tens and fives.

It was another dark night when Jafsie and Colonel Lindbergh drove to the Bronx. They found the dark greenhouse and the stone with the paper under it. "Cross street and start down Whittemore Avenue."

Leaving Lindbergh in the car, Jafsie crossed the street and

started, empty-handed, down the avenue, between two cemeteries. There was no sound but his own footsteps. No one else moved nor made any sign. Jafsie walked awhile, then stood quite still. No one in sight. No sign. He turned back toward the car and walked a few steps. Then a husky voice called behind him, "Hey doctor! Hey doctor!" The cry could have been heard for blocks.

Jafsie walked toward the sound of the voice and finally saw a figure behind the wall of St. Raymond's Cemetery.

"John?"

"Yes."

John inside the wall and Jafsie outside, they walked along together until they reached a hedge where they could see each other more clearly.

"You get the money?"

"Please let me see the baby first?"

"No. No use in that!"

"We can't get seventy thousand. Can't you make it fifty?"

"Okay. Ve take fifty. Iss Colonel Lindbergh there?"

"He is in the car with the money. I must get a receipt and directions for finding the baby."

"You go get the money. Ve meet here in five minutes."

Jafsie returned and took the shoe box with the money in it from Colonel Lindbergh. He waited awhile, then walked back to the hedge.

In a moment, John materialized out of the dark and took the box out of Jafsie's hand. He handed Jafsie a folded piece of paper.

"Vait a minute," said John, "till I see if it's all right."

He reached into the box, pulled out a handful of bills and fingered them. Impulsively he reached for Jafsie's hand and shook it vigorously. John had a strong hand and callused fingers.

"Your vork iss *perfect!*" he told Jafsie. Then he added, in a lower tone, "Do not read that note for two hours! Else you vill not get the baby!"

Jafsie and Colonel Lindbergh waited as they were bidden. Then they studied the note. Again the crude penciling. The baby, the note said, was "in a boad" and the "boad" was anchored off Gay Head, which was on Martha's Vineyard in Massachusetts. By daylight, Colonel Lindbergh, along with Jafsie, an FBI officer, and a friend, Colonel Breckenridge, had taken a plane for Martha's Vineyard. The first flight along the shorelines near Gay Head revealed no boat with a baby in it. Lindbergh landed and took a smaller plane, with which he flew up and down the whole shoreline of the island. The Coast Guard too sent a cutter there. But no baby was ever found.

Jafsie, bewildered, for he felt he had made a friend of "John," returned to the Bronx and inserted another classified ad in the paper:

"Have you crossed me? Jafsie."

Obviously John had, for there was never a reply. It was more than a month later that the little body was found, where the rain had washed off some of the leaves and dirt. And only then did John Hughes Curtis of Norfolk, who had been reporting "satisfactory contact" from time to time, admit out loud that he had fabricated the whole story. To what end, God knows. He had never asked for money. He was arrested and fined a thousand dollars and went away to hide his face somewhere. And gradually the Lindbergh case was forgotten by the public, so many of whom had woes of their own to reckon with.

Babe Ruth was not making quite so much in salary in 1932 as he had drawn the two years before. But he signed for $75,000 (after refusing to put his uniform on for spring training until he got a contract he liked) and he said he was satisfied. There had been a few faint boos to greet him when he showed up at training camp, perhaps from fans who merely resented one man's putting in his own pocket enough money to keep twenty-five families in comfort. Or it may be that Ruth's devotion to golf while his mates all sweated through the early springtime drills made a few spectators to offend.

On opening day, however, Babe hit two home runs and altogether drove five runs across the plate, to help the Yanks beat Philadelphia 12 to 6. Then the cheers resounded almost exactly as they had in better days. Babe had hoped he would be made manager, after Bob Shawkey had been given his chance and failed. But he seemed to bear no grudge, vowed that Joe McCarthy, fired by the Chicago Cubs and quickly hired by the Yankees, could just tell him what to do and he would do it, and admitted that he was approaching the king row on the board. He hardly expected the Yankees would take the pennant again quite so soon. But he told an audience of schoolboys in Philadelphia that his one ambition now was to play in ten World Series. He had already competed in nine. He also told the boys that they all had it pretty soft, compared to his generation, who had to make their own baseballs and go scouting for a place to play.

But Babe had always had baseballs and a place to play, even if it was behind high brick walls in the Industrial School.

What Babe did not like to admit was that he was noticeably slower. In a spring exhibition at Indianapolis he had actually been thrown out at *first base* on a relay, had made one error, and later had been tagged out at the plate trying to score. On April 17, a snowy day in Boston, he fell sick and had to keep to his hotel room with what the house doctor said was a slight fever and perhaps "incipient influenza." He stayed there after the team had gone and sweated away twelve pounds. When he tried at last to get up and put his clothes on, his fingers would hardly close and his knees buckled. "I'm weak as a cat," he told the sportswriters who had come to cheer him. But when he got back to New York for the home opener, Babe hit a home run. He also chased a foul fly to the stand, flung himself headfirst after it, then plunged right over the rail into the seats. The crowd gasped in horror and wondered if they had seen the end of Ruth's career. But Babe recovered himself quickly and trotted, without a limp, back to his position, grinning at the commotion he had caused. This, he decided, was going to be a great season.

But he hurt his knee in a slide at Washington, the same knee he had damaged the season before when he collided with Red Sox catcher Charlie Berry at the plate. So his visions of another fifty-home-run season were dimmed. The Yankees seemed less likely than ever to take the championship away from the mighty Athletics, who, everyone agreed, owned the best pitching staff in baseball, led by Lefty Grove, who had won thirty-one games the year before and brought his club in so far ahead of the Yanks that their dust had all settled before the Yankees got there.

Besides, the Yankees had not even decided who was going to play the infield. They had Jack Saltgaver at second base, and he was better suited to the Newark club. They had their new "California Italian," Frank Crosetti, at third base and he kept booting ground balls. Everybody knew that Tony Lazzeri and Babe Ruth were a step slower than they used to be. And the only twenty-game winner they owned was a left-handed broomhandle-thin pitcher named Lefty Gomez. But once the season was well started, Lou Gehrig began to attack the ball as if he was trying to break sixty. Lazzeri proved himself still the best second baseman in the circuit, while Frank Crosetti, when he was given a chance to play short, seemed to close off all the middle of the diamond by himself. By May 15, the Yankees had taken charge of first place and they never gave it up. They even scared hell out of the Athletics in early June when Gehrig hit four home runs in the same game against Philadelphia, the first time *that* had been done for thirty-six years. Nor did baseball itself seem in as bad a way as everyone predicted. Crowds at the Yankee Stadium would reach fifty thousand when the Athletics came to town, and hot dogs sold as rapidly as in the days when everybody was getting rich.

Babe's wobbly knee so cut down on his swing and on his speed that by the second month of the season his average had fallen to .263. The club was winning without him, however, and they were able to carry him along until he started to hit again. But he had no sooner got his average back where it belonged than he took another header on the field, this time in the outfield at Comiskey Park, Chicago, when he slipped while chasing a fly ball and then could not get up, with a severe muscle cramp behind his knee. They carried Babe off the field, and again spectators told themselves they had seen the last of Babe on a diamond.

Babe was supposed to be immobilized this time for at least three weeks, which was the same as asking him to go on a bread-and-water diet. Hardly a week had gone by when he went to bat as a pinch hitter against the Red Sox, accepted a free walk to first, and gave way to a pinchrunner. But the very next day he was back in the line up, grimly whacking at every sort of pitch that happened into the strike zone. Altogether, Babe hit forty-one home runs that season, more than earning his reduced salary, and hauled his batting average back up to .341. For the tenth time he led the league in bases on balls. He came in second in home runs, leading Lou Gehrig by seven, but seventeen behind young Jimmy Foxx of Philadelphia. (Chuck Klein of the Phillies led the National League with thirty-eight.) And everyone agreed that the ball this year was a sight deader than the one used in the 1920s, had more prominent seams to help the pitchers, and was a hell of a lot harder to drive out of the park.

The World Series of 1932, which brought Babe to his stated goal of ten, was also the one that seemed to live longest in the game's literature. It even inspired an oil painting showing Babe "calling his shot"—that is, indicating that he was about to drive the next pitch over the center-field wall in Wrigley Field, Chicago—a gesture which old men will insist even today Babe never made, or if he made it never meant it to indicate what he was going to do with the ball. Babe himself, from some reports, did not make that claim on his own until after the legend had become established. But others who were on the scene, including some of Ruth's teammates, will have it no other way: he responded to the hoots of derision from the enemy, they insist, by deliberately choosing the spot where he would send the next pitch and then sending it there with almost the speed and accuracy of a bullet.

The fact is that Babe had done this once before, some years earlier in Boston. Responding to a profane heckler, Babe had indicated that the next pitch was going out of the playing field. And out it went, with all of Babe's might behind it.

There was more than the usual bucketful of bitterness in that 1932 Series between the Yankees and the Cubs. The sorest point between them was surely the fact that the Cubs had Mark Koenig, a Yankee graduate, on the roster, via Detroit and the Pacific Coast League, and when the club had voted the divvy of the World Series loot, they had granted old Mark only half a share. Inasmuch as Mark had admittedly helped win a number of games along the way to the championship (the Cubs' manager conceded that they could not have taken the pennant without him), the Yankees correctly diagnosed this as the dingiest deal of the season. Had the Yanks taken on a player in the home stretch who had come up with a .353 average to help *them* win the flag, he'd have been awarded a full share. (When the Yankees were voting the divvy in the 1923 World Series, they voted a half-share to young Mike Gazella, who had joined the club in mid-season and played in only a few games. But Babe would not permit that. "I won't play in the series at all," he declared, "if you don't vote the kid a full share." The Yankees took another vote and awarded a full share to Gazella.) So the Yankees, from the very moment the clubs faced each other across the field, took pains to remind Koenig what a scrimy collection of nickel-nursing bastards he had fallen among.

The Cubs did not respond directly until the clubs took the field against each other. Then they turned their own loudmouths loose, to detail the doubtful ancestry and myriad personal failings of the Yankee troops. Most of the vituperation was directed at Babe Ruth, whose burgeoning belly and failing legs were celebrated in phrases more notable for indelicacy than for wit. In Chicago, with the Yankees having already won the first two games and needing only two more, the insults from the Chicago dugout grew more virulent. And the Chicago fans, particularly those in the bleachers, earnestly reinforced the efforts of their own heroes by lending voices and flinging missiles.

In batting practice before the game, Babe had dropped some half dozen new baseballs in among the bleacher bugs in right field, so that he was soon inwardly abubble with the conviction that he might "clout one" in the game. As he trotted past the Chicago dugout near first base, he took pains to urge the Cubs not to concern themselves unduly over getting back to New York, because the Series was going to end right here, in Chicago, with back-to-back Yankee victories. Then before entering the Yankee dugout he repeated this cheery message to the Chicago fans nearby, his shoulders trembling with laughter as he spoke.

In the first inning, Babe came to bat with two Yankees already on base. Charlie Root, the Chicago pitcher, was working grimly, pouring all his craft and muscle into every pitch. But Babe swung at the first good pitch as if he was still taking batting practice. Without even an "oof!" to indicate the effort, he patted the pitch into the bleachers, to score three runs at once. As he came back to the dugout after that, he paused to look happily up at the gloomy fans behind the dugout, then greeted them by pursing his lips and blowing a mild raspberry. In the second inning, Babe just missed a home run when his long fly ball fell a few feet short of the wire screen in the outfield. With the Cubs at bat in the fourth inning, Bill Jurges drove a long ball into left field, where Babe tried to block the ball in standard fashion by dropping to one knee in front of it. Babe's knees did not always obey his requests in those days; this time he just did not get down fast enough to hold the drive to a single, as he had meant to. Jurges reached second base on the hit and Chicago soon scored two runs, to tie the game at 4–4.

Some free soul in the stands commented on Ruth's dereliction on this play by flinging a lemon that hit Ruth in the leg. But Babe was not in the least put out. He retrieved and discarded the lemon, then indicated, with much wide gesturing, that he would prefer for the fans to aim their missiles, not at his poor creaking legs, but at his head, which could well withstand the blow.

When Babe came to bat in the fifth inning, Guy Bush, a long-legged, big-eared Chicago pitcher from the deep South who owned a voice like a hog caller's, took a position on the top step of the dug-out and aimed choice indecencies at the back of Babe's neck. The fans all joined to remind Babe of his lack of brilliance in the field. Babe merely grinned.

Charlie Root had no fear of Ruth, despite the earlier home run. He fired his fast ball right into the strike zone. Babe Ruth watched with great interest as it fled past him into the catcher's mitt. Then, almost before the umpire had a chance to confirm Babe's judgment, Babe turned to Bush and held up one finger to indicate that that was strike one. Bush made a megaphone out of his two big hands and howled profanity into Babe's face. Babe took his batting stance again and watched with increased interest as another Charlie Root pitch whistled through the strike zone.

Bush seemed to stretch his long neck almost onto the playing field to impel his next comment toward Babe. But Babe still grin-ning, merely held up two fingers to signal that now it was strike two. Root pretended to ignore all this. He grimly took the sign from the catcher and earnestly delivered the next pitch well outside the strike zone. Babe just cocked an eye at it. The next pitch, too, was too far out to be a strike and Babe promptly turned to Bush to hold up two fingers of his *left* hand to show that the count was even.

But then he made his historic gesture. Was it just a lifting of the fingers of his right hand to note the strike count? Or was it *really* a wave to indicate that the next pitch was going out of the park? More than one writer who was on the scene reported that the Babe gave a sign that meant "This is it! Here it goes now!" And go it surely did, about as far as any man in that day could have driven it, out to where the scoreboard met the bleachers in deepest right center, the longest home run, men said, that they had ever seen hit at Wrigley Field.

When Babe circled the bases after that, laughing, thumbing his nose, yelling dirty words back at Guy Bush and at all the unhappy foemen he passed along the way, the enemy fans stood up and cheered him. Where in the name of God would you ever find the like of this man, who would stand there with two strikes on him and promise to destroy you on the next pitch?

Of course the like of him would *never* appear again. The great bat-ters who followed him earned more ink than he did, what with base-ball becoming a major industry so soon after that and salaries, once

Ruth had shown the way, taking off into executive levels for the men who drew the crowds.

Later heroes acted more like wealthy men, shunning the "dirty-faced little boys" and the clamoring bleacher bugs, casting their lot more often with stage folk and the oil and advertising aristocracy, voting Republican, learning to mouth the bloated phrasings of the new "communications industry," and turning the game of baseball into a part-time job. Babe, who had refused to pose for a picture with President Hoover because he himself was a Democrat and an Al Smith man, who had once taken charge of an unruly gang of young fans and ordered them all into line and kept them there, who insisted that there be no publicity and no pictures on many of his trips to visit ailing poor kids in their homes or in the hospital, who had come back to New York at Christmas time in 1931 to put on a false beard and play Santa Claus to 250 kids from New York hospitals, and who, until the end of his career and past it, played baseball for the fun of it, was never to be compared to men who just hit more home runs than he did, or earned bigger salaries.

Babe's salary in 1933 was again a matter of concern. Everyone, including Babe himself, knew there would be another reduction. But Babe had made up his mind to one thing: he would not take a cut to $50,000. He'd take a dollar more, but not $50,000. So once again the newspapers accepted, or pretended to accept, the picture of two stubborn men girding their loins to battle each other clear to starvation rather than yield a dollar bill one way or the other. Yankee management pretended to find it indecent that Babe would ask for so much when so many had nothing at all. It is more than slightly doubtful, however, that what portion of the truly jobless and hungry even took note of the matter felt that the outcome would affect their own state in the least. Everybody wanted to see Babe Ruth play ball. Who the hell cared about Jake Ruppert's money?

Single young men and women in that era, who might have felt most kinship with an active ballplayer, had more real woe of their own than they found needful to keep their hours full. For there was no home relief for the unmarried. There were the flophouses, the subways, the missions, the empty doorways, the nickels and dimes to be cadged from passersby, or the promise of God knows what in some far-off town to be reached by freight car. There was never any counting the number of young men and women who wandered the country then, or even how many were killed in railroad yards, trying inexpertly to board or disembark from a moving freight train. There were thousands certainly who were brutalized by railroad police—by "brakies" and "yard bulls"—or who were tossed in the overnight tank of some city jail and sentenced only to get out of town the next day and stay out. A few who looked for old-time adventure in hobo-ing about the country learned too soon that competition, even for sleeping room in a boxcar, was often too vicious for a gently raised lad to cope with. And many who had dreams of coming home in later years bronzed by faraway suns and toughened by dealing hand to hand with nature, crept home instead, pale, sick, hungry, and scared by the horrors of the road—the clubbings of the private police, the vermin-ridden jails, the homosexuality, the desperate clinging for very life to the freezing top of a boxcar, the tears that would flow as chilblained hands tried to earn a stingy meal on a woodpile, or tried to work out on a pile of rocks one's penance for owning no visible means of support.

Such folk shed no tears for the troubles of the rich. But the journalistic elite, the gossip columnists, the city hall reporters, the professional athletes, the musical-comedy headliners, the radio stars, the high-stake gamblers, and their like still carried heavy hearts over the fall of Jimmy Walker. This, more than the lot of the wayward poor, seemed to them the deepest tragedy of the season, wrought by that mealy-mouthed governor who obviously had been concerned only with winning the votes of upstate apple knockers and other untailored types. Jimmy had been their darling. So Jimmy *had* taken tribute from bus companies, from men who financed cab companies, and even from Paul Block, a newspaper publisher who vowed that his ten-year-old boy, on learning that poor Jimmy had to make do on $25,000 a year, had suggested daddy do "something nice for him." (Daddy had promptly set up a stock account in Jimmy's name.) Goddamit, that was the American way! Everybody knew a politician had to take graft to get along. What mattered really was that a man be "a prince" and a "right guy"—quick to offer a hand to a friend, determined never to turn in an associate, ready to bandy wisecracks with the smartest mouths in the land.

But actually Jimmy had not always been "a prince" to those whose friendship he could make no use of. He could be arrogant, insulting, overbearing to obvious nobodies who tried to offer their plaints out loud at meetings of the Board of Estimate (which might have waited an hour and a half for Jimmy to make the scene.) He had a gift for dirty names and foul epithets and applied them freely to all who crossed him. He rubbed the citizens' noses in his private derelictions, which were revealed in some detail by Samuel Seabury, counsel for the legislative committee that was assessing Jimmy's stewardship. He reveled in his practical immunity from criticism, ensured by his drinking-buddy relationship with the city press. Every reporter knew that the "unnamed party" to whom Jimmy, according to the committee, had diverted $75,000 of the money he had gathered through extracurricular activity, was really his girl friend Betty Compton. But no one said so. Every newsman knew that when Jimmy made his dramatic and unheralded trip to California he was not *really* going to plead the case of Tom Mooney, a political prisoner since 1916, but just needed an excuse to be there while Betty was in Hollywood. But nobody said that either.

All the insiders and the right guys in the city knew that that wet smack Roosevelt had ruined himself politically when he took the ax to Tammany's own beloved Jimmy. But all the outsiders and wrong guys and jobless and poor and dispossessed and hungry farmers and starving small-business men never heard that at all. They so greatly outnumbered the adepts and the sophisticates that in November 1932, Roosevelt won every state except Maine and Vermont, where it was still deemed a virtue to be up against it most of your life.

Hardly anyone had time to offer blame or praise when Babe Ruth finally settled his 1933 salary dispute for $52,000. For by the time the news was current, the nation's banks had been closed in a dramatic move by the new President to preserve what assets they still clung to.

This bank "holiday" actually had its beginnings in Michigan, although there had been brief bank holidays in less vital states. The bankers in Michigan, in those golden days when every banker was alive to new methods for breeding dollars in the fecund fashion of the Insulls and the Hopsons, had worked out a "holding company" design for their banks. The Detroit Bankers Group and the Guardian Detroit Union group had made it their goal to lay their hands on all the money and credit resources of the state, and between them they had just about managed it. The Detroit Bankers group owned Detroit's First National Bank, with its 140 branch offices, and also owned nine banks outside the city. The Guardian Detroit Union group owned the Guardian National Bank and its thirty-eight city branch offices, and had acquired thirty-six banks outside the city.

These moves were not intended to create (as the promoters argued) "larger and stronger banks" or to extend commercial credit to the millions of credit-hungry Michigan small-business men. When the Guardian Detroit Bank and the National Bank of Commerce joined hands to create the Guardian National Bank of Commerce, they actually turned two strong banks into a weaker bank. The combined capital of the two banks before the merger was $30 million. The capital of the "larger" bank when the two were joined together was $10 million. The master builders had added about ten stories and knocked away two-thirds of the foundation.

As for opening the blessings of bank credit to rugged individualists throughout the state, it eventually turned out, when the bank doctors performed the autopsy, that 85 percent of the bank's capital had been loaned to buy securities. There had been, the penitent bank managers complained, "no demand for commercial loans."

This was fairy tale, of course. The managers had not been out to finance commerce at all but to sell securities—stock first of all in the monstrous holding companies they created, stock that they and other insiders had bought for $20 a share and which sold at one time for $300 a share. And your friendly banker was glad to lend you his depositors' money to buy the stock at that price.

The bankers also sought out other inventions to keep those stock prices rolling upward. What with the many out-of-city banks they had acquired, each of which had innumerable branches of its own, they actually had cornered, in their commercial and savings accounts, four out of every five dollars deposited in the state. There was hardly a grocery store, or a corner lunchroom, or a tool factory, or a lingerie shop, or an automobile factory, for that matter, that did not count on banks in this combine to finance its payroll and keep its working capital liquid. If working men and women of the state had saved any money at all, they had almost certainly saved it in one of these mighty institutions, which illustrated their "strength" by building awesome marble towers in the inner city, where the very tellers' cages seemed made of gold. (The Guardian Union Trust called itself "the cathedral of finance" and dwelt in a thirty-six-story skyscraper costing $12 million, with windows of stained glass.) But this awesome responsibility for the daily well-being of almost every living citizen of the state lay gently indeed on the backs of the chesty, self-adoring fellows who had created these institutions to help them enjoy the "profit aspect of wealth."

Did the holding company need to demonstrate its high "earnings" in order to keep the stock price up? Why, then one of the subsidiary banks was forced to pay dividends it could not afford. Did the insiders need to create a market for the holding-company stock? Then the bank employees all over the state were encouraged (i.e., ordered) to buy the stock themselves on the installment plan.

Did a nosy bank examiner find a load of sour collateral supporting a note? Then the insiders merely created a new subsidiary to borrow money from one of their own and had the subsidiary "buy" the bad note from the bank. They used depositors' money freely to help "straighten out" the politicians who would see that streets and sewers and water lines were laid in barren areas so that mortgages could then be issued and used as the basis for bonds that could be sold to men and women who would borrow from the banks the money to buy them with.

When the tottering steed at last began to fold in on itself, the bankers knew well enough what was happening. But they worked like busy little elves to keep the news from leaking, hoping always that just a few more jabs in the rump might give the corpse life enough to allow them to ride it far enough to get themselves off in safety. When it came time for an annual statement that would reveal the scantiness of the deposits in one bank, they talked a billionaire friend into depositing enough extra millions to make a good show at the year's end. Then he took his money right out of the front window and put it back in his own pocket. They wheedled loans from the Reconstruction Finance Corporation. They used their considerable influence with the press to keep unpleasant facts from oozing into print. And ultimately, when they saw that the jig was definitely up, they talked the governor of the state into the "holiday" that would close *all* the banks in the state—even those few that had escaped their clutches and were in sound condition—so that it would seem almost like an act of God rather than the overdue failure of a lot of banks that had been gutted of their assets by profit-hungry promoters.

After it was done, the talk was of "plunging real-estate values" and the "general collapse" of the securities markets everywhere. But these hearty lads had been busily promoting their own stocks, through accepting them as security for loans of depositors' money, even long after the stock market had been scraping bottom. Millions of the dollars that were supposedly on hand to keep the veins of commerce pulsing were just signs written in the air. They did not exist at all, except in the imagination of some amenable accountant who had "written up" the assets of a subsidiary corporation, or in promises to pay from people who had nothing to pay with.

When the city had four hundred thousand of its working people looking for jobs, the promoters of the Guardian and Detroit groups were still busily weaving their gossamer webs of criss-cross indebtedness to maintain the illusion that the stock they were peddling was chipped from the nation's bedrock. Mayor Frank Murphy, valiantly struggling to feed the thousands of hungry folk in the city, spent $20 million in one year for welfare. Then the city went broke. Property taxes went unpaid. Developers stopped developing the barren lands and stopped paying their debts too. The cathedral of finance saw its cherubim and seraphim stampeding out the open windows like sea birds before a squall, scattering worthless promissory notes. And still the promoters struggled to keep the facade gleaming and cook up new ways for deluding examiners and public into letting them continue to use somebody else's real money to provide an appearance of substance to the phony certificates they were printing in their own back rooms.

The bank holiday seemed a sort of joke at first, or a simple one-day catastrophe, like a blackout or a blizzard, that would give us all something to date our memories with and momentarily make the whole world kin. Inability to get large bills turned into silver gave rise to fairy stories about millionaires who had to borrow nickels from applesellers to make telephone calls. But there were indeed many incongruous sights, as purse-proud folk sent their chauffeurs down to subway change booths to gather collections of silver, and sable-clad ladies waited in line at the Automat to buy handfuls of nickels. (These sources soon ran dry.)

But when the banks failed to open up after a day or two, the situation grew far past a joke. In Detroit during the state holiday, out-of-state banks had been able to rush in gold enough to help meet some payrolls. And the banks there had opened up briefly to allow depositors to take out up to 5 percent of their balances. But in the national bank holiday there was no relief anywhere. Newsboys and shoeshine men had to offer credit to customers. Even dime-a-dance girls accepted IOUs when the dimes had all run out. Farm people brought eggs and butter and winter apples and milk into town to swap for what they needed. The New York *Daily News* turned the whole business into a giant publicity stunt when it invited readers to use any merchandise to the value of fifty cents as admission fee to its Golden Gloves boxing semifinals at Madison Square Garden. Fans brought in underwear, used shirts, hats, canned peaches, monkey wrenches, raw meat, secondhand trousers, smoked herring, onions, toothpaste, books, bedsheets, and boxes of pasta. But what they offered most were jigsaw puzzles, these being the most desired adult toy of the day.

A poor man who wanted to go to the movies and had only a five-dollar bill to get by on, simply could not get in, for there was no change in the ticket booth. Office workers and counter jumpers and laborers all found checks in their pay envelopes, checks they could not cash. Salesmen swapped their samples for food and lodging. Even Macy's, which *always* sold for cash, had to extend credit to its customers; department stores that ran restaurants let their charge customers eat on the cuff.

But nobody was buying haircuts or shaves, ice-cream cones, contraceptives, or cough medicine. Delivery boys went tipless. Commuters without tickets stayed home. Well-to-do people had to take six of something when they needed only one, for change was more precious now than certified checks. Church collection plates began to gather small IOUs scribbled on calling cards. (For a time the churches had been one of the prime sources for small change.) Coffee Pots allowed their patrons to sign their names to the little punch tickets that indicated the price of their meals. But some people just held to their rooms, eating stale scraps and using coffee grounds over again, without cash, newspaper, or charge account.

Imitation money of every sort appeared in random spots over the nation. In the border states, Canadian money became the same as legal tender and Mexican pesos would pass for cash even in cities far north of the line. Several major cities actually printed official scrip, for there was no telling how long the cash drought would last. Small-business men in Greenwich Village organized a sort of cooperative that issued metal tokens through its members that could be passed for cash in all the subscribing stores. "Emergency certificates" in amounts of one to fifty dollars were authorized by New

York State and plans were made to distribute them at the offices of the New York Clearing House. Newspaper editors and legislators began to call aloud for jail terms for any so low as to hoard gold.

Then the Congress, impelled by the frantic cries of constituents, waved through both houses, without taking time to read it (there were no copies made; it was read aloud), a bill that permitted the President and the Secretary of the Treasury to take almost any steps they deemed meet for dealing with the banking crisis. Specifically, it provided for jailing of hoarders and the uttering of new paper money that was backed, not by gold buried in vaults, but by "assets" held by banks. Some $2 billion of this new money was printed, and it was worth of course whatever you could buy with it. The wealthy, who had cornered most of the hard money, now had to dilute their share with this soft stuff, which meant that for a while at least there would be enough to give everybody, even working people and unemployed people, something to spend.

Why did the Hoover-type economists always begrudge even small sums of money to their customers, and why did they imagine that the country could "prosper" when most of it was broke? Their theory flies so directly in the face of common sense that one wonders that its proponents were allowed at large, much less given charge of the nation's faring. Of the business leaders in the eras of Coolidge-Hoover "prosperity," only Charles M. Schwab of Bethlehem Steel urged that the key to national well-being was to "pay as high wages as possible." The Hoover-Mellon-Mills theory was always to jack up tariffs so that foreigners could buy our manufactures but could not sell us theirs, and to squeeze working people so tight that the could not even afford to purchase the goods they made. (Shoeless shoeworkers in New England were no rarity, nor were hungry farmers in the South.)

Other men who endorsed this theory as the key to national greatness, sound sleep, and good digestion were E. F. Hutton, Walter P. Chrysler, and Thomas L. Chadbourne. In 1933 they decided to launch a "movement" that had all the odor of a fascist cabal, calling for repeal of any law that kept business from "governing itself" and for abolition of the income tax. Happily only a dozen or so of their fellow crackpots rallied to this banner, waving checks for $5,000 cash. (Chrysler pledged $150,000.) Apparently, in that era, people's memories being so retentive and all, when E. F. Hutton talked, only E. F. Hutton listened.

Of course many businessmen were finding that the Depression (if only the discontented would still their cries) concealed some silver linings of varying degrees of brightness. The Brooklyn Edison Company, for instance, having merged with Consolidated Gas in 1928 to form Con Edison, was actually doing better in 1933 than the two components had been before the crash. When that bleak year began, Con Edison dividends were up 75 percent. Employment had been slumping in the Depression years and was now only 5 percent ahead of the first year of the merger, so wages did not eat into the take. Three thousand workers were dropped in 1932. (Most of those who remained were earning less than $1,500 a year, or about three times what an average stockholder received for doing nothing.) But Mr. J. C. Parker, president of Con Edison, was deeply involved in a drive for unemployment-relief funds during 1933, beseeching Brooklyn citizens to come up with over a million dollars to alleviate the lot of, among others, the men he had turned on the street that dividends might be fattened. And rates, unlike other prices in the slump, had remained "strong."

To anticipate the day when the national cash drawer would no longer fly open at their touch, certain big businessmen hastened to apply for refunds and abatements on their income taxes. They found the Hoover Administration panting to serve them. The United Fruit Company was granted a refund of $3 million. National Aniline and Chemical asked for and received over a million; Botany Worsted Mills did likewise. As for the Aluminum Company of America, owned by Andy Mellon and his brother, it took back only $91,495 this time.

But Ogden Mills, the new Secretary of the Treasury, did not mean to leave office without effecting some sort of New Deal for himself. Acting as executor of his father's estate, he had filed an income-tax return that, in his capacity as Secretary of the Treasury, he (or his subordinates) had found in order. But then, in his spectral form as executor, Ogden Mills looked back over his work and found it wanting. So he applied to his official self, as Honorable Secretary, for a reassessment. Whereupon Secretary Mills reexamined the efforts of Executor Mills and agreed that grievous errors had been made. To rectify matters, Secretary Mills granted to Executor Mills an abatement of $5,870,000 plus a refund of $45,000—the only time *he* knew of, said Paul Anderson of the St. Louis *Post-Dispatch,* that a man had won money playing solitaire.

Even more generous bounty was heaped upon certain officers of the National City Bank who had owned the foresight to get into the airplane business while they still had good friends in Washington with the power to grant contracts. Frederick Rentschler, chairman of the board of the National City Company, presided over the conception, gestation, and parturition of the Pratt & Whitney Company, which built engines for airplanes, operating with just one customer of any account—the United States government. It was enough to make a man wonder if perhaps the company had been created to take advantage of some strong inside connection. Later, the National City folk effected a merger that turned their baby company into United Aircraft, which soon came up with generous airmail contracts from the government, which brought with them heavy subsidies to nourish the infant industry.

All that might have been well enough, for God knows the people everywhere could have been easily persuaded that a strong aerial navy was as vital to the general weal as a merchant marine. But when the "contracts" were awarded, there was no competitive bidding at all. Instead, the major airlines (which had, thanks to the many official favors granted them, been able to squeeze out all opposition) sat down around a table in the office of Assistant Postmaster General W. Irving Glover and divided the contracts up among themselves, deciding on fees and services without wasteful bickering. These meetings were kept secret. But when the new Administration came in, nosy legislators smelled them out. Whereupon former Postmaster General Walter F. Brown admitted that the meetings *had* been held—but there had been "no collusion." Still, if the greedy fellows had not gathered together in order to collude, what *had* they been up to, goodness knows?

At any rate, once these matters had come out, including the fact that, of the $90 million or more laid out since 1926 in contracts and subsidies, over half had been devoted to such critical expenses as higher salaries, fatter dividends, and more generous travel allowances, President Roosevelt promptly canceled all the contracts. But by this time Fred Rentschler, who had invested $295 of his own money to get Pratt & Whitney off the ground and so start the whole glorious argosy on its six-year flight, had taken in, what with salaries, bonuses, profits and what not, a round $35 million.

Gravy as rich as this made Babe Ruth's thousand-dollar-a-week salary seem hardly worth taking to the bank. But Babe allowed that he was happy with it. He was mostly happy just to be playing base-ball. He loved golf too, and always hastened south ahead of time now to begin hitting golf balls before spring training began. (He once mused that he might become a professional golfer, for there was hardly a man alive who could match the distance and accuracy of his soaring drives. Some associates suggested, however, that Babe might not be able to bend his bulging belly well enough to sink his putts in pro style.)

Babe had played in ten World Series but now he discovered he had "one more" goal to attain before he would be ready to shed his player's uniform: he wanted to hit seven hundred home runs. Whether it be six hundred or seven hundred, what matter? Nobody was ever going to deal in such figures again.

Although slowed down afield and on base and given to easing up on himself in the spring so that he now had to cart his winter-weight body around on those midsummer diamonds, Babe still earned his keep with the Yankees. His batting average ranged above .300 and by mid-June he already had fifteen of the forty-eight home runs required to reach his goal.

Then, to embellish the Century of Progress Exposition in Chicago, the Chicago *Tribune* talked the baseball powers into staging an All-Star game, with the two top managers—gentle Connie Mack and tough John McGraw—managing the American and National League teams respectively, the players to be selected by votes of the fans. Babe, naturally, as the most famous baseball player alive or dead, was chosen among the first. And he made the game his own by driving in two runs with a long home run into the right-field stands at Comiskey Park. That was enough to beat the team from the curve-ball league 4 to 2.

When the season was done, Babe had collected thirty-four home runs and had beaten the Red Sox in the final game, as a *pitcher.* Some people felt that then would have been, artistically, an ideal time for Babe to bow out of active play. He had even hit a home run in the game he pitched, so there was, in stock-market jargon, an up-tick to end on. But Babe had no such fancy. He was fairly well per-suaded, from the gossip he heard around him or read on the sports pages, that somebody soon would offer him a job as manager.

When someone suggested to Jake Ruppert that perhaps he would sign Babe to run the Yankees, the colonel shook his head. Babe could stay on as long as he could lift a bat. He could pinch-hit. He could play just weekends. But he could not take Joe McCarthy's job. But if somebody *else* wanted to hire Ruth, no one would stand in the way.

One man did. Frank Navin of Detroit phoned Ruth and asked him to come talk about it. But Babe was in no rush. He still felt Ruppert might change his mind. And right now he had to play some ball in Honolulu.

New York City, meanwhile, was engaged in some management changes of its own. After Jimmy Walker had abruptly sent his "hereby resign" note to the city clerk and fled to Europe, Tammany had appointed doddering John P. O'Brien to fill the seat until they could warm up someone sexier. O'Brien was supposed to have been an able city corporation counsel at one time. But now he was not even a good ventriloquist's dummy, for he insisted every so often on speaking before he had been told what to say. Once, when asked whom he might select for police commissioner, he replied with the utter ingenuousness that entranced all the newsmen: "I have not had any word on that as yet."

Word from whom?

The newspapers all rejoiced in this Freudian (or Hibernian) slip, for it seemed to say out loud what everyone had always known and no politician would every admit—that boss Jimmy Hines or some such character at Tammany Hall really made the major decisions. Next day, poor old John O'Brien made haste to haul his words back and revise them. He had never said any such thing, he insisted. What he *had* said, and what the newswriters would have heard if they had not been in such haste to make a fool of him was, "I have no word for you on that as yet."

Thereupon the newswriters, to ensure accuracy from then on, took to reporting old John verbatim, so that they managed to give to the world such gems as "We are all Indians, more or less," and "We Irish, Jews, and Italians!"

But John had stepped into another trap immediately as he tried to revise his statement, because he had failed to foresee the obvious follow-up. Whom *did* he have in mind for commissioner, the press asked him. Had he even thought about it?

Why, I have several people in mind!

Who, for instance?

At this point, old John fumbled among the papers on his desk, where through some fantastic mischance, a letter lay that urged the appointment of one Abram J. Engelman as commissioner. And who had written that letter? That question was never asked. But the letter had been written by an unemployed writer to whom Engelman had paid two dollars. The astonished reporters did ask who *Engelman* was, for God's sake. And who had recommended him?

Referring to the letter, O'Brien was able to reply that Engelman was head of the Pedestrian-Motorist Safety League and a long-time student of police matters. And he had been highly recommended!

The newsmen thereupon cantered out to run Engelman to ground. What they found was an impecunious insurance salesman of ingratiating manner who had been writing letters to papers and politicians for the past ten years. As for the Safety League, that existed, as Mayor Hylan had once pointed out, in Engelman's hat.

But Engelman was not to be denied. For another two dollars, he persuaded the writer to issue a statement to the press declaring that the appointment of a member of the uniformed police as commissioner would be "a disaster!" And this statement, to Engelman's utter rapture and the glad amazement of the writer, was printed verbatim on the front page of every newspaper in the city.

Of course with that, the Engelman affair sputtered out and O'Brien soon got word that he was to give the job to an ex-cop named Ed Mulrooney who could be counted on not to deal too roughly with the folk who had won the favor of the district captains.

As for O'Brien, before he was voted out of office in 1934 (thanks to a devious political deal masterminded by Roosevelt) he did not really leave the citizens laughing, as Walker often did. One afternoon, in his rush to get somewhere or other, O'Brien had run down and killed a child with his caravan of screaming police vehicles, and not all the malapropisms in the world could make that sound funny.

The new mayor was a rumpled, overweight little man of Italian and Jewish ancestry, who looked so little like the slickly turned-out politicos to whom the town had grown inured that he was even able to stand in line at a municipal soup kitchen and sample the fare without detection. Fiorello La Guardia had been elected by a minority vote after Franklin Roosevelt had moved Ed Flynn, Democratic boss of the Bronx, to nominate incumbent Mayor Joseph V. McKee to oppose the Tammany candidate, Dim John O'Brien, and had then had another spokesman announce that the White House wanted none of McKee. Roosevelt *did* want La Guardia, but La Guardia was a Republican.

La Guardia was also a man who openly, unashamedly, single-mindedly, and two-fistedly favored the workingman. Early in his first term as mayor he was faced by a strike of restaurant waiters—a strike that was freely described as a Communist conspiracy and was angrily resented by the white-collar folk who found that their "appetites were spoiled" at lunch by the sight of men carrying picket signs outside their pet noontime retreats. With all the men who walked the streets still looking for some better job than peddling razor blades from door to door, it was not difficult to recruit amateur waiters to fill in for men and women who had gone on strike.

But La Guardia, rejoicing in the almost dictatorial power in small matters his new job gave him, simply ordered the health department to examine (as the law provided it should) all the new employees to make sure they carried no contagion. But Fiorello made sure his inspectors scheduled their inspections for the meal hours, with the immediate result of turning lunchtime and dinnertime into a shambles wherever strikebreakers had been employed. (The inspectors also turned up an amazing number of cases of infectious disease among the strikebreakers.)

The restaurant owners, who had been smugly totting up the take as the pickets hardly turned more than a few handfuls from the door, had barely time to gather the breath to scream "Dirty pool!" when they had to cave in and grant the major demands of the strikers. A good thing, too, for the building-department inspectors and the fire-department inspectors were polishing their badges at that very instant, ready to descend on the restaurants as soon as the dinner bell rang.

The next strike La Guardia had to deal with was a walkout of laundry workers, next to food workers the most notoriously underpaid and brutalized in the city. Fiorello was able to settle this one in a matter of minutes. When the laundries complained that the police the mayor had assigned to "keep order" at the laundries were really conducting a blockade and beseeched him to remain "neutral" in the struggle, Fiorello promptly agreed. Then he called the Department of Water Supply and ordered it, in the name of neutrality, to desist from supporting the laundry owners and to turn off their water. That was the end of *that* affair.

It was, however, a brutal winter for most poor citizens. For one thing, it was one of the coldest the city had known. Residents in lower middle-class apartment buildings had long known that the soul so lost to common sense as to forget to cross the superintendent's palm with silver would have no heat sent to his apartment. But until the Little Flower took charge of the city, there was simply no recourse. If you lacked the cash to assuage the super, you could (and most assuredly would) sit and freeze, even while hall radiators spat excess steam. Under Fiorello, however, only a call to the Board of Health was required to send some young Irishman with a glinting eye to the cold apartment to swing his test thermometer about on a string in the first step toward making ready to tag the owner with a summons.

The Federal government had adopted a half dozen emergency stratagems to get money into the hands of those who needed it. At first, cash was put right into the hungry palms. But proper citizens were immediately outraged at the "dole." Then, under various alphabetical agencies, notably the Civil Works Administration and the later Works Progress Administration, the Roosevelt regime began to offer real jobs to men and women in keeping with their skills.

The effect was electrifying. Men offered pick-and-shovel jobs in Iowa actually fought with their fists to lay hold of the tools. Others, reporting for the first time in over a year to real jobs with real weekly pay, sat down and wept. But others kept putting off the dreaded and shameful day when they would have to walk in and apply for a "relief" job, so thoroughly had they been indoctrinated with the faith that none but poltroons, "failures," mendicants, and the physically crippled would accept even disguised "charity."

Once the giving of jobs—real jobs even though the pay was minimal—became standard practice for the government, it developed increasing opposition until hardly a dollar could be appropriated without appeasing along the way many a special interest that feared it might divert a dollar from its own till. The very business mouthpieces who had denounced the "dole" now discovered that it was not so bad after all. Putting people to work making or building things to be given away would surely begin to eat into their own markets, or decrease the "labor pool" from which low-paid workers might be dipped, or remove the pressure some workers felt to put up with substandard conditions and overlong hours.

Still, nearly all the well-fed were in favor of stiffening the spines of the poor. "If relief is to be given," said General Robert E. Wood of Sears, Roebuck, "it must be on a bare subsistence allowance." General Wood, who was noted for his "liberal" views, also declared that he did not agree with the "philosophy of the city social worker" that "nobody should be allowed to starve."

Henry Ford held that riding freight trains all around the country, as so many young people were doing, "was the best education in the world." Winthrop W. Aldrich, head of the Chase National Bank, called for the immediate elimination of work relief. He and his kind all seemed to feel that even permitting Civilian Conservation Corps kids to build roads into the woodland where no one would think of doing such a job for profit somehow took a few pennies of potential profit from industry. Profit for industry, rather than the general welfare, seemed to these folk the proper concern of the body politic.

Fortunately, the new President did not agree with them, although he did have to cope with their hired mouthpieces, not only in the press but in Congress. And so men and women who wanted to work, even those who had been schooled in such nonprofitable endeavors as writing, the dance, and acting on the stage, were offered an opportunity to work steadily, for scant wages, at the profession they had been trained for.

But Fiorello too had to deal with the people he needed to buy the city bonds and provide its daily pence. So he felt constrained before long, as reformers invariably must, to illustrate his devotion to the American Way and his violent distaste for radicals of any stripe. When the wretched folk who had rejoiced in the CWA jobs were suddenly dumped back, at the behest of right-wing legislators, onto emergency relief at a ten-dollar reduction in monthly income, there was an immediate uproar. It had been difficult enough to feed a family on fifty dollars a month. To attempt it on forty dollars was slow-motion suicide. Relief clients therefore organized into a sort of union, usually with the aid of some Communist adviser, and began to stage angry, not to say desperate, protests. Fiorello, who had been named a Communist too many times himself, undertook at once to prove his Americanism by naming the organizers "yellow dogs" and "fakers." He also forgave the police promptly for clubbing into submission the protesters who gathered outside relief headquarters to express their dismay.

The boss of the New York police then was a National Guard general named John F. O'Ryan, a man so steeped in right-wing, not to say fascist, philosophy that one wonders that Fiorello, regardless of his need to appease the conservatives, was able to stomach the man's existence, for O'Ryan was something more than a law-and-order man. He had urged that enlisted men never be called for jury duty, inasmuch as they were "like children" and could never tell spit from shinola in a courtroom. He organized a special rifle squad of police who, he vowed, would intimidate any agitators "as soon as they appeared on the scene." He had created this special squad, he admitted, "in anticipation of labor trouble." O'Ryan also, when questioned about the brutal clubbing of protesters at the relief headquarters, bragged that he had put some cops on trial—not for using their nightsticks too freely on unarmed men and women who had gathered to protest starvation but "for failure to use all the force at their disposal." (As a member of a board of inquiry looking into the outrages of military "justice" in the American Expeditionary Forces in France, O'Ryan had given his approval of sentences of as much as twenty-five years at hard labor for being two or three days AWOL after the armistice.)

Eventually, late in 1934, Fiorello fired O'Ryan, but not until after the iron-skulled general had been turned loose on the taxi strikers and had clubbed down a good many more than even some bankers thought necessary.

PART VIII

A Long Farewell

THE spring of 1934 had offered many signs of happy days at hand. Two million more Americans were working again after months without jobs. Retail trade showed gains up to 25 percent over the year before. Construction was up 36 percent. And more passenger cars were being built than during any Depression year.

Babe Ruth signed to play baseball for $35,000. But hardly anyone took note of what he was going to get. He was growing old, and not even he expected to keep pulling down a thousand dollars a week. He had all sorts of sources of side income. He lived like royalty regardless of what his paycheck said. And he could still hit baseballs a long way.

When he came back from Hawaii, Babe had been offered a chance to manage the Yankee farm club in Newark, run by his long-time admirer George Weiss, but Babe would not even consider the offer. Those *other* guys—Cobb and Speaker and Johnson and Ott and Frisch and Hornsby and Terry and Traynor—*they* had been hired to manage in the big leagues without any minor-league apprenticeship. Were they any bigger than *me?*

Of course not. Had there been any such thing as Baseball Incarnate, and not merely a convocation of greedy and small-minded men who all owned franchises at the same time, Babe would have been offered a club of his own, even if he contributed not much more than carrying the lineup card out to the umpire. For Babe had been the making of modern baseball, had boosted salaries, increased attendance all over the land, inspired little boys everywhere to take to hitting baseballs with sticks, glorified the game until even high-class hotels learned to brag of the ball clubs that stayed there, and altered the technique of hitting to such a degree that batsmen ever afterward would go to the plate with the notion of driving the first good pitch as far as it would go.

When the 1934 baseball season began, there was much open talk of Ruth's inability to run the base lines or cover a proper share of ground in the outfield. Early in the season he was hit on the knee by a pitch and had to stay out of the lineup for a while or limit himself to one or two trips to the plate.

Babe found that some clubs, most often the Philadelphia Athletics, had begun to overshift on him, putting the shortstop on the "wrong" side of second base and moving the third baseman over into the shortstop's position. So he took to shortening up his grip on the bat even more, in order to wield it with more accuracy, and he set out to poke a baseball now and then down the third-base line where nobody could reach it. When he reached first base safely in this manner he would stand there grinning as happily as if he had just bounced a rubber ball off a playmate's head.

Hard luck this season seemed to ride close to Babe's heels. One of his mightiest home runs, hit halfway up in the right center-field bleachers, was thrown away one day when the game at the Yankee Stadium was ended by rain after four innings. His failing legs had already stolen a previous home run from him when a four-hundred-foot drive that bounced off the bleacher rail in center allowed him time enough only to reach third base. Two years earlier he'd have made it all the way around. Early in June, when he faced a Philadelphia rookie left-handed pitcher named Mort Flohr, who was throwing his very first pitch in the big leagues, Babe took the pitch on the right wrist and found himself benched again. It did not take him long to get enough use of the wrist so that he could swing a bat effectively. But it was a longer time before he could sign autographs, because Babe wrote with his right hand even though he threw with

270

his left. And no one in baseball ever signed as many autographs as Babe Ruth did.

In June, a sports columnist named Richards Vidmer took a private poll of all the Yankee players and reported they had voted unanimously (but anonymously) that Ruth ought to be taken out of the lineup for good. Babe was making it tough on the fielders who had to cover part of his share of the outfield, was holding up runners who followed him on the base lines—and was just not hitting the ball as often as he should to hold a big-league job.

But Babe soon afterward made two running catches in the outfield, either one of which could have been credited with saving the game, and made them on his craft and judgment rather than his speed, for he knew where most batters were likely to hit and he could line up a fly ball almost the instant he heard it ring off the bat.

The very next day, five thousand kids in the left-field pavilion (the seats in left field at the stadium had not yet been covered), outraged when Ruth was not listed in the lineup, set up a high-pitched chant: "We want Ruth! We want Ruth!" Just how the players would have voted on benching Ruth after that was never recorded, but some of them must have been reminded that the big man, slowed down or not, was still the chief reason why many fans paid their way into the park. (Ruth did come up to pinch-hit that day, to the loud delight of all his young fans. But he struck out.)

By June 24, when Babe had been at bat twenty-four times in a row without hitting safely, the grumbling against his presence in the lineup began to grow audible in the clubhouse, particularly among the younger players. On that day, batting against Sad Sam Jones of Chicago, Babe hit a home run with the bases full, accounting for four runs and winning the ball game. A few days later he went to bat three times and made a double, a single, and a home run. He also saved the ball game again with a running plunging grab of a fly ball that endangered his creaking knees. After that there was less talk of putting the old bull out to pasture. He finished the season with a batting average of only .288, low for Babe but a respectable mark indeed for some who in later decades would aspire to his crown. He hit twenty-two home runs, giving him altogether 708 for his career.

It was taken for granted by fans and writers everywhere that Babe would not play baseball any more. He made one final approach to Ruppert and was told again there was no chance of his replacing Joe McCarthy as manager of the New York club. At the World Series in St. Louis that fall Babe told anyone who wanted to know that he would never sign another player contract. Then he took off for Japan, where he would lead an American All-Star club through that land where baseball—or *beisu boru*—had infected an even larger share of the populace than it had in the United States, or at least had developed into a more virulent fever.

Perhaps it was the trip to Japan that persuaded Babe he had merely to sit tight and let baseball-club owners woo him. For no other American had ever won such frantic adoration in Japan. Sixty-five thousand men, women, and children gathered at the Meiji Shrine Stadium to watch him. Five games in Tokyo drew a total of over two hundred thousand fans. Extra police were needed to keep the screaming crowd from bearing Babe right to the ground. Tirelessly, grinning down into the upturned grinning faces, Babe signed autograph after autograph, until his fingers simply would not close any longer on the pen.

The trip to Japan, while it must have filled Babe's heart full with the conviction that the world was still his own, brought an estrangement that was never healed until the other man was within months of his death. During the voyage Babe fell out with his pal Lou Gehrig, and the two did not exchange polite words again for almost five years. Lou was far too abstemious ever to have served as a playmate for Babe. But the two were good friends and had barnstormed through the United States together, Babe leading the Bustin Babes and Gehrig the Larrupin Lous. What went on between them involved a girl, as quarrels with Babe often did. But as no one alive knows the whole truth of it, there is no need to offer conjectures about it. It was a bitter falling out that a few years earlier might have led to a bloody fist fight. It ended in tears on July 4, 1939, Lou Gehrig Day at Yankee Stadium, when Babe, before an oversize crowd, put both arms around Lou's neck and hugged him. Next June Gehrig died.

Many not at all famous folk had died in the bitter winter of 1933–34, including an eighteen-month-old boy named John Blatcher, a victim of pneumonia, who gasped his last few breaths in a shabby bedroom behind the firehouse at Freeport, Long Island. His father, just returned to work after months without a job, could not afford twenty-four dollars a day for an oxygen tent. Many an aged citizen died that winter too, without much notice being taken except by their neighbors and perhaps the welfare investigator, all of whom knew that it was hunger and the driving cold (below zero in the city for the first time in the memory of some citizens) and not merely old age that had driven the life out of the shrunken bodies.

Then there was John Dillinger, the most notorious bank robber in the nation, who died in midsummer outside a movie house under the guns of FBI men who had decided to take no chances of further escapes by this "most wanted" villain. John had successfully found his way out of two jails and had bragged there was not a lockup in the nation that could hold him. He had had a face-lift to make him look less like the pictures on the wanted posters, and had grown a mustache to hide his grim mouth. But three FBI men found him, and when Dillinger started to run, they just opened fire all at once and hit Dillinger so many times he could hardly have lived more than a second. They consigned him then to the one lockup from which no man had ever escaped alive—the grave. There was joy in many hearts to see the end of a man who had stolen so much from so many banks. But Dillinger, along with his companions, had taken somewhat less than half a million dollars, a very small fraction of what the Detroit bankers had gathered among them. But that Detroit robbery had been managed quietly, without guns or threats of violence, and the only deaths had been those of inconsequential folk, who committed suicide when they discovered they had been ruined.

A score or more of young men and women, whose names were barely even recorded at the time, were shot down in the South when the cotton-textile mills there burst into a wild walkout. It was called a strike. But in many places it was merely a spontaneous explosion, of such devastating power that it intimidated even some of the leaders of the textile union. Indeed, many disciplined union members refused to join the walkout because their leaders had not given the word. Mills where there had not been even a whisper of union talk and where no agitator had ever intruded to rouse the workers to a rage just suddenly burst open at every gate as working men and women, lintheads all, stormed out in resistance to the stretch-out.

Stretch-out. That was the fighting word. Wages had been desperate enough, for the new "minimum" wage agreed on by the Industry Board set up under the National Industrial Recovery Act had soon become the maximum wage for even the loom fixers, the elite of the skilled workers in the mill. The millowners, cynically "regulating" themselves under the new rules that called for a five-day week and a floor on wages, simply moved to get more out of every worker for every dollar spent in wages. Before they had finished (smirking all the while at their allegiance to the "Blue Eagle" rules) they had cut the pay rate down below what it had been in the depths of the Hoover days. They did this by requiring men and women who had been wont to strain their muscles to weariness intending, for instance, twenty-two looms to look out for fifty-six.

This, said the industry's spokesmen, was merely "putting a skilled worker on a skilled job and asking others to take over his unskilled duties." But it was killing millworkers or driving them to frenzies of effort to earn that "minimum" wage. So they turned in desperation to the only weapon they had—the walkout.

Before many days had passed they had closed about half the mills in the South. And the operators had brought in special guards, had sought for and received National Guard companies and squads of "deputies" to "keep order," had set up machine guns around the mills and had made ramparts of bales of cotton. Union organizers who undertook to rally the workers were arrested, beaten, or fired on. Pickets were dispersed with clubs and guns—and pickets fought back too with clubs and rocks. Many of the millworkers were hill people, independent, jealous of their rights, fearless in battle. But courage was no match for machine guns. One flying squadron of union organizers, approaching a mill in a car, was methodically gunned down without warning. All six of the people in the car were killed.

With their brethren already in the field, the cotton-textile workers in the North could not stand idly by. The union there called workers out in a dozen mills throughout Massachusetts and Rhode Island. Wages there had never sunk to the five dollars and ten dollars a month some Southern lintheads took home. But work that should have paid twenty-five dollars a week was often bringing only ten. And the stretch-out was adopted everywhere.

There was talk of Communism and of violence in the North, but compared to the state of belligerence in the South, the Northern end of the strike seemed like a Sunday bird walk. What violence there was—and two workers did lose their lives—could be laid, not to Communist agitation but to the presence of roused-up and trigger-happy lawmen who looked on all strikers as outlaws nearly as deep-dyed as Dillinger.

The governor of Rhode Island, Theodore Francis Green, who, at the first sign of the strike had sent his natty Guardsmen into the field with steel helmets, bayonets, and backpacks full of tear-gas grenades, suddenly began to find bad guys on every roof. He called the legislature into session to seek permission to ask for Federal troops. The state senate quickly passed the bill he wanted, but the house cagily set it on the table.

"But what we are facing," the governor quavered, "is not a strike at all but a Communist uprising!"

He ordered that "every known Communist" in the state be arrested forthwith.

President Roosevelt, however, called the fussbudgety governor into a private conference and patted his hand. Then the governor went back and conceded that perhaps the crisis was not quite so critical. He did not round up all the Communists after all, for the American Civil Liberties Union reminded him that that would have been a violation of the Constitution. Anyway, the unions themselves had run the Communists out of their meetings and refused to listen to any talk of violence. There was only one Communist they would put up with and that was Ann Burlak, the notorious Red Flame, who worked mostly in Fall River and New Bedford, across the line in Massachusetts, although she did dare now and then to challenge Governor Green's dragnet.

To meet the Red Flame then was to suffer a sudden letdown. Newswriters who hastened to interview her and draw from her lips raucous cries for armed uprising and take-over of the government were stunned to find themselves face to face with a slender, exceedingly pretty, almost shy blonde young lady who in some other place and circumstances might have been groomed into a movie star. Annie, as the millworkers called her, was no bomb thrower at all, just a well-read and well-spoken girl, polite as a schoolmarm, who would offer you a clear, disarming gaze and a handshake meaty as a man's. The millworkers who listened to her would almost all agree that her "ideas were wrong" but they just knew her heart was right. And when she told them the facts of life in the mills they knew she spoke the truth. Communist she may have been, but just let any lawman set out to rough up little Annie and the millworkers would have dismembered him.

The strike, for all its extent and anger, petered out soon in a welter of promises and agreements that the millowners had no intention of honoring. And it may have been that many strikers began to wonder if it had been so smart to eschew all violence. Perhaps some even asked themselves if perhaps Annie's "ideas" had been right. At any rate, the temper of the workers when the strike was called off augured not much good for the leadership of the old A.F.L., who had hailed the settlement as a mighty victory.

Except for the taxi strike, which might have been won by the strikers had not a Communist-controlled local voted down the compromise agreement and forced an industry-wide strike, New Yorkers were not too much alarmed at labor troubles. The taxi strike, which saw some cabs turned over and burned, while others had their windows and windshields demolished at the height of the theater hour, did scare the hell out of many citizens of every social level. But that was over soon. The strike of the Dugan Bakery deliverymen, which silenced the clop-clop-clop of one of the last collections of horse-drawn vehicles in the town, created no great stir. Much more was made, in the midtown offices and the "men's bars" where advertising men, stockbrokers, radio executives, and other peaked-lapel types foregathered, of the alarming photographic accident in a Camel cigarette ad that made it appear that a famous steeplechase rider was exposing himself. This, combined with the suggestion (ascribed to the rider) that it was possible when you were "all in" to get a "lift (!)" with a Camel, set most of the well-dressed males in town to roaring.

And the capture of Bruno Richard Hauptmann, kidnap-killer of the Lindbergh baby, excited everyone high and low. It almost seemed as if, with Roosevelt and La Guardia waking and watching over us all, we might some day find the world running aright, as it had of course in our fathers' day. For Hauptmann, a German ex-convict who was in the country illegally, had been captured by the New York City police, as the result of two years' patient tracking down of each of the gold-certificate ransom bills that appeared in the city. Going off the gold standard in 1934 had made these certificates stand out like flags.

The police made a map and put pins in it, and traced lines to enclose the pins, each pin marking a spot where a bill had been passed. The police discovered that garages and filling stations were the spots where the bills were changed most frequently, that the changing of the ransom bills seemed concentrated in the Fordham section of the Bronx, and that the bills appeared faster and faster as the time since the kidnapping grew longer. The police urged filling-station attendants to note and mark on the bills the license numbers of cars whose drivers offered them. Ultimately one gas station deposited a bill carrying a license number that belonged to Hauptmann. The bank showed it to police. What interested police most about this bill was that when the attendant questioned him about using one of the out-of-date certificates, Hauptmann had bragged: "I got a hundred more of dose tings at home!"

He had, too. They were hidden in holes bored in the end of a two-by-four in Hauptmann's garage, along with a pistol. On a panel inside a closet in Hauptmann's two-story Bronx home, the address and telephone number of "Jafsie"—the intermediary—were written in pencil. And a piece of wood missing from the floor of Hauptmann's attic had been used to build the kidnap ladder. Besides, Hauptmann, when arrested, had one of the ransom bills in his pocket.

With the capture of Hauptmann, newspaper editors seemed ready to pitch every other news story out the window. What did it matter who was to blame that the *Morro Castle* of the Ward Line had caught fire at midnight off Ashury Park and had burned to a hulk with the loss of 124 lives? Did anyone in New York fret about the progress of the textile strike? Who had time to note that the Dean brothers, pitching almost every day, had led the St. Louis Cardinals roaring up to overtake the New York Giants at the finish line? Here was a tale to make each separate hair upon a reader's scalp stand up like quills upon the fretful porcupine.

It is not certain that all or even most readers were able to maintain their excitement at full pitch as the Lindberg case moved to trial. But it did fill the New York papers full, with even the *voir dire* examination of the jury panel set forth word by word, and all the challenges and byplay and possible improper influences recounted in headline, subhead, and story.

At the Hunterdon County courthouse in Flemington, New Jersey, there was a stampede of visitors that resembled the first day at a world's fair. The Union Hotel across from the courthouse, the only hotel in town, shrewdly and swiftly doubled the capacity of its bar. Pickpockets hastened to town to await the pushing crowds. One man made up little souvenir "kidnap ladders," pretending they were "duplicates" of the one found under the baby's window, and sold them for a quarter each. And the portly sheriff of the county made up "passes" of admittance for which he charged fees of five dollars (for balcony) and ten dollars (for main floor). Newspaper reporters, of whom there were more than three hundred assigned to the story, including correspondents from London and Paris, had to buy passes, as well as the first-come spectators. A few spectators sold their tickets for as much as ten times what they paid. All this cash was required, the sheriff declared, to defray the cost of the many new benches that had to be set up to accommodate the tourists. And applications for passes came from as far off as Arizona. When one newspaper expressed outrage at this swindle, the sheriff silenced its complaints by letting the reporters from *that* paper in for nothing.

The trial soon took on the stature of a major sports event, with "action" available from bookies or in man-to-man bets in every barroom or cigar store in town. (The odds favored conviction.) Hawkers sold pictures of every principal in the case, including the jurors. One enterprising metalworker stamped out copper mementos of the trial and sold them for a few cents each. Autographs were sought from everyone: reporters, court officers, lawyers on both sides, witnesses, even from Lindbergh and Hauptmann (practically the only two who refused to sign). To underline the sporting aspect of the event, one small boy approached defense attorney Edward J. Reilly and asked him to autograph a *baseball.* Reilly graciously consented.

Reilly, sometimes called "The Bull of Brooklyn," was easily the most flamboyant figure at the trial. In morning coat, striped trousers, and glittering shoes, with a fresh white carnation always in his lapel, Reilly by turns bullied prosecution witnesses and attempted sweetly to seduce them into self-contradiction. His reputation had been made in the criminal courts of New York, where he often depended as much on "straightening out" a convenient witness or employing a little political muscle on a district attorney or a judge, as he did on his brand of beer-hall oratory. He had standard tricks he had employed so often that reporters could almost forecast the moment when he would spring them on the judge and jury.

Red-faced, extravagant in gesture and resonant of voice, Reilly, far from his native turf, sometimes seemed like the top man in a vaudeville skit. His effect on the opposing witnesses was minimal. During his wild-swinging cross-examination of Colonel Lindbergh, in which he dropped dark hints of sinister forces that might have been unleashed by enemies Lindbergh had made in his youth, the spectators sometimes laughed at Reilly's questions and applauded Lindbergh's good-humored replies. Still, Reilly persisted in his standard gambit of requiring his client, at some point in the trial, to shout "liar!" at a prosecution witness. Reilly had Hauptmann try this first when a cab driver, asked to identify the man who had paid him a dollar to take a note to Dr. Jafsie Condon, pointed at Hauptmann and said, "That's the man!" Hauptmann dutifully responded, "You're a liar!" But only a few people in close proximity to the defense table even heard him. After Reilly harangued the court in vain to have the court stenographer "correct the record" to show Hauptmann's response, he decided to try again.

His next chance came when an officer of the Department of Justice told of finding ransom money in Hauptmann's garage. This time Hauptmann came right out of his chair and began to move woodenly toward the witness. Hauptmann was an emotionless man and he delivered his lines with about as much fervor as if he were reading newspaper headlines to his wife. But this time he did speak loudly:

"Stop your lying, Mr. Sisk!" he declaimed. "You are not telling the truth! You are a liar!"

Inasmuch as the defense never charged that the money was *not* found in the garage, this all seemed so obviously synthetic it is doubtful if a single juror was stirred, even though court officers did rush forward to prevent Hauptmann from reaching the witness. But Reilly gave it one more try. When a former neighbor from the Bronx testified that Hauptmann had been limping for two days after the date of the kidnapping, *Mrs.* Hauptmann rose up from her spectator's seat and screamed, in thoroughly convincing style, "That's a lie! You're a liar!"

Mrs. Hauptmann's presence in town, with her blond, chubby, curly-haired little boy, won a fair amount of sympathy for Hauptmann, even though the betting odds remained heavily for conviction. The local people, except those who were profiting from the trial—the hotel owner, the renters of rooms (the hotel owner had taken options on most of the empty rooms in town), the souvenir sellers, and the pickpockets—actually grew rather bored with the spectacle and could walk right by the courthouse without an extra glance. Even in the courtroom, attendance began to thin out once Jafsie had testified.

This strange old fellow with the inextinguishable smile and the American flag in his lapel held even the defense attorneys half hypnotized as he rambled on about physical conditioning, sensible diet, correct grammar, and training of the memory. Despite his happy smile, he took himself with utmost seriousness, brought his own bodyguard and luncheon companions with him to Flemington, and even visited the jail one day to try to talk Hauptmann into confessing. Jafsie promised Hauptmann he would intercede with Roosevelt to save Hauptmann from the electric chair in return for a full confession. Hauptmann listened stonily and answered not a word.

With Jafsie off the stand, much of the juice went out of the trial and the sheriff had empty seats to peddle after lunch every day. He thereupon took to issuing half-day passes, to keep all the seats warm. (Some of the "seats" were merely leaning room in the rear, or places on the windowsills and radiators.) Reilly's arm-waving efforts to involve all the prosecution witnesses in some sort of plot to stage the kidnapping turned to vapor. Hauptmann's story that a man named Fisch, who had gone to Germany and died, had been the real source of the ransom money was promptly deflated when Fisch's relatives were brought in to testify that Hauptmann had actually given money to Fisch. Besides, no more ransom money made its appearance anywhere once Hauptmann was in jail.

So the case went to the jury, and lawyers and reporters relaxed in the courtroom while awaiting the verdict. Ed Reilly, still neatly creased and slickly barbered, with his glowing red face and fresh carnation giving him the appearance of a wedding guest, stood up before the bench and delivered a barroom version of "When Irish Eyes Are Smiling." Then he took over the witness chair and gave his impersonation of some of the prosecution witnesses, supplying questions and answers in falsetto tones. The prosecutor, New Jersey Attorney General David T. Wilentz, moved to a seat in the jury box and suggested that he might better have sat there through the trial. (There had been a scramble of sorts to get on the jury, with one old man trying hard to pretend he was young enough to serve. When asked how old he was he said, "Past middle age." But how old? "Past sixty." Now, you must know how old you are! "Well, sixty-eight. Last week." He was too old, by statute, to serve on the jury and was excused.)

Reporters and spectators, while the jury was out, played games and staged picnics throughout the room. Milk cartons, straws, bottles, sandwich wrappings, and remains of cigars and stubbed-out cigarettes cluttered all the open spaces. Some men gathered in clusters to roll dice. The judge, meanwhile, was reading law in his chambers. (In Japan, Babe Ruth reported, pitchers who were taken out of the box did not go to the locker room but back to the bullpen for more practice.)

Hauptmann, of course, was found guilty. Immediately jurors were invited, at fees of several hundred dollars each, to make public appearances in theaters, to write books, or to allow newspaper ghosts to write the individual stories of each juror. The trial had been a really monstrous show, replete with so many violations of ethics, the Constitution, and the simple rules of decency that there was hardly any recounting them. Defense testimony had been analyzed and dismantled in the *New York Law Journal;* secret sound movies of the trial had been made; witnesses had been sneaked into the jail to peek at Hauptmann in preparation for identifying him; it had even been planned to drive Hauptmann's old green Dodge into the courthouse, but it could not get through the door.

Still, everyone (except Governor Harold Hoffman of New Jersey, who held up execution for a time) was convinced of Hauptmann's guilt and all were satified with the outcome. All, that is, except the good ladies from the Salvation Army, who were deeply hurt that Hauptmann had not been permitted to come down from his cell to join in their periodic singing of "Revive Us Again!" and other pet hymns. Why, they even had a man once who had killed a *whole family* in Queens, and *he* had been allowed to come join the sing!

About the time the trial ended, Babe Ruth had reached Paris on his long way back from Tokyo. There had been much talk at home about his being made someone's manager, but he had had no offers. (It came out much later that Larry MacPhail, then owner of the Cincinnati Reds, had sought Colonel Ruppert's permission to offer Ruth the managership of the Reds. Ruppert, who had vowed he "would not stand in Ruth's way," stood in the way this time by refusing permission.) When Connie Mack returned from the Orient, he had told sportswriters that Babe would make any club a fine manager. He had done a great job of managing the tourists on shipboard and on the diamond, said Connie, and he certainly should remain in the major leagues. But when someone put it to Connie that perhaps Babe might join the Philadelphia club to understudy Connie himself and eventually take over, Connie said no. Babe had nothing more to learn about baseball and should not have to understudy anybody, Connie declared. Besides, as for himself, he meant to keep on managing the club until he was eighty. (He quit when he was eighty-eight.)

Jake Ruppert said Ruth would be offered a contract at, say, $25,000. But Babe, in Paris, vowed he was all through with the Yankees and would play no more for anyone. He rejoiced in his triumphs throughout the Orient. But he did not believe the Japanese would ever play major-league baseball. They just did not grow big enough to hit the ball long distances. (Babe on the trip had outhit everyone, even Lou Gehrig and Jimmy Foxx.) And as for those lovely girls on Bali, they were not for Babe. "Too chesty!" he declared.

So Babe and the Yankees were divorced right then. (Mary Pickford and Doug Fairbanks were divorced after a three-minute hearing about the same time, six thousand miles away in California.) And Babe planned to play golf, and maybe write a book, and wait for the telephone to ring.

The telephone rang not long afterward. James Michael Curley, now governor of Massachusetts, was the man at the other end of the line. Worried about the state of the Boston Braves (they had leased their park to a dog-racing outfit, and had then been refused the use of Fenway Park too, and only got Braves Field back when the National League refused to allow the dogs to have it), Curley decided they needed a major attraction; so he called Babe and asked if he might be interested in managing in Boston. Babe was indeed. And Emil Fuchs, the frantic owner of the foundering Braves, felt his heart leap up at the notion. There was one difficulty: he already had signed Bill McKechnie as manager.

But Babe could come as vice-president, could play some ball, draw in great crowds, "assist" McKechnie—and who knows, maybe even take Bill's place some day. So Babe was offered a new contract, after Jake Ruppert had granted him his unconditional release. The salary was said to be $25,000, plus a percentage of the increase in the gate.

The gate did increase, immediately. At spring training, in St. Petersburg, Florida, where the Yankees had long held their own camp, Babe drew a crowd of 6,500 when he first appeared in a Boston uniform. The Yankees, playing in Tampa, drew 384. Still, Bill McKechnie had his doubts about Babe's playing any more baseball. "He's too slow to play the outfield," said Bill. "And he can't move around enough to play first base."

But Judge Fuchs said Babe should play, so Babe played. And for a time it looked as if Fuchs was right. When the Braves reached Newark to play the Yankee farm club there, Babe hit two enormous home runs, one of them well over five hundred feet long. And when they opened the season in Boston, on a typical clammy cold Boston spring afternoon, twenty-five thousand fans turned out to watch Babe's debut in the curve-ball league. (In his youth, one recalls, he wanted no truck with National Leaguers at all.) Coming to bat with one man on base, Babe hit a crackling single off Carl Hubbell, the man who had humiliated him by striking him out in the All-Star game the season before. Babe sent one run over the plate with that blow, scored another run himself, and then drove in two more runs with a home run over the right-field fence to beat the Giants 4 to 2. Babe had scored two of the Braves' runs and driven in the others. Judge Fuchs, who had been cheered by the rich gates of the exhibition season (they had actually offset all expenses), lay on his pillow that night to dream of golden days ahead, with all fear of bankruptcy fled.

But Babe *was* too slow. He made two hits in a game against the Dodgers. But he covered not much more space in the outfield than he could have spread a bedsheet over. And he needed to drive a ball just about to the fence to make it safely to first. Soon he was not driving the ball into safe territory at all, and fans who had screamed in near delirium at his first appearance began to boo when he took his place in the field. Regularly now he found himself lifted for a pinch runner or given a defensive replacement in the outfield.

Babe had told the sportswriters when the season began that he "never felt better in my life."

"My legs haven't bothered me one bit!" he insisted. "And Bill McKechnie is a great guy to work for!"

The sportswriters however told each other (or so they all insisted afterward) that it had been a mistake to bring the aged Babe to Boston, where he would slow up the club on the field and "disrupt discipline" off the field. It is a fact that Babe no longer paid any mind to curfews or training rules, feeling perhaps that he had long since paid his dues in that department and might be allowed now to live his own life. He grew fat. His belly actually got in his way now so he could not get down after ground balls. (It was the size of his belly and his consequent inability to field bunts that had persuaded old Cy Young to quit this same club, after twenty-two seasons in the majors, some quarter century before.)

But Babe had one more great moment ahead. It would have been the logical time for him to retire from play, for it was a spectacular show, such as only Babe and one or two of his imitators could have staged. And it was staged in Pittsburgh, where home runs were hard to come by and where some mighty pitchers still labored.

One member of the Pittsburgh club that day was a man who had shared a locker room with Ruth since Babe's early days in Boston, and had sometimes ridden the night circuit with Ruth and had long been his intimate. This was Waite Hoyt, mighty right-handed pitcher from Brooklyn, who was himself drawing near the end of the track. When, in the clubhouse meeting before the game with the Braves, the Pittsburgh pitchers had brushed aside any suggestion that they needed to plan any strategy for Babe, Waite warned them that the old lion still had strength in his forward feet.

"He has no batting weakness," he warned them.

"Ah, shucks" (or something like that), said big-eared Guy Bush. "I got that guy out in the '32 Series by throwing him sinkers."

"So did Charlie Root," said Hoyt. "And Charlie's sinker landed in the center-field bleachers."

The first pitcher to face Ruth that day in May 1935 was Red Lucas, a veteran right-hander who was working his twelfth season in the majors. Lucas fired his hard one at Babe, and Babe, swinging as easily as if he were drawing a line with a stick, poked the pitch high and far over the seats in right field—and again there were men ready to swear that it was the longest home run ever seen.

When Ruth next came to bat, there was a new pitcher, Bill Swift, who was having his best year in baseball. A hulking right-hander, Bill fed Babe fast balls. And Babe put one of those into the seats in the centerfield. Swift was out of the game when Babe came up in the seventh inning. The new pitcher was Guy Bush, an eighteen-game winner the season before, the man who knew just how to get Ruth out and the one who had taunted Babe into his "called shot" in Chicago in 1932. He wound up with an exaggerated motion and flipped his fast ball past the Babe. He put two quick strikes on Ruth and hopped around the mound like a wound-up toy. Then he put on an especially fancy windup and came in with the killer—the fall-away sinker that was supposed to leave Babe floundering. But Babe offered nary a flounder. Instead he cracked the trick pitch right out of the playing field and jogged all the way around the bases again.

The trouble is that, after that triumph, which seemed to reclaim his status once again, Babe could not bring himself to quit. He laughed merrily in the clubhouse and saw himself going back up to the plate again and again to "hit a couple" and then sit down and watch the youngsters finish the game. But instead he began to ground out once more or pop weakly to the infield and watch the ball without the heart to run it out.

The Braves pitchers began to gripe about him now, for they saw too many sure outs fall safely in the field that Babe should have been covering. The young players openly made fun of him or told the sportwriters the old goat ought to move over and admit he was through.

There were other great names in baseball now. The Dean brothers, Dizzy and Paul, consistently earned more ink than Babe did, not merely with their dazzling victories on the mound but with their antics on and off the field. Dizzy Dean had even found the gall to visit the St. Mary's Industrial School in Baltimore, where Babe had spent his youth, and tell the assembled kids there that, while Babe had long been the greatest ballplayer in the land, now it was Dizzy Dean who occupied the throne.

To grown-up fans, however, Babe remained the king. When the Braves traveled through the West, it was Babe who caused attendance to swell. But before the summer had even begun, Babe was himself beginning to doubt if he would ever attain his goal with the Braves. He was aware of the hostility of the press and of his teammates. He resented the manner in which Fuchs tried to cash in on his fame—signing him up to go visit a store where the owner has bought five hundred tickets and then stand there and sign all the tickets. The hell with that racket, said Babe. He was not going to turn into a ticket hustler after all he had accomplished in the game.

Then one day Babe had to chase a foul fly a long, long way in left field. He wound up against the rail, his eyes bulging, his heart hammering against his ribs, and his breath escaping in raucous moans, while his legs seemed to have turned to papier-mâché and he had to clutch the rail to stay erect.

"Jesus," he said after that. "I got to stop this before I kill myself!"

Babe sought out Judge Fuchs then to tell him he wanted to resign his job. "O God, no!" said the frantic judge. "You can't quit! I've got a big advance sale on the Western trip and you've *got* to show up. If I don't make that extra dough . . . well, if you throw in the sponge now I'll have to do the same thing. I'll be finished."

So Babe played on and made no more hay at all at bat. His movements in the field became more and more limited. He took himself out of ball games and often put himself into the lineup to pinch-hit, only to take himself out again for a pinch runner if he got on base. But he had no quarrel with McKechnie, whom he counted as a close friend—his only real buddy on the Braves.

In early June 1935, Babe was invited to come to New York to attend a banquet on board the *Normandie,* the great new flagship of the French Line that was on the way to setting a new record for a transatlantic voyage. Babe was to appear there, along with Mayor La Guardia and other lions, to be the official representative of baseball. Having already missed two games because of bad knees and fearing that his ailment might be "water on the knee," Babe felt he would do his club more good down there getting his picture in the paper than he would sitting on the bench watching them lose to the Dodgers. An exhibition game was scheduled in Haverhill for the day before the banquet, and Babe was ready to attend that.

"I'll hobble around there to please the crowd," he said. "But I'm in no shape to play a league game."

Still, Judge Fuchs insisted that Babe would have to stay in Boston, even if he just slid up and down on the bench. Babe lost his temper then and told the good judge what he thought about his whole chintzy operation, including his habit of running his veterans ragged to hawk baseball tickets about town. During the game that day, Babe sulked on the bench, after sending word up to the press box that he would have an announcement to make when the game was over. But he could not wait until the end of the game. In the eighth inning, with the Braves leading the Giants 2 to 0, Babe sent word to the writers that he would see them right away. He made for the locker room, and when the writers gathered, he led them to a small room at one side and closed the door.

"I hate like hell to do this and say this," he told them, "but I am going on the voluntary retired list. I don't mean I'm going to retire from baseball. But I'm not going to play any more for the Braves."

Then Babe called the promoter in Haverhill and told him he had quit. The man let out a cry of dismay. He had already advanced $600 to Fuchs on the strength of this game. What the hell would he do? Babe assured the man that he would be there if Fuchs would allow it. Fuchs said he would not. If Babe wanted to play for Haverhill, that would be O.K. And Fuchs would put a kid pitcher on the mound and bet Babe would never get a hit off him. Babe was damned if he would lend himself to public humiliation of that sort and he made ready to go back to New York. Fuchs announced he had given Babe his unconditional release.

That night, Saturday, Bill McKechnie called Babe to tell him how sorry he was that he was leaving. Next morning Bill showed up at the Brunswick Hotel, where Babe was staying, and helped him gather up his gear for the auto trip to New York. They walked together, along with some reporters, out to the sidewalk in the June sun. Bill and Babe exchanged a long long handshake and promised each other they would soon meet again. At a nearby hotel, there was a wedding reception for a Boston sportswriter and his new bride, and the gaiety had spilled out to the street. One of the guests, spotting Babe on the sidewalk, rushed up and flung a shower of confetti over his head. Babe absently brushed a little of it off and tried to smile.

"I bet this is the first time a guy ever got confetti thrown on him when he was fired," he muttered.

There was no sound of music nor any gaiety at Babe's departure, nor any speeches recounting the thousand great deeds he had done. The reporters watched him stonily, most of them ready to write that it was a good thing for the club that he was gone. Bill McKechnie held Babe's arm awhile, and gave him a final pat or two. Then Babe, his face solemn, climbed into his car and made slowly off into the Commonwealth Avenue traffic.

The story made headlines in Boston and New York. But more people were stirred just then by the fact that the Supreme Court had knocked down the National Recovery Act, with its minimum wage, its five-day week, and its consumer-protection standards. A family of operators who sought to peddle substandard chicken and pay substandard wages had their right to do so under the Constitution affirmed by the court. And now more than half the nation wondered uneasily if the entire New Deal structure would come tumbling down and leave them naked to the wind, without any Works Progress Administration to sustain them, or unemployment insurance to ease them, or bank deposit insurance to protect their savings, or government mortgage loans to hold on to their homes.

In smaller matters, especially in Boston, all was as it should be. Ladies who wished to swim at the municipal bathhouses were outraged at the long-skirted 1910-style suits that were offered and refused to accept them. And a mysterious fellow of similar mind roamed the streets of Cambridge at night with a razor in his hand, slashing the skirts of young ladies and ripping them off.

Baseball fans, with none of Ruth's exploits to bemuse them, dwelt for only a short time on the problem of what evil days he might yet fall upon. He seemed cozily situated in his big apartment on West Eighty-eighth Street and Riverside Drive, with a good wife to look after him and no cares to beset him. But his anger still simmered, especially when he read of statements by Fuchs that hinted at dark revelations Fuchs might be "forced" to make now that Ruth had spoken his mind so plainly. Ruth might have made good, said Fuchs, if he had buckled down and got into condition. But as it was, he just *had* to get rid of him.

"My God!" Babe roared. "I let the guy talk me into the deal! He told me he had $50,000 in advance commitments and if I didn't sign up, he was finished!"

But the sportswriters reminded Babe, who was surrounded now by neighbors who had come to rejoice in his return, that McKechnie, too, had said Babe should have been let go earlier, that he was "undermining discipline" and was "guilty of actions I would forbid to other players." And McKechnie even said, the writers told Babe, that *he* had recommended Babe be fired.

"No such a God damn thing!" Babe exclaimed. "Bill was a good buddy of mine. He was the only one that came to see me off. He never gave out any crap like that."

The writers showed Babe the "official" release, issued after Fuchs had called McKechnie into conference. This was the only point in the whole controversy at which Babe seemed to lose his aplomb. His whole face sagged, as if he might start to cry. Not Bill McKechnie! He could still feel that affectionate hand on his shoulder. For all his street smartness, for all his having made his own way since he was in his teens, Babe was still not worldly-wise enough to know that men can learn to knife friends in the back when a job is at stake. But Bill McKechnie! Babe thought of all he and Bill had said to each other in that farewell meeting on Sunday morning. And to think that all the time . . . Babe was too shaken even to feel anger.

Then Babe was off the front pages, and even out of the newspaper altogether, and baseball fans turned to delight themselves in the reckless doings of Dizzy Dean, who had won thirty games the year before and looked likely to do it again, who had staged a one-man strike to win a salary raise for his brother, and who had taunted the whole city of Detroit as he stood on the pitcher's mound on the way to winning the final game of the 1934 World Series.

Dizzy's latest was his battle with his own clubmates in Pittsburgh, when he accused the whole lot of "laying down" on him and letting the Pirates rock him for four runs in a single inning. To get even then, he had started to lob the ball over the plate so the Pittsburgh batters could blast it. And when his teammates called him names for that, he had challenged them all to battle.

Tough Ducky Medwick had taken Dizzy up on the challenge and had charged up to meet him near the first-base line. The two were held apart, but Ducky then hustled to the bat rack and picked out a weapon. Paul Dean jumped up and laid a hand on Ducky.

"Don't hit him with no bat!" he walled. "I don't care what you do with your fists. But don't hit him with no bat!"

Then, torn between love of his devoted but wrongheaded brother and loyalty to his ball club, Paul slumped to the bench and burst into tears.

Epilogue

WHETHER the fates that had the country in their keeping planned it thus or not, an era seemed to end when Babe Ruth's playing career was over. For almost at that instant, the plain people of the nation were made to realize that they would never, by merely delegating to a strong President the power to put forces back into balance, return the Ship of State to the tranquil course they always supposed their fathers had plotted. When the nine solemn old men who comprised the Supreme Court decided that the right of moneyed folk to exploit their customers and hired hands could be neither abridged nor denied, they were signaling the working people of the country that it was time to take some of the power back. There would be no more cozy accommodations between the lords of industry and the lords of labor, no more "settlements" that spelled further postponement of the better day the union had promised, when boss and workingman would sit down beneath the evergreen palm and share the same dessert.

For after this came the sitdown strikes that ripped the old American Federation of Labor from ears to ankles and brought in the new industrial unions that multiplied the strength of organized labor by ten. From almost that time forth, the people set out not merely to plug a few leaks in the ship or get its gear back to working but to redesign it and radically change its course. Beginning with the fateful decision that destroyed the NRA, the electorate undertook to make the general welfare the "business" of the United States and to establish the principle that when the working citizenry was sore beset it was the duty of the government to offer aid.

Even some of the crackpot schemes men had devised for enriching everyone at no expense to anyone else seemed suddenly to have run their course. One such was the chain-letter craze that had spread like a contagion through the country. This device was meant to ensure that any participant who took care not to "break the chain" would be made rich eventually by receiving money through the mail from men and women he had never heard of. Typically, some innocent would find in the mail a letter from an acquaintance asking that he send money—some letters required only a dime, some as much as a dollar—to the person whose name and address headed an enclosed list. Then he was to copy the letter and list and mail it to three others, putting his own name at the bottom of the list and leaving off the top name. Eventually, he was assured, through the magic of geometric progression, he would receive untold sums in the mail.

About the time Babe Ruth stopped playing professional baseball, this craze was petering out. Its demise was never better celebrated than in Marblehead, Massachusetts, where Leonard Thorner, an employee of the city engineering department, opened a stack of letters one day and found green bills totaling over $10,000 tumbling out of every envelope. And every damn bill, Thorner noted sourly, was stage money, such as could be bought at the five-and-ten. The wise guys he worked with were responsible for that, said Thorner. But he mailed out no more chain letters.

To hear the rich folk tell it in those days, the common people of the land were equally fed up with the stage-money phoniness of "boondoggling." That was the name Clare Booth applied to the creating of jobs by the government, with no tribute of profit to any entrepreneur. With all the newspapers and all the news magazines and all the thinkers-out-loud on the radio ridiculing the "waste" of home relief and WPA (where loafers spent their days, it was reported, merely leaning on shovels), there seemed no doubt at all that the "Madman" in the White House would soon be sent packing. Young folk in Wall Street, who once sputtered with rage at Roosevelt's name, felt they could afford to laugh indulgently at his utter ignorance of finance, for his days were surely numbered. In some business circles, employees were occasionally warned to keep their "New Deal notions" to themselves. Sometimes they were merely eased out and quietly blacklisted. But there was such ferment among the common people—the millworkers, the black folk of the South and North, the garment workers of the cities, the steel and rubber workers, the factory hands in the auto and electrical industry—as the nation had never known before. Of a sudden the meek had grown tired of waiting to inherit the earth and decided to lay hold of it. The auto workers, who had been spied on, stretched out, and brutalized so that (in at least one plant) 25 percent of the payroll could be found in the first-aid room every day, turned suddenly to tigers who took over the plants and defied the whole world to oust them. Black sharecroppers who had "yassuh'd" and "nossuh'd" their way through endless dreary days of cringing before the boss dared to unionize and offer some sort of resistance to the white man's "law." Even office workers, who had been brought up to prize their white collars above their thin pay envelopes, began to identify with the "lower classes" long enough to learn that in union there is strength.

Communist "intellectuals"—including some of the very ones who had railed against the "fascist threat" that Roosevelt posed—leapt forward with their eyes alight to lead embattled workers and unemployed in an assault on some fanciful Winter Palace. (In Ohio, a Communist named Louis Budenz, leading a ragged army of the unemployed to the State House in Columbus a few seasons earlier, had exhorted this minor multitude: "We must take over the government and establish a Workers' and Farmers' Republic!")

Still the wearers of pinkie rings and pleated pants, comforted each day by the cheerful tidings vouchsafed them in their favored editorial columns, or by the formulations of such acknowledged know-it-alls as David Lawrence and Edwin C. Hill, never questioned that the New Deal was the same as done with. And when the *Literary Digest,* by polling all the people who had telephones, came up with the prediction that a Republican landslide was already astir, they felt as if they had seen *that* coming all along. The *intelligent* men and women of the country were not going to stand by any longer and allow "thrift" to be penalized nor incentive to be dampened, neither yet the lazy and the ne'er-do-well to suckle without fee forever at the public breast.

So when Roosevelt was returned to office in a smashing landslide of his own, along with an overwhelmingly Democratic Congress, there were such cries of anger and dismay among the rich that it seemed for a time as if they might all pick up their paper money and secede. A few of them actually did, and some others began in all seriousness to plot armed resistance and assassination. In those days it was never considered treasonous at all for a man who made his living by the sweat of other brows to mutter sourly about "taking a rifle and shooting that sonofabitch in Washington."

But Babe Ruth, despite his current wealth, had never been anything but a Democrat, as all poor people had been where he came from. So he remained true to his origins, even though he could not have told you his Senators' names and might even have had to address the President as Doc.

Babe of course did not withdraw from public life. He still accepted offers to come talk to groups of boys or give out prizes at baseball tournaments. He played golf winter and summer, and took up bowling to fill some of his evenings. He even traveled to northern New York periodically to auction off the teams at a golf tournament at the Champlain Hotel near Plattsburg. No one seeing him at this time would have found him any different from the rambunctious young man of his palmy days—except that he dressed more tastefully and could speak in public without awkwardness. He still would come to the tavern dining room in the early morn and merrily rattle the doors to get the place open, so he could sit down to his pork-chop breakfast. He still sat at the bar at night and took delight in peppering friends with peanuts and bits of popcorn, crouching and pretending to hide, after a missile hit its mark, like a naughty boy in a schoolroom.

He could be grateful that he had a wife who watched over his money for him and at least made an effort to see that he got to bed betimes and ate regular meals. Nor did she try too hard to make him into something he could not be. Babe, one friend said, retained the sexual appetites and attitudes of an Airedale, who after frisking about the town, visiting whatever kennels might have made him welcome, would come bounding home bright-eyed, seeking no other greeting than a pat on the head and assurances that he was a very,

very good boy. When he had traveled with the Yankees, Babe often brought two or three girls for company, placing them on different floors in the hotel and arranging with some pal to make the necessary phone call that would allow him to plead a date with the trainer at the ball park, whereupon he would progress from one room to another a few floors below. After he left baseball he had to find other excuses to go dashing out to make his rounds—a need, for instance, to "buy a Sunday paper," or to get a rubdown at the New York Athletic Club, where he had the desk clerk primed to tell any inquiring female that he had "gone up to the second floor" (where ladies were not permitted) when actually he had simply hustled in the front door and out the back.

Jake Ruppert died in 1939. Babe was present to hold the old man's hand until nearly the end, and to weep that, for the first time in his life, Ruppert had called him "Babe" instead of "Root." For the funeral Babe appeared in a fedora, a special honor for his old boss, like wearing a hat with plumes.

Babe taught baseball to small boys or talked to them about "success." He talked on radio too, giving advice on ballplaying and offering anecdotes from his own career. And characteristically, he became so rapt in his discussion one time that he forgot his surroundings completely. He had taken off his leather jacket so he might whack it to imitate the sound of a well-pitched ball hitting the catcher's glove. *Whack!* went his fist into the leather. Then, "Jesus Christ!" he screamed into the cringing microphone. "I broke the goddam cigars!"

Some people will say that the cigars he kept almost constantly in his mouth, or the fat-bowled pipe he chugged at when he sat in his leather chair at home and contemplated his baseball trophies, eventually proved his undoing. But Babe had no inkling, in his retirement, that he was anything but strong and full of life. His stomach had always troubled him, for he habitually provided it with more than it could comfortably hold. But he never developed the sort of swollen gut that causes some fat men to waddle. His girth increased and he could not easily bend all the way over. But he still moved around the golf course or at the top of the bowling alley with comfort and grace.

Before Jake Ruppert died, Babe Ruth had made just one more effort to find a place for himself in organized baseball, when he let Colonel Larry MacPhail hire him as a coach for the Brooklyn Dodgers in 1938. Babe even put on a Dodger uniform and played in two exhibition games that year. He hit a single in one, or at least made a safe hit on which he stopped at first base. In the other he hit a three-bagger—that is, he drove a ball, in the Elmira ball park, that traveled so far Babe was able to quit at first base and allow another runner to take over for him. The pinch runner, Jesse Haines, ran all the way to third base before they got the ball back.

At Brooklyn, Babe suffered one final humiliation. He found himself sharing the locker room again with the ballplayer he most despised, Leo Durocher. And Durocher no longer looked on Babe as an object of awe, nor did he pant for a chance to carry Babe's glove, as he might have done in his days with the Yanks. Instead, Durocher let Babe have the rough side of his tongue. Once he and Babe actually charged each other and would have had it out on the locker-room floor had not burly Burleigh Grimes grabbed them and by main strength held them apart until their anger had spluttered out. Next season Durocher was made manager and Babe did not come back.

Babe appeared in public again as one of the charter members of the new Baseball Hall of Fame, a kind of glorified trophy room built in the town where baseball was not invented. The crowd that came to Cooperstown that day to observe the installation saw Babe make his final appearance in an organized baseball game. In the exhibition that marked the induction ceremonies, Babe came to bat as a pinch hitter and managed only a feeble pop fly that the pitcher caught easily. The crowd yelled as if Babe had clouted the ball over the fence. Babe wore a big-league uniform once more in the motion picture based (very loosely indeed) on Lou Gehrig's life. Gary Cooper, even though he threw the ball like a girl, made an acceptable Gehrig. But what actor could ever have provided anything but a sorry substitute for the Babe?

Babe found himself too old to serve in the Second World War, just as he had been too married to serve in the First. But whenever he was wanted to solicit funds or blood for the Red Cross or sell war bonds or simply talk to soldiers, Babe said yes and perhaps gave as much of his time with as little fuss about it as any celebrity alive. After the war, Babe took a trip to Mexico, to visit with the Pasquel brothers, who were trying to build a major baseball league in that land where fans threw firecrackers at players who failed them. Babe relished the welcome he received and relished the Mexican food that must have set his poor stomach to crying "enough!" And he came back to this country to predict that the Pasquels would make a success of their venture (they did not) and that the Mexican League would help lift the level of baseball salaries, which, said Babe, were still too damn low. The owners were making plenty, Babe asserted, and were not offering the players a fair share. Unlike many self-made men in other fields, Babe never felt that the nation was on an even keel just because he was riding comfortably. (The semi-official mouthpiece for the club owners, the *Sporting News,* scolded Babe for such treasonable talk.)

Soon after this, Babe began to experience discomfort too severe to be coddled with bicarbonate of soda. He had crippling pains in his neck, and headaches that made him curse. His voice, which had grown gravely of late, became even more scratchy. He had occasional difficulty in swallowing. Late in 1946, Babe was taken to French Hospital for "tests" and stayed there three months. Doctors severed nerves to block the pain but found that he suffered from inoperable cancer, which they could do no more than retard a little. As the weeks went by and Babe did not emerge from the hospital, men and women all over the world heard that he might be near death. Priests led their flocks in prayers thousands of miles away and in languages Babe could never have understood. The hospital mail room began to take on the appearance of the locker room at Yankee Stadium, with letters and postcards addressed to Babe Ruth arriving by the hundreds every day.

While it was still winter, Babe came out of the hospital to go home. There were writers from a dozen papers and magazines to meet him then and to get some word from his own lips of what the state of his health might be. Babe looked at them, tried to grin, could not speak at all, then held out his poor arms, shrunken now until they seemed like a little boy's. Babe tried again to speak but sobs took his breath away and he could just stand there weeping.

Still Babe's illness did not prevent him from offering what strength and time he could spare to the one cause he was still devoted to— teaching baseball to kids. He still traveled around the nation to give out awards at American Legion baseball tournaments. He tried to play golf, and still showed up on the Florida golf courses to meet and talk with friends. His face had sunken to a caricature, with only the broad nose still recognizable. His clothing hung on his dwindling frame as if from a rack. But he grinned, and in the hoarse whisper that was all he had left, he could still make jokes and hail old friends as "Dago" or "Chicken Neck" or just plain "Stud."

He had to be dosed regularly with morphine to quiet the unbearable pain. And for a short time he even had to be admitted to the Neurological Hospital at the Columbia Medical Center to regulate the dosage. When he came out, he was invited to the twenty-fifth anniversary celebration at Yankee Stadium, where old teammates met him and helped him push his feeble arms and legs into his old Yankee uniform, now far too wide for him at every point. His number 3 was about to be retired—never to be used by any Yankee player again. And his uniform was to be donated to the Hall of Fame, to be encased in glass there and stared at by visitors who had never seen him play. Weak as he was, retaining no more than a hoarse whisper of a voice, Babe still made his way to the microphone and offered a simple and gracious speech of thanks for the roaring tribute he had received from the crowd.

Babe always seemed grateful that men and women, and especially small boys, cheered him or sought his autograph. To the end of his days he never acquired the swagger, the self-importance, or the aloofness that some modern heroes seem to feel is best suited to their station in life. One of his oldest friends, Waite Hoyt, a pitcher with the Red Sox when Babe was pitching for that club, and a pitcher with the Yankees when Babe was hitting home runs there, recalls a visit Babe made to Cincinnati when he had only a short time to live, yet still could afford the time to attend an American Legion baseball ceremony. Waite and his wife visited Babe and Claire in their hotel, while Babe sat unspeaking, head down, assiduously attending his glass of beer, that being just about the only "food" he enjoyed then, for he could swallow nothing solid. When it became clear that Babe had no vigor left, Waite and his wife rose to go. But Babe halted them.

"Wait a minute," he whispered. "I got something for you."

Slowly he found his way to the small refrigerator and took from it a single orchid in a tiny glass vase. He held this out to Mrs. Hoyt.

"There," he said. "Now don't forget old Babe!"

Talking of this long afterward, Waite Hoyt stopped and mused a while.

"You know," he murmured finally, "he was really *nice!*"

Index